Using the Instructor's Manual

The teaching aids and suggestions in this Instructor's Manual (IM) are organized by chapter. Each chapter contains the following components:

Chapter Overview:	Provides a short synopsis of chapter content.
Chapter Goals:	Describe the major learning outcomes for the chapter.
Chapter Outline:	Contains a detailed description of chapter topics organized by major headings.
Transparencies:	Contain a list of transparencies available in the Transparencies Packet for the text.
Teaching Suggestions:	Provide concrete ideas for ways to present topics in a thoughtful and interactive way.
Journal Starters:	Provide prompts to encourage students to write about chapter topics from a personal perspective.
Increasing Understanding Feedback:	Contains Increasing Understanding Questions from the text's Companion Web site, as well as feedback for these questions.
Reflect on This Feedback:	Includes Reflect on This questions from the text, as well as feedback for these questions (also found on the text's Companion Website).
Classroom Windows Feedback:	Chapters 1, 2, 6, 7, 10, 11, 12, and 13 contain a boxed feature called Classroom Windows, focusing on actual footage of real-life teachers working with students. These are available in both CD-ROM, which comes with the text, and videotapes for the instructor. These are also referenced in the IM under Teaching Suggestions and described in the Multimedia Guide section of the IM. Feedback for discussion questions linked to this feature can be found in the IM for each chapter as well as the text's Companion Website.
Video Perspectives Feedback:	Chapters 3, 4, 5, 8, and 9 contain a feature called Video Perspectives. These 10- to 20-minute video clips taken from ABC News reports about educational issues are also referenced in the IM under Teaching Suggestions and described in the

1

	Multimedia Guide Section of the IM. Feedback for discussion questions linked to this feature can also be found in the text's Companion Website.
Video Discussion Feedback:	In Chapters 1, 2, 4, 7, 8, 10, and 13, students can view, on the text's Companion Website, short clips of nationally recognized experts in education talking about chapter-related issues. Discussion questions, which appear in the text, as well as feedback for these questions, can be found in the IM (also found in the text's Companion Website).
Self-Assessment Feedback:	Provides questions, along with feedback, for the multiple-choice Self-Assessment Questions found in the Companion Website for each chapter. NOTE: Since students have access to these questions and their feedback on the Companion Website, they cannot be used effectively on quizzes and tests.
PRAXIS Practice Feedback:	Provides feedback for the PRAXIS Practice exercises at the end of each chapter.
Web Site Addresses:	Contain Web site addresses that pertain to relevant chapter topics.

Instructor's Manual and Media Guide
to accompany

Introduction to Teaching
Becoming a Professional

Second Edition

Don Kauchak
University of Utah

Paul Eggen
University of Northern Florida

PEARSON
Merrill
Prentice Hall

Upper Saddle River, New Jersey
Columbus, Ohio

Pearson Prentice Hall™ is a trademark of Pearson Education, Inc.
Pearson® is a registered trademark of Pearson plc
Prentice Hall® is a registered trademark of Pearson Education, Inc.
Merrill® is a registered trademark of Pearson Education, Inc.

Instructors of classes using Kauchak & Eggen, *Introduction to Education: Becoming a Professional, Second Edition,* may reproduce material from the instructor's manual for classroom use.

10 9 8 7 6 5 4 3 2 1

ISBN: 0-13-114980-6

Table of Contents

Chapter 1
Why Become a Teacher?

Overview

Chapter 1 invites readers to analyze their beliefs and motivations about becoming a teacher. In addition to describing the themes for the book, the chapter analyzes reasons for entering teaching and factors that influence those reasons. Reform is introduced and linked to changes in teacher preparation as well as No Child Left Behind. In addition, PRAXIS, portfolios, and INTASC are described and related to entering the profession.

Chapter Goals

This chapter examines

- Why people decide to teach
- Some of the rewards and difficulties in teaching
- The question of teaching as a profession
- How educational reforms will affect your life as a teacher

Chapter Outline

I. Do I Want to Be a Teacher?
II. Rewards and Difficulties in Teaching
    A. Intrinsic Rewards
        1. Emotional Rewards
        2. Intellectual Rewards
    B. Extrinsic Rewards
    C. Difficulties in Teaching
        1. Working Conditions
        2. Salaries
        3. Merit Pay
    D. Private School Employment
    E. Putting Rewards and Difficulties into Perspective
III. The Teaching Profession
    A. Characteristics of Professionalism
        1. A Specialized Body of Knowledge–Extended Training for Licensure
        2. Emphasis on Decision Making
        3. Reflection
        4. Autonomy
        5. Professional Ethics
    B. Are Teachers Professionals?
        1. Lack of Rigorous Training
        2. Lack of a Unique Function
        3. Lack of Autonomy
        4. Lack of Accountability
        5. Putting Professionalism into Perspective
IV. Becoming a Teacher in an Era of Reform
    A. Kentucky Education Reform Act: Statewide Reform
    B. Changes in Teacher Preparation
        1. Competency Testing–PRAXIS: Comprehensive Teaching Testing
        2. Portfolios: Individual Teacher Accountability
    C. INTASC: Standards in Teacher Education

Transparencies

T1.1 (Table 1.1) Responses to Interest in Teaching Inventory
T1.2 (Table 1.2) Beginning and Average Teacher Salaries for Each State
T1.3 (Figure 1.1) Dimensions of Teacher Professionalism
T1.4 (Table 1.3) The INTASC Principles

Teaching Suggestions

I. Do I Want to Be a Teacher?

> The purpose of this section of the chapter is to encourage students to examine and reflect on the reasons they are considering going into teaching.

- Have students respond individually to the survey in the text on the first day of class before they have read the text. Discuss how their responses differed from the averages in the text (see *Transparency 1.1* "Responses to Interest in Teaching Inventory").

- Have students rank order the nine reasons in the text and compare their responses to those in *Transparency 1.1*.

- If your class is large enough, analyze students' responses to the survey by comparing male to female students and elementary to secondary focus. Discuss these differences in class.

- *Discussion Question #4* asks, "For which group of teachers–elementary, middle school, or high school, are emotional rewards likely to be greatest?" Use this as a discussion starter.

- *Journal Starter #1* asks students to analyze themselves in terms of an influential teacher they experienced.

II. Rewards and Difficulties in Teaching

> The purpose of this section of the chapter is to encourage students to analyze the advantages and disadvantages of entering the teaching profession.

- Display *Transparency 1.2* "Beginning and Average Teacher Salaries for Each State." Ask the class to compare your state's salaries to the national beginning teacher average ($30,719), to the national overall average ($44,367 for the 2001–2002 school year), to those of adjoining states, and to the highest and lowest states. Ask students to explain or discuss these differences. Contact your state office of education for updated information on this topic as well as district-by-district comparisons.

- *Discussion Question #2* asks, "Do you believe teaching is more or less rewarding than it was in the past? More or less difficult? Why do you think so?" These questions might be used with small groups first, which could then report to the whole class.

- To encourage students to think about teaching in private schools, ask what the pros and cons are for teaching in these types of schools. Ask whether the positives outweigh the negatives.

- Show the video segment "Classrooms in Action: The Real World of Teaching," contained in the *Classroom Windows* video that accompanies this text. This segment also appears on the CD-ROM that accompanies the text along with the following discussion questions, which can be used to encourage student discussion:

  1. For which of the three teachers are the emotional rewards likely to be the greatest? Explain why you think so.

  2. For which of the three teachers are the intellectual rewards likely to be the greatest? Explain why you think so.

  3. Based on what you saw in the episodes, which teacher do you believe has the most difficult job? Explain why you think so.

  4. For which teacher is knowledge of content most important? Pedagogical content knowledge? General pedagogical knowledge? Knowledge of learners and learning? Explain why you think so.

  5. How much autonomy do you believe each teacher had in designing and conducting his or her lessons? Explain why you think so.

  6. To what extent do you believe each teacher demonstrated the characteristics of a professional? Explain your assessment.

  Feedback for these can be found later in this chapter.

- Encourage students to analyze how the media portray teachers. Assign different groups of students to view, discuss, and report back to the group on the movies listed below. Ask them to address the following issues/questions: How realistic was the portrayal of teaching and teachers? What did you learn about the rewards and pitfalls of teaching? What did you learn about students? What did you learn about schools? Would you recommend the film to others?

  Films: *Children of a Lesser God, Dangerous Minds, Dead Poets Society, Lean on Me, Mr. Holland's Opus, Music of the Heart, Stand and Deliver*, and *The Water Is Wide*

- *Journal Starter #2* asks students to analyze themselves in terms of their personal strengths and liabilities in relation to teaching.

III. The Teaching Profession

The purpose of this section of the chapter is to help students understand how the movement toward professionalism will affect their lives as teachers.

- *Discussion Questions #6* and *#7* ask students to analyze and evaluate the movement toward professionalism in education.

- *Going into Schools #1* asks students to interview teachers about a number of topics, including the rewards of teaching, teacher professionalism, and the kinds of knowledge required to be a teacher. Use the results as a discussion starter.

IV. Becoming a Teacher in an Era of Reform

- **Ask students to bring articles from local newspapers that describe local reform initiatives. Ask how these are similar to and different from national reform efforts.**

- **Contact your state office of education's teacher certification office to find out about recent changes in teacher licensure. Share these with your class, and ask them to compare state standards with national initiatives.**

- **If your state requires the PRAXIS Series, obtain information on it from your college or university's testing center, and share sample items with your students. Have them decide which kind(s) of professional knowledge each taps. Do the same if an alternate test is used. Point out that PRAXIS Practice Exercises are found at the end of each chapter. Do the one in this chapter with your class.**

- **If you have access to professional portfolios prepared by graduates of your program share them with the class. Or ask your colleagues to identify a graduating senior with an exemplary portfolio. Ask him or her to visit your class to share and explain the portfolio.**

- ***Transparency T1.4,* " The INTASC Principles," provides a brief description of the 10 INTASC principles. Point out that the Portfolio Activities at the end of each chapter are linked to these.**

- **The *You Take A Position* feature in this chapter asks students to take a personal position on high-stakes tests and accountability. Use this assignment to organize a debate on the topic.**

- **The articles by Kohn (2000) and Hirsch (2000) could also serve as an information base for this debate or a discussion on this topic.**

V. Exploring Diversity: Cultural Minorities and High-Stakes Testing

- **Discuss the pros and cons of high-stakes testing for minorities. Ask for suggestions on how to minimize the negative effects of testing.**

VI. Decision Making: Defining Yourself as a Professional

The purpose of this section of the chapter is to encourage prospective teachers to reflect on chapter content and relate it to their own personal lives.

- **This section encourages students to ask themselves, "Do I want to be a teacher?" It also asks them to consider how the following trends will influence their lives as teachers:**

    - **Increased emphasis on teacher knowledge**
    - **Increased emphasis on testing and accountability**
    - **Teacher professionalism**

Journal Starters

1. Do you remember any teachers that had a powerful impact on your life as a student? What did they do and how did they affect you? What positive aspects of these teachers would you like to incorporate in your teaching? How would these make you different as a teacher?

2. Why do you think you want to become a teacher? What positive experiences do you think you'll have as a teacher? What challenges do you think you'll face? What assets do you bring personally to teaching? What liabilities? What aspects of your personality will help you as a teacher? What aspects will hinder you?

Increasing Understanding: Questions and Feedback

1.1
In Table 1.1 we see that the lowest average response on the Interest in Teaching Inventory is for Item 4, and the highest average responses are for Items 5 and 6. Are these consistent or inconsistent results? Explain your thinking in your answer.
1.1
These results are consistent (or are certainly not inconsistent). For instance, individuals may consider another career, such as a job in the business world, and later feel that they aren't as fulfilled as they would like to be. They might then turn to teaching because they want to work with young people and/or make a contribution to society.

1.2
Consider medicine, law, and engineering, three other prominent professions. Are the extrinsic rewards in teaching likely to be higher or lower than they are in these professions? Explain.
1.2
This is a difficult question to answer precisely, because all professions will have both intrinsic and extrinsic rewards. Extrinsic rewards, such as desirable vacation periods and having work hours that match the school hours of their own children, are important extrinsic rewards for teachers. On the other hand, teachers' salaries tend to be lower than the salaries in other professions, so salaries are not likely to be more extrinsically rewarding for teachers than are for members of other professions. The specific answer to the question will depend on student needs and values. If desirable vacations are important, the extrinsic rewards in teaching will be greater than in other professions. If money is of primary importance, another profession might be preferable.

1.3
How does your state compare with the national averages for salaries? How about neighboring states? What does this tell you about regional trends in terms of teachers' salaries?
1.3
In general, teachers' salaries are highest in the eastern and midwestern parts of the country and lower in the southern and western regions.

1.4
As you anticipate a teaching career, do you believe working in the profession is more or less difficult than it was ten years ago? Explain.
1.4
The question asks students to describe their beliefs, which means that technically it doesn't have a right or wrong answer. However, evidence indicates that teaching is likely to be more difficult than it was 10 years ago. Two primary reasons for this exist. First, students are more diverse than they ever have been in the past, and teachers are likely to have a number of students in their classes whose first language is not English. Second, many students are coming to school with fewer school-related experiences than they have had in the past. The number of students living in poverty is increasing, and parents are spending 40 percent less time with their children than they spent a

generation ago.

1.5

What kind of teacher knowledge is primarily involved in effective questioning? How do the other forms of knowledge also influence a teacher's decision-making during interactive questioning?

1.5

Teacher questioning primarily involves general pedagogical knowledge, which is an understanding of general principles of instruction and classroom management. The other forms of teacher knowledge are involved also. Teachers need to have a knowledge of content to frame their questions. They also need an understanding of pedagogical content knowledge, to make the content understandable to students. Finally, they need a knowledge of learners and learning to effectively frame the question and respond appropriately to student answers or nonanswers.

1.6

One of your students is obviously more interested in her friends than in the topic you're teaching, and you can't seem to keep her from talking. You call on her; she doesn't hear the question. Should you reprimand her, repeat the question, or go on to another student? Explain your reasoning. (The feedback for this question will give you a research-based answer.)

1.6

Research suggests that you should repeat the question, which both pulls her back into the lesson and maintains the flow of instruction. Reprimanding her disrupts this flow, and going on to another student implicitly condones her behavior.

1.7

What is the relationship between teachers' knowledge of this code of ethics and the other components of teacher professionalism such as decision making, reflection, and autonomy?

1.7

Teachers' understanding of this code of ethics provides a knowledge base for professional decision making and reflection. In addition, because the code of ethics requires professional interpretation, it also encourages teacher autonomy.

1.8

Analyze the ten INTASC principles in Table 1.3 in terms of the different kinds of professional knowledge described earlier. Which are emphasized the most? the least?

1.8

Principle 1, Knowledge of Subject, is clearly related to Knowledge of Content. The second principle, Learning and Human Development, is related to Knowledge of Learning and Learners. Principles 3, 5, 6, 7, and 8 are most closely related to General Pedagogical Knowledge, while Principle 4 is related to Pedagogical Content Knowledge.

Reflect on This: Questions and Feedback
(These can also be found on the Companion Website: www.prenhall.com/kauchak .)

An Ethical Dilemma

1. Item 6 of Principle I of the NEA Code of Ethics says the teacher "shall not on the basis of race, color, creed, sex, national origin, marital status, political or religious beliefs, family, social or cultural background, or sexual orientation unfairly grant any advantage to a student." Is giving Maria a passing grade a violation of this code?

We don't think necessarily so. The Code of Ethics provides general guidelines for teacher actions; teachers must factor in a number of factors in arriving at educational decisions.

2. Does the fact that Maria both has a learning disability and struggles with English influence your decision in Question 1?

Both of these factors could have an influence on teachers' decision making.

3. Are grades and standards absolute, or should they be adjusted in cases like Maria's?

Grades and standards provide guidelines to both teachers and students about acceptable levels of performance. Teachers should use these flexibly in their professional decision making.

4. What would you do in this situation?

This decision should be driven by the question, "What is in the student's best interest?" Each teacher, when faced with decisions such as these, should ask this central question.

Classroom Windows: Questions and Feedback

Classrooms in Action: The Real World of Teaching

1. For which of the three teachers are the emotional rewards likely to be the greatest? Explain why you think so.

Although emotional rewards are important for each level–elementary, middle, and secondary teachers–they are likely to be the greatest for Rebecca, the kindergarten teacher, because young children are spontaneous, open, and genuine. Comments such as "I like to play in the mud," which one little boy said in the episode, illustrate these characteristics. On the other hand, a great many emotional rewards exist for middle and secondary teachers as well. They simply weren't as observable in these episodes.

2. For which of the three teachers are the intellectual rewards likely to be the greatest? Explain why you think so.

The intellectual rewards can be important for both Scott, the middle school teacher who taught Bernoulli's Principle, and Sue, the high school teacher who was working with her students on The Scarlet Letter. *Bernoulli's Principle has a great deal of real-world application, and* The Scarlet Letter *is a classic piece of literature. Studying either or both can be very stimulating. It is difficult to say that the intellectual rewards will be greater for Scott than Sue, or vice versa.*

3. Based on what you saw in the episodes, which teacher do you believe has the most difficult job? Explain why you think so.

As with many topics and issues in education, people's opinions with respect to a question such as this one will vary. For instance, attracting and maintaining the attention of small children is difficult, so in this regard Rebecca's job is demanding. With respect to planning, Scott probably had the most difficult job, since he had to gather the funnels and balls, distribute them to the students efficiently so time wasn't wasted, and then teach a challenging topic. Sue's job was probably least physically demanding, since she had no materials to gather. All three teachers' jobs were demanding in the sense that they needed to think clearly about their goals and the means of helping students reach the goals.

4. For which teacher is knowledge of content most important? Pedagogical content knowledge? General pedagogical knowledge? Knowledge of learners and learning? Explain why you think so.

Knowledge of content was probably most important for both Scott and Sue. He needed to thoroughly understand Bernoulli's Principle, and Sue needed to have a deep understanding of the novel. Pedagogical content knowledge was most important for Scott. He understood that he could illustrate Bernoulli's Principle by having the students blow over and between the papers and blow through the funnel. General pedagogical knowledge was important for all three teachers. All needed to be skilled in organizing their lessons, using their time efficiently, and questioning. Knowledge of learners and learning was also important for all three teachers. Rebecca needed to understand the way kindergartners think, Scott needed to realize that, for middle school students, concrete examples are essential for comprehending a challenging topic, and Sue needed to know that her students had to be in active roles to learn as much as possible about the novel.

5. How much autonomy do you believe each teacher had in designing and conducting his or her lesson? Explain why you think so.

Each teacher had virtually total autonomy in designing and conducting his or her lesson. Selecting the topics and deciding how the topics would be taught were decisions the teachers alone made.

6. To what extent do you believe each teacher demonstrated the characteristics of a professional? Explain your assessment.

Based on the evidence we have from the video episodes, the teachers demonstrated the characteristics of professionals. They demonstrated specialized knowledge, each was a licensed teacher (although we don't have evidence for that conclusion from the video), and most importantly, they demonstrated a great deal of decision making and autonomy in their teaching.

Video Discussion Questions and Feedback

(These video clips are available on the text's Companion Website. See the *Video Discussion* section in the Media Guide for a complete description of these videos.)

1. Dr. Urie Triesman is a professor of mathematics at the University of Texas at Austin and Director of the Charles A. Dana Center for Math and Science Education. His work focuses on school reform and ways that schools can be helped to improve. He is concerned that individual school and teacher autonomy often conflicts with centralized testing programs. What does Dr. Triesman believe is the proper balance between these two forces? Do you think centralized testing jeopardizes school and teacher autonomy? Explain why you believe it does or does not.

Dr. Triesman believes that strong central control through testing produces accountability. However, he believes that individual schools should have freedom to decide how to meet these external standards.

2. Theodore Sizer is the director of the Coalition for Effective Schools, which attempts to reform high schools. As we've seen in this chapter, testing is being proposed as a major reform tool. In Dr. Sizer's opinion what questions should people ask when they consider using standardized tests to assess student learning? Do you think Dr. Sizer's cautions are justified?

Dr. Sizer advocates constant assessment but cautions against the mindless use of standardized tests. When considering using standardized tests, teachers should ask whether they measure deep understanding or trivial knowledge. In addition, teachers should ask whether the tests measure important knowledge and whether they are effective in predicting students' future performance in an area.

Self-Assessment Questions
(Note: Students have access to these questions and their feedback on the text's Companion Website.)

1. You're a sixth-grade math teacher in your first year of teaching. Of the following the best example of an intrinsic reward for you is likely to be
   a.   a salary supplement for sponsoring a computer club.
   b.   the fact that you get to decide how you want to teach each of your topics.
   c.   a 2-week winter holiday vacation.
   d.   looking forward to tenure after your third year of teaching.

2. You're a fifth-grade teacher in your fourth year of teaching. Which of the following is the best example of an intellectual reward in teaching?
   a.   Receiving tenure after you complete your third year of teaching
   b.   Having your students bring in information on global warming that they've gathered for a project on environmental awareness
   c.   Having one of your students come up to you and say, "I used to hate science, but now I really like it."
   d.   Receiving a salary supplement for being a grade-level chairperson

3. Which of the following is closest to the average yearly teacher salary in the United States?
   a. $30,000
   b. $40,000
   c. $50,000
   d. $60,000

4. You're anticipating your first job. Of the following which is closest to the salary you can expect in your first year?
   a. $20,000
   b. $25,000
   c. $30,000
   d. $35,000

5. Which of the following is the most commonly cited reason that teachers prefer to teach in a private school rather than a public school?
   a.   Smaller classes
   b.   Higher salaries
   c.   A larger administrative staff (that provides more support)
   d.   Less parental interference

6. Which of the following is considered to be a characteristic of a profession?
   a.   A wide range of generalized knowledge
   b.   Certification based on life experiences
   c.   Autonomy on the job
   d.   Supervision and support by superiors

7. Understanding that middle school students need concrete examples to best understand the topics they study is best described as
   a.   knowledge of content.
   b.   pedagogical content knowledge.
   c.   general pedagogical knowledge.
   d.   knowledge of learners and learning.

8. Consider the following statement: "The educator strives to help each student realize his or her potential as a worthy and effective member of society."

Of the following which is the best description of the statement?
   a.   It is a statement describing the characteristics of teachers as professionals.
   b.   It is a statement describing the intrinsic rewards in teaching.
   c.   It is a statement describing a principle from a Code of Ethics.
   d.   It is a statement describing the autonomy of teachers as they practice their craft.

Use the following vignette for Items 9 and 10:

Eighth graders at Landrom Middle School have to pass a state-mandated test called the Basic Skills Assessment Inventory (BSAI) which focuses on reading, writing, and math. Students are not allowed to begin high school until they meet a minimum level on the test.

9. Of the following the BSAI is best described as a(n)
   a.   high-stakes test.
   b.   educational reform.
   c.   type of accountability.
   d.   prescribed standard.

10. Teachers at Landrom are responsible for students' performance on the BSAI. Holding teachers responsible in this way best illustrates
   a.   standards-based education.
   b.   teacher autonomy.
   c.   educational reform.
   d.   accountability.

Self-Assessment Feedback

1.	b	Being able to make your own decisions about how you will teach the topics you want your students to understand is rewarding. Each of the other choices is an extrinsic reward.
2.	b	Receiving tenure (choice a) and a salary supplement (choice d) are extrinsic rewards, and having a student tell you that this is the first time she ever liked science (choice c) is an emotional reward.
3.	b	The average teacher salary in the United States in 2000–2001 was $43,250, so $40,000 is the closest approximation of the choices given.
4.	c	The average beginning salary for teachers in the United States ($28,986) is closest to $30,000.
5.	a	Smaller classes are commonly cited as a reason people choose to teach in private schools. Salaries in private schools tend to be lower (choice b), the administrative staffs tend to be smaller (choice c), and parental involvement is greater in private schools (choice d).
6.	c	Autonomy is one characteristic of a profession. Professional knowledge is specialized as opposed to general (choice a), licensure is based on specific training (choice b), and supervision by a superior is the opposite of autonomy (choice d).
7.	d	Understanding that students need concrete examples is an example of knowledge of learners and learning.
8.	c	This is a principle from teachers' code of ethics.
9.	a	Since students are not allowed to begin high school until they reach a minimum score on the BSAI, it is a high-stakes test.
10.	d	Making teachers responsible for student performance on the BSAI illustrates accountability.

PRAXIS Practice: Questions and Feedback

Student Instructions: Analyze the case in terms of the following characteristics of professionalism. In your analysis identify specific parts of the case that related to professionalism, and explain the connection.

1. Specialized Body of Knowledge

A specialized body of knowledge was suggested by Marissa's comment about the value of research in her professional decision making.

2. Training for Licensure

Marissa's studies were aimed at obtaining an additional endorsement or area of certification.

3. Decision Making

Marissa decided what was best for her students based upon her knowledge of their needs (context) and her understanding of the research about how students learn.

4. Reflection

After taking classes, Marissa thought about her reading curriculum and wondered if it was meeting the needs of her students.

5. Autonomy

Though Marissa was given a reading curriculum to implement, she chose to adapt it to better meet the needs of her students.

6. Professional Ethics

A major component of professional ethics is commitment to students. Marissa evidenced this commitment by placing their learning above district guidelines. While perhaps controversial and even potentially professionally damaging, her actions say a great deal about her commitment to the students she works with.

Useful Website Addresses

Web Links for Chapter Terms

curriculum: http://www.ascd.org/

ethics: http://www.nea.org/aboutnea/code.html

high-stakes tests
http://www.aera.net/about/policy/stakes.htm
http://www.apa.org/pubinfo/testing.html
http://www.wrightslaw.com/info/highstak.index.htm
http://www.aasa.org/publications/sa/2000_12/contents.htm

merit pay
http://www.educationpolicy.org/MLcolumn/MLcolumn-071700.htm

http://www.education-world.com/a_issues/issues099.shtml
http://www.edweek.org/ew/newstory.cfm?slug=42neatest_web.h20

professional portfolio
http://teacher.scholastic.com/professional/futureteachers/professional_port.htm
http://www.nbpts.org/standards/index.cfm
http://electronicportfolios.com/

professionalism
http://wakingbear.com/profess.htm
http://www.renaissance.com.pk/jlauref972.html
http://www.nbpts.org/about/coreprops.cfm

reflection
http://www.ed.gov/databases/ERIC_Digests/ed346319.html
http://www.ncpublicschools.org/pbl/pblreflect.htm
http://www.ncpublicschools.org/mentoring_novice_teachers/downloads/module5.pdf

reforms
http://www.goodschools.gwu.edu/
http://www.ed.gov/nclb/landing.jhtml?src=ln

standards
http://www.educatorsresources.com/webpages/certif.html
http://www.ed.gov/pubs/IASA/newsletters/standards/pt1.html

standards by state: http://edstandards.org/Standards.html#State

standards-based education
http://cresst96.cse.ucla.edu/products/newsletters/policypaper.pdf
http://www.nbpts.org/

highly qualified teachers
http://www2.edtrust.org/NR/rdonlyres/C638111D-04E3-4C0D-9F68-20E7009498A6/0/tellingthetruthteachers.pdf

Web Links for "Teaching in an Era of Reform"

Accountability

Adequate Yearly Progress: http://www.ed.gov/nclb/accountability/ayp/edpicks.jhtml?src=ln

Getting Results: http://www.ed.gov/nclb/accountability/results/edpicks.jhtml?src=ln

Achievement Gap: http://www.ed.gov/nclb/accountability/achieve/edpicks.jhtml?src=ln

State Improvement Lists: http://www.ed.gov/nclb/accountability/state/edpicks.jhtml?src=ln

State Standards: http://www.ed.gov/nclb/accountability/standards/edpicks.jhtml?src=ln

Accountability Gains: http://www.educationnext.org/20022/9.html

Accountability in Education: What Can Be Learned from History?:
http://www.pathsoflearning.org/library/accountability.cfm

High-Stakes Testing

AERA Position Statement Concerning High-Stakes Testing in PreK–12 Education
http://www.aera.net/about/policy/stakes.htm

Alliance for Childhood: High-stakes Testing Summary
http://www.allianceforchildhood.net/news/exec_summary_histake_test.htm

Appropriate Use of High-Stakes Testing in Our Nation's Schools: http://www.apa.org/pubinfo/testing.html

High-stakes: Will Misguided Tests Use Doom the Standards Movement?
http://www.aasa.org/publications/sa/2000_12/contents.htm

International Reading Association on High-stakes Testing: http://www.reading.org/positions/high_stakes.html

National Council of Teachers of English Urging Reconsideration of High-stakes Testing
http://www.ncte.org/resolutions/highstakes002000.shtml

National Council of Teachers of Mathematics on High-stakes Testing
http://www.nctm.org/about/position_statements/highstakes.htm

National Forum Policy Statement: High-stakes Testing: http://www.mgforum.org/highstakes/page1.htm

Position Statements on High-stakes Testing: http://www.mncare.homestead.com/Resolutions.html

The Use of Tests as Part of High-Stakes Decision Making for Students: A Resource Guide for Educators and Policy
Makers: http://www.ed.gov/offices/OCR/testing/index1.html

Wrightslaw High-stakes Testing: http://www.wrightslaw.com/info/highstak.index.htm

Web Links for "Exploring Diversity: Cultural Minorities and High-Stakes Testing"

Standards, Tests, and Civil Rights: http://www.edweek.org/ew/ew_printstory.cfm?slug=11taylor.h20

The Impact of High-stakes Testing Policies on Minority and Disadvantaged Students
http://www.aypf.org/forumbriefs/2000/fb010700.htm

High-Stakes Tests May Worsen Educational Outcomes for Minorities and Girls
http://www.gse.harvard.edu/news/features/her10112001.html

Time Out from Testing: http://www.timeoutfromtesting.org/articles.php

Additional Chapter Web Links

Certification

Links to State Education Agencies: http://www.ncate.org/standard/m_stds.htm

Educator's Resources: Certification Information: http://www.educatorsresources.com/webpages/certif.html
Certification for Practicing Teachers: National Board for Professional Teaching Standards : http://www.nbpts.org/
Educational Testing Service: http://www.ets.org

Professional Organizations

American Alliance for Health, Physical Education, Recreation and Dance: http://www.aahperd.org/
American Association of School Librarians: http://www.ala.org/
American Association of Teachers of French: http://aatf.utsa.edu/
American Association of Teachers of German: http://www.aatg.org/
The American Council of the Teaching of Foreign Language: http://www.actfl.org/
American Federation of Teachers: http://www.aft.org/
Association for the Advancement of Computing in Education: http://curry.edschool.virginia.edu/aace/site/
Association for Career and Technical Education: http://www. acteonline.org/
Association for Education Communications and Technology: http://www.aect.org
Association of American Geographers: http://www.aag.org/
Association of Physics Teachers: http://www.aapt.org/aaptgeneral/geneinfo.html
Center for Civic Education : http://www.civiced.org/
The Council for Exceptional Children: http://www.cec.sped.org
The International Reading Association: http://www.ira.org
International Society for Technology in Education: http://www.iste.org.
Music Educators National Association: http://www.menc.org/
Music Teachers National Association: http://www.mtna.org/
The National Art Education Association: http://www.naea-reston.org/
The National Association for the Education of Young Children: http://www.naeyc.org/
National Association of Biology Teachers: http://www.nabt.org/
National Board for Professional Teaching Standards : http://www.nbpts.org
The National Council for the Social Studies: http://www.ncss.org
The National Council of Teachers of Mathematics: http://www.nctm.org
The National Council of Teachers of English: http://www.ncte.org
The National Dance Association: http://www.aahperd.org/nda/nda-main.html
National Education Association: http://www.nea.org/
The National Science Teachers Association: http://www.nsta.org

Professionalism

American Federation of Teachers: http://www.aft.org/
American Society for Ethics in Education: http://www.edethics.org/
Center for Education Reform: http://edreform.com/
MCREL Standards: http://www.mcrel.org/topics/topics.asp?topicsid=14
National Education Association Code of Ethics for the Profession: http://www.nea.org/aboutnea/code.html
National Teachers Hall of Fame: http://www.nthf.org
National Assessment of Educational Progress: The Nation's Report Card
http://nces.ed.gov/nationsreportcard/site/home.asp
On the Commitment to Professionalism in Teaching: http://www.nbpts.org/standards/
Teaching as a Career: http://www.aft.org/career/index.html
What to Look for in a Teacher Preparation Program: http://www.ncate.org/future/lookfor.htm

Teacher Quality

Eliminating Barriers to Improving Teaching: http://www.ed.gov/inits/teachers/barriers2000/Barriers2000.pdf

National Center for Educational Statistics: Teacher Quality: http://nces.ed.gov/fastfacts/display.asp?id=58
National Council for Teacher Quality: http://www.nctq.org/
No Child Left Behind Act of 2001: http://www.ed.gov/offices/OESE/esea/index.html
Promising Practices: New Ways to Improve Teacher Quality: http://www.ed.gov/pubs/PromPractice/index.html
Teacher Quality: http://www.edexcellence.net/topics/teachers.html
Teacher Quality and Student Achievement: A Review of State Policy Evidence: http://olam.ed.asu.edu/epaa/v8n1/
Teacher Quality: A Report on the Preparation and Qualifications of Public School Teachers
http://nces.ed.gov/pubsearch/pubsinfo.asp?pubid=1999080

Chapter 2
The Teaching Profession

Overview

In Chapter 2 we analyze teaching through the lens of time, comparing elementary and secondary schools, as well as schools in other countries. The chapter also discusses the complexities and multiple roles of teaching and analyzes the current teaching force.

Chapter Goals

This chapter examines

- What it is like to be a teacher
- The different roles that teachers perform
- Who your colleagues will be
- How increased emphasis on professionalism will affect your life as a teacher

Chapter Outline

I. Teaching: A Time Perspective
- A.   The School Year–Lengthening the School Year
- B.   Teaching in an Era of Reform: The Modified Calendar Issue
- C.   The School Week
- D.   A Typical Work Day–Class Scheduling
- E.   Grade Level Differences
- F.   Comparisons with Other Countries

II. Decision Making: Responding to the Complexities of Teaching
- A.   Characteristics of Classrooms
  - 1.   Multidimensional
  - 2.   Simultaneous
  - 3.   Immediate
  - 4.   Unpredictable
  - 5.   Public
- B.   The Multiple Roles of Teaching
  - 1.   Caring Professional
    - a.   Communicating Caring.
  - 2.   Creator of Productive Learning Environments
  - 3.   Ambassador to the Public
    - a.   Barriers to Parental Involvement
    - b.   Strategies for Involving Parents
  - 4.   Collaborative Colleague
  - 5.   Learner and Reflective Practitioner

III. Who Are Your Colleagues?
- A.   Gender
- B.   Age
- C.   Race/ethnicity
- D.   Exploring Diversity: Minority Teachers and What They Bring to the Profession
  - 1.   Minorities as Role Models
  - 2.   Minorities as Effective Instructors

18

       3.   Minority Teachers Bring Unique Perspectives to the Profession
    E.   New Teachers–What Happens to New Teachers?
IV. Decision Making: Defining Yourself as a Professional

Transparencies

T2.1 (Table 2.1) How Teachers Spend Their Time
T2.2 (Table 2.2) Public School Teachers' Gender by Assignment

Teaching Suggestions

I. Teaching: A Time Perspective

The purpose of this section is to help students analyze teaching using a time perspective.

- **Ask students to write down their schedules for a typical week. How much time is devoted to studies? to work? to play? Use this to initiate a discussion on teachers' work weeks.**

- **Display *Transparency 2.1* "How Teachers Spend Their Time." *Discussion Question #1* asks how students would modify this if they could.**

- **To focus students on the topic of year-round schools, ask if any have attended these schools and what kind of experience they had. Also ask them to discuss the advantages and disadvantages of year-round schools from both the students' perspective and the teachers' perspective.**

- **Discussion Question #2 asks students to judge the relative merits of different time alternatives. Ask students to volunteer their own personal experiences with these different options. This topic works well as a small-groups-report-to-whole class activity in which the different groups list advantages and disadvantages for each.**

- **Going into Schools #1 asks students to interview teachers about local experiments with time and scheduling. Have students report their findings to the whole class.**

- **Going into Schools #2 asks students to interview teachers about how their school day differs from *Transparency 2.1* "How Teachers Spend Their Time." Have students report their findings, and compare results across grade levels and districts.**

II. Decision Making: Responding to the Complexities of Teaching

- **To provide students with direct experience in this area at the beginning of this section, ask them to evaluate the different options that Ken. Ask them to select the two or three best and worst and explain their choices . Have them do this in small groups and report back to the whole class.**

- **Show the video segment "Classroom Windows: The Real World of Teaching" contained in the *Classroom Windows* video for Chapter 1 that accompanies this text. The video contains segments of teachers at three levels–elementary, middle school, and high school. Ask students to identify instances in each lesson that illustrate the following characteristics of classrooms: multidimensional, simultaneous, immediate, unpredictable, and public. Does the prevalence of these dimensions change with grade level?**

- *Discussion Question #3* asks whether the complexities of teaching are likely to become greater or less in the future.

- *Journal Starter #1* asks students to analyze themselves in terms of these complexities of teaching.

- In terms of the multiple roles of teaching, ask students to identify a teacher in their past who was caring. How did these teachers demonstrate caring? List the different ways, and ask the class to identify patterns by grouping common items.

- *Discussion Question #4* asks whether teacher caring is more important at some levels than others. Ask how outward manifestations of caring might be different at different grade levels.

- Show the video segment "Classroom Windows: The Real World of Teaching" from Chapter 1, and ask students to identify how each teacher displayed caring.

- The *Reflect on This* section that appears in the book's Website (www.prenhall.com/kauchak) describes a situation in which eliciting parent involvement is a problem. Use this case and the questions that follow it in small groups, which can then report to the whole class.

- *Journal Starter #2* asks students to analyze their own personal strengths and weaknesses in terms of these multiple roles.

IV. Who Are Your Colleagues?

The purpose of this section is to help students understand themselves in relation to the rest of the teaching workforce they'll be joining.

- Display *Transparency 2.2* "Public School Teachers' Gender by Assignment." *Increasing Understanding 2.9* asks how prospective teachers could use this information to strategically locate a teaching position.

- To encourage students to personalize the information, ask whether age or gender influences the effectiveness of a teacher (research suggests neither does).

- The Video Discussion featuring Urie Triesman has some interesting perspectives on new teachers' professional development.

Journal Starters

1. Encourage students to think about the complexities of teaching in terms of themselves and their own personal strengths and weaknesses: Which of the complexities of teaching will be most challenging for you? Which will be least challenging? Why? How good are you at doing multiple things at any one time? Do you enjoy juggling multiple tasks? Where in your past experience have you done this before? Were you successful? What implications do your responses have for your future success in and satisfaction with teaching?

2. Encourage students to think about themselves in terms of the multiple roles of teaching: Which of the multiple roles of teaching will be most rewarding for you? Which will be most challenging? How do your responses to these questions reflect your personal strengths and weaknesses? How do they relate to where you plan to teach and what you plan to teach?

Increasing Understanding: Questions and Feedback

2.1

In what kind of districts or schools are you most likely to encounter year-round schools? Why? What implications might these have for you personally?

2.1

Year-round schools are most likely to be found in school districts with growing student populations. There will be jobs in districts like these, but you may be asked to teach year round.

2.2

The time figures in Table 2.1 are averages for all teachers. How might these figures change for teachers working in learning, enrichment, or pull-out programs? How might they change for teachers in self-contained classrooms? What implications might this have for a person considering different types of teaching positions?

2.2

Teachers working in learning, enrichment, and pull-out programs would probably have less time working with students and more time spent in coordinating activities with peers and doing desk and routine work. Teachers in self-contained classrooms would probably have more time to work with students and less time interacting with peers. Students should think about these differences and decide whether they are important to them.

2.3

Reexamine Table 2.1, which describes how teachers spend their time. Which of the time categories are subject to the dimension of immediacy? Explain.

2.3

Virtually all of the categories involving working with students are subject to immediacy. Students typically require constant and immediate attention from teachers; this is one factor that makes teaching so draining. Peer interactions can sometimes require immediacy (i.e., if an emergency arises), but peer interactions usually can be scheduled in advance.

2.4

How does the caring dimension of teaching relate to how teachers spend their time during the day? See Table 2.1. In terms of this table, what are some different ways that teachers show they care? Explain.

2.4

Teachers can show caring in several ways: through their immediate interactions with students; through working with peers on students' problems; and also at their desks as they take extra time to grade and comment on student work.

2.5

Identify at least two teacher roles that Tangia demonstrated in working with her students.

2.5

By attempting to work with all of her students, Tangia displayed characteristics of a caring professional. She also attempted to create a productive learning environment.

2.6

How was caring illustrated in this teaching episode?

2.6

Caring was best illustrated in her attention to individual students during interactive teaching. She created space for the one student to respond and then called on a second student who had waited patiently.

2.7

Refer again to Table 2.1. Identify an additional barrier to increased home–school cooperation. What are some things teachers can do to overcome this barrier?

2.7

From a teacher perspective time is a major barrier to increased home–school cooperation. When teachers are interacting with students, it is difficult to meet with parents or caregivers. A major way teachers can increase their accessibility is letting parents know when teachers are available during desk and consultation periods.

2.8

How does reflection relate to the different dimensions of professionalism–which include a specialized body of knowledge, extended training for licensure, autonomy, and ethical standards–that were discussed in Chapter 1?

2.8

Effective reflection requires professional knowledge; you can't think in a conceptual vacuum. The concepts you learn during your teacher education program–an extended period of training for licensure–will provide you with the conceptual tools to reflect on your practice. Reflection also provides you with opportunities to think about and incorporate ethical standards in your teaching. Finally, autonomy implies freedom. But it also requires thoughtful professional monitoring–an important aspect of reflection.

2.9

How could a beginning teacher use the information in Table 2.2 to maximize the possibility of obtaining a teaching position? What are the advantages and disadvantages of this strategy?

2.9

Prospective teachers can use gender imbalances to increase their prospects for a teaching position. For example, males might seek an elementary education position, and females might look for a social studies position. However, this shouldn't be the primary factor in deciding on the level or teaching area to pursue. Other factors such as interest in working with different-age students as well as interest in a content area are probably more important.

2.10

What are some possible reasons for the decline in the percentage of minority teachers? Is the percentage of minority teachers likely to increase or decrease in the future? Why?

2.10

Probably the most powerful force working against recruiting more minorities into teaching is increased opportunities in higher-paying business jobs. This problem is likely to increase in the future as more corporations, seeking to diversify their work force, become willing to pay top dollar for minority applicants.

Reflect on This: Questions and Feedback
(These can also be found on the Companion Website: www.prenhall.com/kauchak .)

Parent–Teacher Conference

1. What are some possible reasons that more parents didn't come to talk with you?

A number of factors may have influenced attendance rates. Since the school was inner city, economic, cultural, and language barriers may have been factors. In addition, student achievement may have been a factor since few of the parents of your C, D, or F students came.

2. In hindsight what might you have done differently prior to the conferences?

You might have enlisted the aid of your ESL students to help you translate your invitation into students' home languages. You also might have established home-school links earlier, rewarding students who brought back invitations that were signed by parents.

3. What can you do now to establish better linkages to your students' homes?

Try, try, and try again. Some possible strategies include calling homes, home visits, and notes to parents in students' home languages. You might also ask experienced teachers what works for them.

Classroom Windows: Questions and Feedback

Working with Parents: A Parent–Teacher Conference

1. What did DeVonne do to prepare for the conference? Why was this important?

DeVonne gathered all the information she had with respect to the student's performance, which was to be the topic of the conference. She went into the conference armed with factual data.

2. In an attempt to break the ice in the conference, what did DeVonne do to put the parent at ease?

DeVonne thanked the parent for coming in, and she began the discussion by saying some positive things about the student. Beginning a conference on a positive note is important in setting the tone for a conference.

3. When the parent became somewhat defensive and attempted to divert responsibility for the problems from the student to DeVonne, what did DeVonne do in response?

DeVonne used her factual data to support the conclusions she had made about the student. Having data available, that can be shared with parents is probably the most effective mechanism for dealing with parents who are defensive or even potentially hostile.

4. Offer an assessment of DeVonne's handling of the conference. Provide a rationale for your assessment based on your observations of the episode.

DeVonne handled the conference well. She planned carefully, she had ample data to support her conclusions, and she maintained a positive tone throughout the conference.

Video Discussion Questions and Feedback

1. Dr. Urie Triesman is a professor of mathematics at the University of Texas at Austin and Director of the Charles A. Dana Center for Math and Science Education. He believes teachers and their professional development are central to school reform. What does Dr. Triesman believe are some concrete things teachers can do within their own schools to further their professional development? Which do you think have the most potential for furthering teachers' professional development?

Dr. Triesman believes that teachers should continually think about the quality of the learning in their school and classroom. This means that teachers must be learners and must participate with other teachers in their school in a community of learners. To do this, young teachers need to find excellent teachers as mentors who can help them with their professional development.

2. As we saw in this chapter, involving parents is important for school success. How does Dr. Triesman believe that parents can be enlisted as political allies in school reform efforts? Which of these strategies would be most useful to you as a teacher?

First, Dr. Triesman believes that all parents need to be informed about their schools. In addition, schools need to take an active role in recruiting parents as helpers and contributors in schools and classrooms and should make every effort to get as many parents as possible involved in their children's education.

3. Dr. John Goodlad is professor emeritus and codirector of the Center for Renewal at the University of Washington and president of the Independent Institute for Educational Inquiry. He believes that caring is essential to effective teaching. What does Dr. Goodlad feel are some concrete ways in which teachers can structure their classrooms to facilitate the development of caring relationships? Which of these strategies will be most useful to you as a teacher?

First, Dr. Goodlad recommends structuring the classroom so that teachers have an opportunity to get to know each student one to one and face to face. Also, he recommends sharing programs that allow each child to tell about themselves, their feelings, and their fears. These strategies are harder to implement at the secondary level, but even there teachers can take time at the beginning of the term to let students tell about themselves.

Self-Assessment Questions
(Note: Students have access to these questions and their feedback on the text's Companion Website.)

1. Which of the following is **NOT** an obstacle to year-round schooling?
   a. Money needed to redesign schools
   b. Teachers wanting summers free for other pursuits
   c. Teachers' unions
   d. Parents

2. In terms of teachers' work patterns, which is most accurate?
   a. Elementary teachers work longer hours and get paid more.
   b. Elementary teachers work fewer hours and get paid less.
   c. Elementary and secondary teachers work the same number of hours per week.
   d. Secondary teachers work more but get paid less.

3. Of a typical teacher's workday which dimension occupies the least amount of time?
   a. Instruction
   b. Interactions with colleagues
   c. Desk and routine work
   d. Testing and monitoring

4. Compared to their Asian counterparts, U.S. teachers
   a. spend more time teaching and less time governing their schools.
   b. work longer school days but get paid more.
   c. spend less time teaching but spend more time governing their schools.
   d. work shorter hours but are paid less.

5. Block schedules are becoming popular because they
   a. minimize disruptions and provide increased instructional time.
   b. create opportunities for teachers to get to know their students better.
   c. make integrating different curriculum areas easier.
   d. decrease teachers' planning loads.

6. A teacher says, "This test is important so you all need to study for it." In the silence after this statement the whole class can hear one student say, "Who cares?" Which of the following dimensions of classroom life applies **LEAST** to the teacher's situation?
   a. Unpredictable
   b. Immediate
   c. Public
   d. Multidimensional

7. Which of the following is **NOT** a benefit of increased parental involvement?
    a.   Better attendance rates
    b.   Decreased teacher workloads
    c.   Higher academic achievement
    d.   More positive student attitudes

8. Which of the following is **NOT** a barrier to greater parental involvement?
    a.   Culture
    b.   Economic concerns
    c.   Language
    d.   Politics

9. Which of the following is **NOT** a factor in the increased demand for teachers in the next ten years?
    a.   Attempts to decrease class size
    b.   Increased expenditures for education
    c.   Increased standards for teachers
    d.   Increased school-age populations

10. New teachers are more likely to be
    a.   female and less likely to be married.
    b.   male and more likely to be married.
    c.   female and more likely to be minority.
    d.   male and less likely to be minority.

Self-Assessment Feedback

1. c   Teachers' unions have not been a major obstacle to year-round schools.
2. b   Secondary teachers work longer hours because of extracurricular activities, for which they are paid an additional stipend.
3. d   Instruction (27.5%), interactions with colleagues (25.6%), desk and routine work (20.0%) all occupy a greater percentage of a teacher's day than testing and monitoring (10.1%).
4. a   U.S. teachers spend more time teaching and are less involved in school governance.
5. a   Block schedules are popular because they minimize disruptions and provide increased amounts of continuous instructional time.
6. d   This situation is least multidimensional because the teacher is not attempting to do a number of things at once.
7. b   Increased parental involvement typically requires more teacher time and effort, but the benefits are well worth the effort.
8. d   Culture, economic concerns, and language are all potential barriers to increased parental involvement.
9. c   Increased standards for teachers is not a cause for increased teacher demand.
10. a   New teachers are more likely to be female and not married.

PRAXIS Practice: Questions and Feedback

1. Identify at least three characteristics of classrooms that were illustrated in the case study. Which of the characteristics was most prominently illustrated?

Each of the characteristics of classrooms was illustrated in the case study with unpredictable being the most prominently illustrated. Judy, of course, didn't anticipate the balloon blowing off the top of the bottle (she used too much vinegar and baking soda). The event was also immediate and public. She had to immediately respond to the event, and the students observed to see how she would handle it. Being a pro, she responded with humor, and she turned the entire incident into a learning experience. Having the students stop their writing, take a bathroom break, be seated and ready to start science in 5 minutes, and Judy's having her demonstration ready illustrate the multidimensional and simultaneous natures of classrooms.

2. Describe one way that Judy demonstrated the teaching role of caring professional.

Judy demonstrated the role of caring professional by spending extra time each morning with Cassie and Manuel to help them develop their language skills and keep up with the rest of the class.

3. Identify two examples from the case study that illustrated Judy in the role of creator of productive learning environments.

First, Judy's classroom environment was orderly. For example, the students took their bathroom break and were back in their seats and ready to begin in five minutes. Second, Judy had an effective learning activity (in spite of her unpredictable event). She first reviewed the concept of physical change, and she then used her demonstration to illustrate chemical change. She actively involved the students, and she emphasized that reasons for answers were as important as the answers themselves.

4. Describe how Judy demonstrated the role of ambassador to the public.

Judy's letter to parents illustrates her understanding of the need to be an ambassador to the public. Most teachers send a letter home at the beginning of the year, but Judy went two steps further. First, her letter told parents what her plans were for the second semester, and second, she had a Spanish version of the letter for her Spanish-speaking parents.

5. Describe how Judy demonstrated the teaching role of collaborative colleague.

Judy demonstrated the role of collaborative colleague in her grade-level meeting. When Kim was critical of the proposed curriculum, Judy offered a compromise that allowed them to use the curriculum because of its emphasis on problem solving while still providing the practice in basic skills that the team agreed was needed.

Useful Web Site Addresses
Web Links for Chapter Terms

What happens to new teachers?
http://www.ed.gov/pubs/FirstYear/index.html
http://www.educationworld.com/a_curr/curr152.shtml
http://www.rcdaschools.org/newteach.htm

teacher satisfaction
http://www.edfacilities.org/pubs/teachersurvey.pdf
http://www.tppf.org/education/sacont/sacont.htm
http://education.guardian.co.uk/teachershortage/story/0,7348,873823,00.html

alternating-day block schedule
http://www.menc.org/publication/articles/block/blocksch.htm
http://wilsontxt.hwwilson.com/pdffull/03461/LBVG7/LFT.pdf
http://www.ncssfl.org/block.htm

block scheduling
http://www.ericfacility.net/ericdigests/ed393156.html
http://education.umn.edu/carei/Blockscheduling/default.html
http://www.education-world.com/a_admin/admin029.shtml
http://www.educationworld.com/a_issues/issues/issues057.shtml

four-by-four block schedule
http://www.menc.org/publication/articles/block/blocksch.htm
http://www.aft.org/publications/american_teacher/sept99/block.html

modified school calendar
http://www.educationworld.com/parents/issues/trends.shtml#calendar
http://www.educationworld.com/a_issues/issues056.shtml

overlapping
http://cty.jhu.edu/teaching/classroom/preventing%20misbehavior.htm
http://inset.ul.ie/cm/prev/alert.htm
http://www.pecentral.org/climate/april99article.html

productive learning environment
http://www.learning.gov.ab.ca/ClassSize/sec4c.asp

reflective practitioner
http://www.ncpublicschools.org/mentoring_novice_teachers/downloads/module5.pdf
http://educ.queensu.ca/~russellt/howteach/schon87.htm

withitness
http://cty.jhu.edu/teaching/classroom/preventing%20misbehavior.htm
http://inset.ul.ie/cm/prev/alert.htm
http://www.pecentral.org/climate/april99article.html

Web Links for "Teaching in an Era of Reform: The Modified Calendar Issue"

Alternative School Calendars: Smart Idea or Senseless Experiment?
http://www.educationworld.com/a_issues/issues056.shtml

Around the Block: The Benefits and Challenges of Block Scheduling
http://www.educationworld.com/a_issues/issues/issues057.shtml

Background on Block Scheduling and Foreign Languages: http://www.ncssfl.org/block.htm

Block Scheduling: http://www.ericfacility.net/ericdigests/ed393156.html

Block Scheduling: A Solution or a Problem?: http://www.education-world.com/a_admin/admin029.shtml

Block Scheduling: Look Before You Leap: http://www.aft.org/publications/american_teacher/sept99/block.html

Center for Applied Research and Educational Improvement: Block Scheduling
http://education.umn.edu/carei/Blockscheduling/default.html

Education World: School Calendar: http://www.educationworld.com/parents/issues/trends.shtml#calendar

How an Alternating-Day Schedule Empowers Teachers
http://wilsontxt.hwwilson.com/pdffull/03461/LBVG7/LFT.pdf

Scheduling Resources: http://www.menc.org/publication/articles/block/blocksch.htm

Web Links for "Exploring Diversity: Minority Teachers and What They Bring to the Profession"

Digest of Education Statistics Tables and Figures 2002: http://nces.ed.gov/programs/digest/

The Importance of Diversity: http://www.recruitingteachers.org/findteachers/diversity.html

Increasing Minority Participation in the Teaching Profession
http://www.ed.gov/databases/ERIC_Digests/ed270527.html

Latino and Minority-Language Teacher Projects: http://www-bcf.usc.edu/~cmmr/LTP.html

Recruiting African American Teachers Requires Collaboration, Cooperation
http://www.blackissues.com/083001/dlstword.cfm

Recruiting and Retaining Minority Teachers: Programs That Work!
http://www.educationworld.com/a_admin/admin213.shtml

Recruiting Teachers for the 21st Century: The Foundation for Educational Equity
http://www.teachingquality.org/resources/pdfs/Recruiting%20Teachers%20for%20the%2021st%20Century.pdf

Recruitment and Retention of Minority Teachers in Vocational Education
http://www.ed.gov/databases/ERIC_Digests/ed368889.html

Supply and Demand of Teachers of Color: http://www.ericfacility.net/databases/ERIC_Digests/ed390875.html

Teachers for Today and Tomorrow: http://www.ascd.org/readingroom/edlead/0105/bintrim.html

The Teacher–Student Mismatch: http://www.ascd.org/publications/ed_lead/199904/latham.html

Additional Chapter Links

The Teaching Profession

Teacher Talk
http://education.indiana.edu/cas/tt/tthmpg.html
This site contains basic teaching tips for inexperienced teachers, ideas that can be immediately implemented in the classroom, new ideas in teaching methodologies for all teachers, and a forum for experienced teachers to share their expertise and topics with colleagues around the world.

Teachers Helping Teachers
http://www.pacificnet.net/~mandel//index.html
This site connects you to other teachers for help on lesson plans, professional planning, and similar types of issues.

Gallup Organization
http://www.gallup.com/
You'll find valuable information about teachers' as well as the public's attitudes toward education.

The Association for Supervision and Curriculum Development
http://www.ascd.org
This site contains a number of valuable resources for beginning as well as experienced teachers.

Job Satisfaction Among America's Teachers
http://nces.ed.gov/pubs97/97471.html
This report by the National Center for Educational Statistics investigates factors that influence teachers' job satisfaction.

Chapter 3
Learner Diversity:
Differences in Today's Students

Overview

Learner diversity is described as both a challenge and an opportunity facing tomorrow's teacher. Cultural differences, differences in background knowledge, and language differences are explained and analyzed. This cultural diversity, including language differences, requires different curricular and instructional adaptations. In addition, efforts to help males and females and students with exceptionalities reach their full potential pose additional challenges.

Chapter Goals

This chapter examines

- Cultural diversity and its influence on student learning
- How gender influences teacher and student interactions
- How schools accommodate ability differences in learners
- Student learning styles and how they influence school success
- How schools and teachers can help students with exceptionalities succeed in schools

Chapter Outline

I. Cultural Diversity
    A.   Cultural Attitudes and Values
    B.   Cultural Interaction Patterns
    C.   Educational Responses to Cultural Diversity
        1.   Multicultural Controversies
        2.   Culturally Responsive Teaching
            a.   Accepting and Valuing Differences
            b.   Accommodating Different Cultural Interaction Patterns
            c.   Building on Students' Backgrounds
    D.   Language Diversity
        1.   Language Diversity: The Government's Response
        2.   Language Diversity: Schools' Responses
    E.   Teaching in an Era of Reform: The Bilingual Education Issue
    F.   Language Diversity: Implications for Teachers
II   Gender
    A.   Gender and Society
    B.   Gender and Schooling
        1.   Gender and Career Choices
        2.   Single-Gender Classrooms and Schools
        3.   Gender and Schooling: Implications for Teachers
    C.   Sexual Harassment
III.   Ability Differences
    A.   What Is Intelligence?
    B.   Changes in Views of Intelligence
    C.   Ability: Nature Versus Nurture

Transparencies

T 3.1   (Figure 3.2) Changes in School-Age Population, 2000–2020
T 3.2   (Table 3.1) Different Programs for ELL Students
T 3.3   (Figure 3.3) Sexual Harassment in U.S. Schools
T 3.4   (Table 3.2) Gardner's Eight Intelligences
T 3.5   (Table 3.3) Acceleration and Enrichment Options for Students Who Are Gifted and Talented

Teaching Suggestions

I. Cultural Diversity

The purpose of this section is to introduce students to cultural diversity and to encourage them to start thinking about how this dimension of diversity will affect them and their teaching.

- **■**   *Transparency 3.1* **"Changes in School-Age Population, 2000–2020" contains demographic information about the future school-age population. Ask what implications these changes will have for them as teachers.**

- **■**   **The** *Reflect on This* **feature in this section contains a concrete example of cultural discontinuities between cultures and schools and provides opportunities for students to use the information in this section in a problem-solving format.**

- **■**   *Transparency 3.2* **"Different Programs for ELL Students" describes different approaches to teaching ELL students. Discuss how these different programs are found in your particular area or state.**

- **■**   **Invite a teacher who works in either an ELL or bilingual program to share his or her experiences in that program.**

- **■**   *Portfolio Activity 3.2* **asks students to gather demographic information about cultural minorities and ELL students in your area or state. Ask students to report back and compare these figures to national statistics and trends.**

- **■**   *Journal Starter #1* **asks students to examine their own culture and how it influenced them as students and developing individuals.**

II. Gender

The purpose of this section is to help students understand how gender-related issues can affect them as teachers.

- The demographic information at the beginning of this section can be used to frame a discussion of the ways that gender influences students and their learning. Ask whether the schools do a poorer job educating boys or girls.

- Use the gender ratios in this class to initiate a discussion of gender stereotypic roles and professions.

- *Increasing Understanding 3.7* asks whether the teachers in single-gender classrooms should match the gender of students. This might provide a good discussion starter on the pros and cons of single-gender classrooms as well as on how gender influences teachers and teaching.

- *Transparency 3.3* "Sexual Harassment in U.S. Schools" contains information on the occurrence of different forms of sexual harassment in U.S. schools. Ask students if any of them have ever experienced sexual harassment. Ask how this problem differs at different grade levels.

III. Ability Differences

The purpose of this section is to help students understand how ability differences will influence their teaching.

- Display *Transparency 3.4* "Gardner's Eight Intelligences." Ask which are most important for school success. Which are least important? Ask which are most important for teaching success. Which are least important?

- Discuss the pros and cons of ability grouping. Ask if anyone in the class has ever personally experienced it (almost all have, most didn't realize it, and some may have been in lower tracks).

- *Going into Schools #6* asks students to investigate different ways that teachers accommodate learning differences in schools. Ask students to share their results in class.

- *Journal Starter #2* asks students to analyze themselves in terms of ability and multiple intelligences.

IV. Learning Styles

The purpose of this section is to help students become knowledgeable about and sensitive to the different learning styles of their future students.

- To introduce this topic, ask how many like small-group work. How many prefer to learn alone or by lecture? This provides a concrete example of students' learning-style preferences and also frames a teacher's dilemma in working with students with different learning styles or preferences.

- Caution students that the topic of learning styles, while intuitively sensible, has little research support. Point out that this is not because students don't learn differently, but researchers haven't been able to describe these important differences in valid or reliable ways.

- *Increasing Understanding 3.12* asks students to compare cognitive and cultural learning styles from a nature–nurture perspective.

V. Students with Exceptionalities

The purpose of this section is to introduce students to the field of exceptionalities and make them aware of their future roles and responsibilities in this area.

- Locate a textbook on this topic (e.g., Hardman et al., 2002; Heward, 2003), and provide a thumbnail sketch of the history of the field.

- To frame the problem of categorization, ask students to pick one category (e.g., female, elementary ed major) that describes them. Ask what things this category captures and includes. Ask what important parts of them it doesn't address? Help them see parallels with categorizing students on just one dimension.

- *Transparency 3.5* "Acceleration and Enrichment Options for Students Who Are Gifted and Talented" contains information about working with students with this exceptionality. Use this information to initiate a discussion on the classroom teacher's role in the process of working with these students.

- The *Video Perspectives* feature for this chapter, "Safe Haven: Helping Emotionally Troubled Kids Get Back on Track," describes a live-in facility for students with exceptionalities. Use the discussion questions to stimulate students' thinking about this problem.

Journal Starters

1. Encourage students to think about themselves in terms of ethnic and cultural diversity: How have your own culture and ethnicity influenced your school experiences? What types of experiences have you had with other cultures in schools? What did you learn from these experiences? What languages other than English do you speak? What difficulties did you encounter in learning this language? What did your experiences in learning this language tell you about the bilingual education debate? How can you use your personal knowledge of cultural diversity in your teaching?

2. Encourage students to think about themselves in terms of ability differences: How intelligent are you? How do you know? How did your intelligence influence your school success? What types of multiple intelligences are you good at? Which ones are you weaker at? How did these strengths and weaknesses influence your school success? How did they affect your happiness as a person? How will they influence your success and satisfaction as a teacher?

Increasing Understanding Questions and Feedback

3.1
What ethnic group or groups do you belong to? How is this evidenced in the foods you eat, the holidays you celebrate, and the language spoken in your community?
3.1
The answers to this question will, of course, vary with the individual, but ethnic influences are found in every part of our country.

3.2

How do the foods Americans eat reflect this growing cultural diversity?

3.2

America's diet–as evidenced by foods like pizza, tacos, and sushi, as well as the growing number of ethnic restaurants all across the U.S.–attests to the growing cultural diversity in the U.S.

3.3

Use Americans' eating habits to explain why the "mosaic" or "tossed salad" metaphors are more accurate than the "melting pot" one.

3.3

The cultural diversity found in Americans' diet suggests that different cultural groups are maintaining their cultural identities rather than being blended into a homogeneous stew.

3.4

To which metaphor–"melting pot" or "tossed salad"–does the concept of accommodation without assimilation most closely relate? Explain.

3.4

Accommodation without assimilation suggests maintaining strong elements of a student's core cultural values and would be more related to the "tossed salad" metaphor.

3.5

In the opening case study for this chapter, what did Shannon do to build upon her students' cultural backgrounds? Provide at least two specific examples.

3.5

Shannon had students report on their home countries and also encouraged them to bring to class cultural artifacts from their home countries.

3.6

Which approach to helping ELL students is most culturally responsive? Least? Explain why in each case.

3.6

Maintenance programs are most culturally responsive because they attempt to retain students' first language. ELL programs are least culturally responsive because their goal is to teach English as quickly as possible.

3.7

In single-gender classrooms and schools should the teachers match the gender of the students or be different? Explain alternate positions, using the information in this section.

3.7

One position would argue that the teachers should match the gender of students in single-gender classrooms. This would minimize any problems resulting from gender imbalances or inequities. Another position would argue that an opposite-sex teacher would help minimize any narrowing of perspectives or biases in single-gender classrooms.

3.8

If experience is crucial to performance on tests of learning ability, how might performance be affected by growing up in a minority culture?

3.8

No test is culture free since the content reflects a test-taker's past exposure to culturally embedded experiences. If a cultural minority student has not been exposed to the experiences tapped by the test, test performance will suffer.

3.9

If educators believed in Gardner's theory, what would an elementary-level report card look like? A high school report card?

3.9

At both levels the report card would be multidimensional, reflecting students' progress or growth in the different areas of intelligence. This already occurs to some degree at the elementary level, where students are evaluated on the "ability to get along with others" and "ability to monitor one's own work and progress." The secondary level, with its heavy emphasis on learning academic subjects, would require greater changes.

3.10

Based on his theory of multiple intelligences, would Howard Gardner favor ability grouping? Explain why or why not. How might he modify ability grouping?

3.10

He would not favor ability grouping in its current form because presently it reflects grouping students along one narrow dimension–academic learning. He might modify it by recommending alternate forms of grouping based on different types of intelligence–like interpersonal intelligence, or the ability to work with and get along with others. An alternative might be to purposefully group diverse students together on these dimensions so students could learn from each other. Teachers already do this in cooperative learning, where they place students with differing degrees of interpersonal skills together.

3.11

Would a field-independent person more likely be impulsive or reflective? Why?

3.11

A field-independent person, because of his or her ability and inclination to break complex problems into their constituent parts, would be more likely to be reflective.

3.12

From the nature–nurture perspective, how are cognitive and cultural learning styles different?

3.12

Though not mutually exclusive, cognitive learning styles are more likely to result from genetic causes (nature), and cultural learning styles are more likely to result from learned behaviors (nurture).

3.13

Using information from previous sections in the chapter, explain why standardized testing might miss many minorities who are gifted and talented.

3.13

Standardized testing, to a large extent, tests a student's exposure to background experiences. If the background experiences of cultural minorities are different from those tapped by standardized tests, these students may not do well on them.

3.14

Identify at least one similarity and one difference between learning disabilities and mental retardation.

3.14

In terms of similarities, both are exceptionalities that result in lowered school achievement. A student with a learning disability typically has average intelligence, and the disability manifests itself in a specific area. Mental retardation, by contrast, is typically not subject or area specific and results from lower cognitive functioning.

3.15

Identify at least one similarity and one difference between learning disabilities and behavior disorders.

3.15

Both learning disabilities and behavior disorders interfere with learning in the classroom. Learning disabilities are typically cognitive in orientation, interfering with students' ability to learn new information. Behavior disorders, by contrast, are more affective in nature and involve problems in monitoring behavior.

Reflect on This: Questions and Feedback
(These can also be found on the Companion Website: www.prenhall.com/kauchak .)

How Cultural Differences Affect Learning

1. What cultural differences were encountered that could potentially affect the way these students would benefit from American classrooms?

Time is a major cultural difference that could interfere with learning since schools are run by tight time clocks. In addition, schools emphasize quiet conformity versus rough-and-tumble individualism.

2. What would you do if you were at the awards ceremony?

This is an individual decision, but in real life the educator became so personally disturbed with the chaos that she actually hushed the children. This caused quite a bit of individual turmoil for the teacher because she felt tugged between two cultures.

3. What adaptations could a teacher make to help students such as these learn better in classrooms?

The concept of accommodation without assimilation is valuable here. This suggests that the teacher help students understand how schools require different ways of acting than their homes. For example, she might talk with them about the importance of punctuality for students. In doing this, the teacher should be careful not to devalue students' home culture.

Video Perspectives: Questions and Feedback

Safe Haven: Helping Emotionally Troubled Kids Get Back on Track

1. How well would these students function in regular schools and classrooms?

Based on their past experiences, it is highly unlikely they would be able to function in regular schools or classrooms. The demands of classroom life plus stresses caused by other students would be overwhelming.

2. What are the advantages and disadvantages of this approach to helping students with special needs versus inclusion?

A self-contained day school provides the structure and nurturing that these students need to survive. What this approach lacks is opportunities for these students to learn to function in the real world. A major goal of the curriculum at this school would focus on transitioning into regular schools, colleges, and jobs.

3. How could schools and classrooms be adapted to help these students make a successful transition back into a regular classroom?

Inclusion suggests that students spend as much time as possible in regular classroom settings. It does not rule out supplementary instruction, such as small-group sessions with similar students to ease the transition. In addition, the teacher would have help from an IEP team, in designing the classroom to maximize student adjustment and success. School counselors, psychologists, and social workers would be valuable to the teacher in this process.

Self-Assessment Questions
(Note: Students have access to these questions and their feedback on the text's Companion Website.)

1. In the near future the school-age population is likely to see what trend?
    a.   Significant decreases in all populations
    b.   An increase in the minority population while the white population remains stable or declines
    c.   An increase in the white population while the minority population remains stable
    d.   Zero growth for any population

2. The Supreme Court decision *Lau v. Nichols* resulted in
    a.   the free and appropriate education of children with disabilities.
    b.   the requirement of special language programs for limited-English students.
    c.   the creation and maintenance of programs for the gifted and talented.
    d.   early intervention for education of children with special needs.

3. Magnet schools are
    a.   private schools that receive public support because they resolve problems of school segregation.
    b.   public schools with high-quality, specialized programs.
    c.   public schools that attract minority students.
    d.   public schools that enroll students from a narrowly defined geographic area.

4. Gender bias in the schools is specifically forbidden by
    a.   the Bill of Rights of the U.S. Constitution.
    b.   *Brown v. Board of Education.*
    c.   Title IX of the Educational Amendment Act.
    d.   Title I.

5. Inclusion refers to
    a.   including students with exceptionalities in as many school activities as possible.
    b.   including students with exceptionalities in every classroom.
    c.   including parents in their child(ren)'s education.
    d.   including non-English speakers in the regular classroom.

6. Which type of second-language program is **LEAST** compatible with the concept of assimilation?
    a.   Maintenance
    b.   Transition
    c.   Immersion
    d.   ESL

7. Which of the following accurately describes gender differences in the schools?
    a.   Girls score higher on SAT and ACT exams.
    b.   Boys are less likely to be involved in discipline problems.
    c.   Girls receive lower grades than boys.
    d.   Boys are more likely to be involved in remedial classes.

8. Which of the following is **NOT** true about sexual harassment in the schools?
    a.   Girls are more likely to be sexually harassed.
    b.   Most cases of sexual harassment are reported.
    c.   The most common form of sexual harassment is verbal.
    d.   Students are often unaware of sexual harassment policies in their schools.

9. Which of the following is **NOT** true of ability grouping?
   a.   Ability grouping is detrimental to low-ability students' achievement.
   b.   Ability grouping results in lowered motivation and self-esteem for lower groups.
   c.   Cultural minorities tend to be overrepresented in lower groups.
   d.   Ability grouping is prevalent because it's easier for teachers.

10. The major difference between mainstreaming and inclusion is that
   a.   mainstreaming is primarily aimed at the mildly disabled.
   b.   inclusion is a more comprehensive approach to dealing with students with exceptionalities than mainstreaming.
   c.   mainstreaming is more focused on achieving a least restrictive environment.
   d.   inclusion is primarily focused on classroom adaptations.

Self-Assessment Feedback

1. b   Schools will most likely see an increase in all minority populations while the white population will stay stable or decline.
2. b   The *Lau v. Nichols* decision resulted in requiring special language programs for limited-English students.
3. b   Magnet schools attempt to achieve integration through high-quality specialty programs.
4. c   Gender discrimination is specifically addressed in Title IX of the Educational Amendment Act.
5. a   The thrust of inclusion is to integrate students with exceptionalities in as many school activities as possible. This may not mean that they'll be in every classroom.
6. a   Maintenance programs are least compatible with assimilation because they attempt to retain students' native language.
7. d   Boys are more likely to be involved in remedial classes.
8. b   Only 7 percent of sexual harassment cases are reported.
9. d   Ability grouping is actually more difficult for teachers because it creates logistical problems.
10. b   Inclusion is a more comprehensive approach that attempts to adapt the whole school campus to the needs of students with exceptionalities.

PRAXIS Practice Questions and Feedback

1. To what extent did Diane display culturally responsive teaching in her lesson?

Diane's teaching was culturally responsive in several ways. She included all students in her lesson on an equal basis, and she had established a classroom climate where all students felt that they were welcome and that they belonged there. In addition, she built on students' background knowledge by using concrete examples that were familiar to them.

2. To what extent did Diane's teaching reflect sensitivity to gender issues?

Diane's teaching was sensitive to gender issues in several ways. First, she made an active attempt to involve all students—boys and girls—equally in the lesson. (We counted 9 responses from boys and 10 from girls.) In addition, she reminded students of the importance of all students participating.

3. What did Diane do to accommodate differences in learning ability and learning styles?

Diane did several things to accommodate differences in learning ability and style. First, she used a number of open-ended questions that ensured success and invited all students to respond. Second, she provided Sean with extra support in answering his question. Third, she provided opportunities for students to work together and also gave them a choice in who would report back to the group. Finally, she gave Todd extra help and support with the writing assignment.

Useful Web Site Addresses

Web Links for Chapter Terms

ability grouping
http://www.education-world.com/a_admin/admin009.shtml
http://www.gifted.uconn.edu/kulik.html

acceleration
http://www.pps.k12.or.us/depts/tag/instruction/acceleration_article.shtml
http://cty.jhu.edu/imagine/accel.html

adaptive fit
http://www.findarticles.com/cf_dls/m0HDG/3_22/102909956/p1/article.jhtml

between-class ability grouping
http://www.ncrel.org/sdrs/areas/issues/content/cntareas/science/ma1group.htm
http://www.donet.com/~eprice/sdallan.htm

behavior disorder
http://www.nichcy.org/pubs/factshe/fs19txt.htm
http://www.nichcy.org/pubs/factshe/fs5txt.htm
http://specialed.about.com/cs/behaviordisorders/
http://www.mentalhealth.org/publications/allpubs/CA-0006/default.asp
http://db.education-world.com/perl/browse?cat_id=5160

culturally responsive teaching
http://www.nccic.org/faqs/clrteaching.html
http://knowledgeloom.org/resources.jsp?location=6&tool=-1&bpinterid=1110&spotlightid=1110
http://www.nwrel.org/cfc/frc/beyus10.html

disability
http://www.ed.gov/offices/OSERS/Policy/IDEA/regs.html
http://www.ideapractices.org/
http://www.ncd.gov/
http://www.nichcy.org/index.html
http://www.disabilityinfo.gov/
http://www.dredf.org/
http://www.kidsource.com/kidsource/pages/dis.learning.html

English as a Second Language (ESL)
http://www.cal.org/resources/faqs/index.html
http://iteslj.org/
http://www.tesol.edu/

enrichment
http://journals.sped.org/EC/Archive_Articles/VOL.33NO.4MARAPR2001_TEC_Article7.pdf
http://www.education-world.com/a_curr/curr101.shtml

ethnicity
http://ethics.acusd.edu/Applied/race/
http://folk.uio.no/geirthe/Ethnicity.html
http://cfdev.georgetown.edu/cndls/asw/aswsub.cfm?head1=Race%2C%20Ethnicity%2C%20and%20Identity

exceptionality
http://www.ed.gov/about/offices/list/osers/osep/index.html?src=mr

field dependent/independent
http://www.eltnewsletter.com/back/June2002/art1022002.htm
http://tip.psychology.org/styles.html

gender-role identity
http://www.gender.org.uk/about/00_defin.htm

gifted and talented
http://www.ucc.uconn.edu/~wwwgt/nrcgt.html
http://www.kidsource.com/kidsource/pages/ed.gifted.html
http://www.nagc.org/

immersion programs
http://www.cal.org/resources/digest/0101twi.html
http://www.ericfacility.net/databases/ERIC_Digests/ed363141.html

impulsive students
http://www.school-for-champions.com/education/hyperactive.htm
http://childdevelopmentinfo.com/learning/teacher.shtml

inclusion
http://www.edweek.org/context/topics/issuespage.cfm?id=47
http://www.circleofinclusion.org/
http://www.uni.edu/coe/inclusion/

learning disability
http://www.nichcy.org/pubs/factshe/fs7txt.htm
http://www.ldonline.org/
http://www.ncld.org/
http://www.ldanatl.org/

learning style
http://www.learningstyles.net/
http://www.support4learning.org.uk/education/lstyles.htm
http://www.garysturt.free-online.co.uk/learnsty.htm
http://falcon.jmu.edu/~ramseyil/learningstyles.htm
http://www.virtualschool.edu/mon/Academia/KierseyLearningStyles.html
http://core.ecu.edu/vel/itc/tutorials/learningstyles.htm#2

least restrictive environment
http://www.lrecoalition.org/
http://www.wrightslaw.com/info/lre.index.htm
http://ericec.org/digests/e629.html

maintenance language programs
http://www.ncela.gwu.edu/miscpubs/nabe/brj/v17/17_12_medina.pdf

mental retardation
http://www.nichcy.org/pubs/factshe/fs8txt.htm
http://www.dddcec.org/
http://www.aamr.org/
http://www.thearc.org/

metacognition
http://www.ncrel.org/sdrs/areas/issues/students/learning/lr1metn.htm
http://www.gse.buffalo.edu/fas/shuell/cep564/Metacog.htm
http://www.ericfacility.net/ericdigests/ed327218.html

multiple intelligences
http://pzweb.harvard.edu/PIs/HG_MI_after_20_years.pdf
http://pzweb.harvard.edu/PIs/HG.htm
http://www.education-world.com/a_curr/curr054.shtml
http://www.edwebproject.org/edref.mi.intro.html
http://www.infed.org/thinkers/gardner.htm

reflective students
http://www.thejournal.com/magazine/vault/A1367.cfm
http://www.hrm.strath.ac.uk/teaching/classes/full-time-41939/lectures/lrngstyles.pdf

sexual harassment
http://www.ed.gov/about/offices/list/ocr/sexharassresources.html?exp=0
http://www.oct.ca/english/ps/september_1999/harrass.htm
http://www.wiu.edu/library/govpubs/guides/sexhared.htm

single-gender classes and schools
http://www.cbsnews.com/stories/2002/05/09/politics/main508465.shtml
http://www.womensenews.org/article.cfm/dyn/aid/571/context/cover/
http://www.edweek.org/ew/newstory.cfm?slug=36gender.h21
http://www.washtimes.com/national/20020919-80076932.htm
http://www.newsmax.com/archives/articles/2002/5/2/155112.shtml
http://www.theatlantic.com/issues/98apr/singsex.htm

special education
http://www.ed.gov/about/offices/list/osers/osep/index.html?src=mr
http://www.wrightslaw.com/
http://www.dssc.org/frc/
http://www.special-ed-careers.org/
http://www.nichcy.org/index.html
http://www.cec.sped.org

tracking
http://papers.nber.org/papers/w7854
http://archive.aclu.org/students/slequal.html
http://www.ed.gov/news/pressreleases/2001/10/10052001j.html
http://www.specialednews.com/conflict/conflictnews/CADREstatetracking020500.html
http://www.edweek.org/ew/vol-16/37olsen.h16

http://www.ericfacility.net/ericdigests/ed290542.html
http://middleweb.com/Whlcktrack.html

transition programs
http://www.transitioncoalition.org/bestpractices/session1.php3?page=session1_1
http://www.nichcy.org/transitn.asp
http://www.lawhelp.org/documents/110131725.pdf?stateabbrev=/MN/

within-class ability grouping
http://www.ericfacility.net/databases/ERIC_Digests/ed290542.html
http://www.scre.ac.uk/rie/nl60/nl60harlen.html
http://chiron.valdosta.edu/whuitt/edpsyc/grouping.html

Web Links for "Teaching in an Era of Reform: The Bilingual Education Issue"

Ask National Clearinghouse for Bilingual Education: Frequently Asked Questions
http://www.ncbe.gwu.edu/askncbe/faqs/

Bilingual Education: http://www.nasbe.org/Policy_Updates.html

Bilingual Education: An Overview: http://www.nea.org/issues/bilingual/

Bilingual Education: http://www.edweek.org/context/topics/issuespage.cfm?id=8

Bilingual Resources on the Internet: gopher://scilibx.ucsc.edu/7waissrc%3a/.WAIS/ERIC_archive.src?bilingual

Bush Plan Could Alter Bilingual Education: http://www.edweek.org/ew/ewstory.cfm?slug=23biling.h20

English Learners–Language and Culture in the Classroom: http://www.cde.ca.gov/el/

ERIC Clearinghouse on Language and Linguistics: FAQS: http://www.cal.org/ericcll/faqs/

Frequently Asked Questions on Bilingual Education: http://www.ed.gov/offices/OBEMLA/q_a1.html

Frequently Asked Questions on the Rights of Limited-English Proficient Students
http://www.ed.gov/offices/OCR/qa-ell.html

Massachusetts Voters May Get Choice on Bilingual Education
http://www.edweek.org/ew/newstory.cfm?slug=43biling.h21&keywords=teaching

Resources for English Teachers: http://goldmine.cde.ca.gov/cilbranch/bien/bien.htm

Will Star 2000 Kill Bilingual Education?: http://www.education-world.com/a_issues/issues121.shtml

Additional Chapter Web Links

English Only

California Referendum Mandates English-Only: http://www.rethinkingschools.org/archive/12_03/langmn.shtml

English for the Children: http://www.onenation.org/
English Only: ACLU Briefing Paper: http://www.aclu.org/library/pbp6.html
The English-Only Movement: http://ourworld.compuserve.com/homepages/JWCRAWFORD/engonly.htm
English-Only Movement: Its Consequences on the Education of Language-Minority Children
http://www.ed.gov/databases/ERIC_Digests/ed427326.html
A Lawmaker's Firsthand View of the Bilingual Issue
http://www.humnet.ucla.edu/humnet/linguistics/people/grads/macswan/LAT15.htm
Proposition 227: Anti-Bilingual Education Initiative in California
http://ourworld.compuserve.com/homepages/jwcrawford/unz.htm

Equity and Diversity

Critical Issue: Educating Teachers for Diversity: http://www.ncrel.org/skrs/areas/issues/educatrs/presrvce/pe300.htm
Equity and Diversity: http://nici-mc2.org/pgs/equity/equity.htm
Multicultural Pavillion: Teacher's Corner: http://curry.edschool.Virginia.EDU:80/go/multicultural/teachers.html
Multiple Intelligences: Theory and Practice in the K–12 Classroom
http://www.indiana.edu/~eric_rec/ieo/bibs/multiple.html
The National Association for Multicultural Education (NAME): http://www.nameorg.org/
Stories, Cases, and Vignettes: http://www.enc.org/topics/equity/stories/

Gender Equity

The American Association of University Women: http://www.aauw.org/
Beyond Title IX: Gender Equity Issues in Schools: http://www.maec.org/beyond.html
ERIC on Gender Equity: http://www.teach-nology.com/litined/equity/gender/
Gender Equity in Schools: A Primer: http://www.american.edu/sadker/genderequity.htm
Gender Equity Websites: http://civic.bev.net/aauw/gequity.html

Chapter 4
Changes in American Society:
Their Influences on Today's Schools

Overview

Changing societal trends are analyzed in terms of the changing American family and shifts in demographic and socioeconomic patterns. Challenges facing modern youth–including alcohol and drug use, violence, suicide, child abuse, and increased sexuality–are analyzed. Educational efforts to assist American youth in facing these changes and challenges are described in terms of community, school, and instructional efforts.

Chapter Goals

This chapter examines

- Changes in families that pose challenges to our students
- Changes in economic conditions that can influence learning and teaching
- Changes in student characteristics that impact student readiness to learn
- Ways that schools respond to challenges facing our students

Chapter Outline

I. A Changing Society
    A. The Changing American Family
        1. Child Care
        2. Latchkey Children
    B. Changing Socioeconomic Patterns
        1. Poverty
        2. Homelessness
        3. Socioeconomic Status and School Success
    C. Changing Student Populations
        1. Changing Sexuality
            a. Teenage Pregnancy
            b. Sexually Transmitted Diseases
            c. Homosexuality
            d. Sex Education
        2. Increasing Use of Alcohol and Other Drugs
        3. Increasing Crime and Violence–School Uniforms
        4. Bullying
        5. Schoolwide Safety Programs
    D. Teaching in an Era of Reform: The Zero Tolerance Issue
    E. Video Perspectives: Action, Reaction, and Zero Tolerance
        1. School Violence and Teachers
        2. Increasing Suicide
        3. Increasing Awareness of Child Abuse
II. Students Placed At-Risk
    A. It Takes a Village: The Community-Based Approach to Working with Children Placed At-Risk
    B. Students Placed At-Risk: Promoting Resilience
        1. Effective Schools for Students Placed At-Risk
        2. Effective Teachers for Students Placed At-Risk: Professional Responses
        3. Effective Instruction Structure and Support

III.   Decision Making: Defining Yourself as a Professional

Transparencies

T 4.1 (Figure 4.2) Poverty Levels by Ethnicity
T 4.2 (Figure 4.3) Changes in the Student Population
T 4.3 (Figure 4.4) Student Drug and Alcohol Use: Percentage of High School Seniors Reporting Use in the Previous 30 Days
T 4.4 (Table 4.1)   Characteristics of Students Placed At-Risk

Teaching Suggestions

I. A Changing Society

The purpose of this section is to help students understand the demographic changes and the changing student populations occurring in U.S. society and how these changes will affect their teaching.

- **To personalize the information in this section, ask students to anonymously describe on paper the kind of family structure they grew up in. Tally the information, and share with students. Ask how it is similar to and different from national statistics. What implications does this have for them as teachers?**

- **Point out that the SES categories presented in the text are not neat and clean, with overlap and transitional categories like upper- and lower-middle class. Ask how culture or ethnicity interacts with SES.**

- **_Transparency 4.1_ "Poverty Levels by Ethnicity" contains information about links between poverty and ethnicity. Ask students to explain these links. What are the implications for teaching?**

- **The Sandham (2000) article in _Education Week_ provides a powerful description of what schools can do to deal with homelessness. If available, share this information with students.**

- **_Journal Starter #1_ asks students to reflect on their own backgrounds and think about how this could influence them as teachers.**

- **_Transparency 4.2_ provides an overview of "Changes in the Student Population." Which of these is most important at the teaching levels students are interested in? in different locales where they plan to teach? How are their content areas (e.g., health or biology) affected by these changes?**

- **Ask students if they knew anyone in high school who became pregnant. How was it handled? What happened to the mother? What happened to the father? What should schools do with this problem?**

- **_Discussion Question #3_ asks what role the school should play in dealing with teenage sexuality.**

- **Refer to the national statistics on drug and alcohol use in the text. Ask students to conjecture how these figures compare to those in the schools they'll be working in. What implications do these differences have for them as teachers?**

- Recently the American Bar Association came out against zero tolerance programs because of problems with their implementation (see *Education Week, 20*[24], Feb. 28, 2001, p. 3.).

- *You Take a Position* in the *Teaching in an Era of Reform* section asks students to take a position on zero tolerance. Ask students on different sides of the issue to share their perspectives.

- The video "Action, Reaction, and Zero Tolerance" in the chapter's *Video Perspectives* section contains several true stories about zero tolerance programs across the nation.

- *Reflect on This* in this section asks students to deal with a case of child abuse. Use this case to initiate a discussion on the topic.

II. Students Placed At-Risk

- *Transparency 4.4* "Characteristics of Students Placed At-Risk" describes both characteristics of and educational problems of students placed at-risk. Emphasize the cautions in the text about negative stereotyping and low teacher expectations.

- Invite a teacher who works with at-risk students to share his or her experiences with those students.

- *Going into Schools #1* asks students to interview a student who is at-risk. We have found this assignment a powerful way to humanize and personalize this topic. We have also asked our students to work with the student over time as a tutor/mentor. This has also been an effective strategy to help our students learn about these students more deeply.

- *Going into Schools #2, #3,* and *#4* ask students to interview a teacher and counselor and observe students placed at-risk in the classroom. We suggest dividing the assignments up among students and having them work in small groups to report their findings to the class.

- The *Reflect on This* feature in this section asks students to think about curricular and instructional modifications for working with students placed at-risk.

- *Journal Starter #2* asks students to think about their own experiences with students placed at-risk and ways schools and teachers could do a better job of meeting the needs of these students.

Journal Starters

1. Encourage students to think about societal changes in terms of their own experiences growing up: How does your own personal background prepare you for these societal changes and changes in the school population? What type of family did you grow up in? What was the SES level of your family? Did you know students in high school who were sexually active? Did you know students who used alcohol or other drugs? How did these affect their performance in school? Were your schools safe from violence? How did this influence your attitudes toward school?

2. Encourage students to think about themselves in terms of what they've learned about students placed at-risk: How will your past experiences with students placed at-risk influence you as a teacher? Were there students placed at-risk in your high school? Did you know them? Were they in any of your classes? How well were they integrated into school life? Did they participate in sports or other extracurricular activities? What could the school and

teachers have done to make the school and the classrooms in it more inviting and nurturant places for these students?

Increasing Understanding: Questions and Feedback

4.1 Identify at least two things teachers could do to help parents work with their children more effectively on homework and other academic activities.

4.1

Teachers can do a number of things to help parents help their children with schoolwork. At the beginning of the year they can send a letter home explaining their class and inviting questions from parents. Early on at Back to School Night teachers can communicate their accessibility and willingness to help. At this meeting they can also provide concrete suggestions about ways parents can help their children. Teachers can also send home weekly notes, letting parents know what their children are studying. These are just a few suggestions–you may have others.

4.2 Where do you think most new teaching positions will occur, in schools populated by students from upper-, middle-, or lower-SES backgrounds? Why do you think so?

4.2

Most new teaching positions occur in low-SES schools. These are often the most challenging places to work and often have the highest rates of teacher turnover.

4.3 What is the most effective thing teachers can do to demonstrate that they care about a student?

4.3

Giving their own time and personal attention is the most powerful way that teachers can demonstrate caring.

4.4 What do "instructional structure" and "motivational support" mean? Give an example of each to illustrate your explanation.

4.4

Structure means providing scaffolding so that students are successful in their learning tasks. Motivational support involves encouraging students through feedback. For example, a writing assignment of four paragraphs could be broken down into four separate ones with individual due dates (structure). The teacher would then read and provide positive feedback about what the student did well and what still needs additional work (motivational support).

4.5 Identify one advantage and one disadvantage of home instruction for teenage mothers. Do the same for in-school programs.

4.5

Advantages of home instruction for teenage mothers include one-on-one instruction and the convenience of home visits. A disadvantage is missing the social dimensions of learning as well as being isolated from extracurricular activities. An advantage of in-school programs is the social support to finish school. A disadvantage is the potential negative stigma of teenage parenting.

4.6 What could teachers do on the first day of class to minimize peer sexual harassment? Throughout the school year?

4.6

Teachers can help prevent peer sexual harassment by including it as one of the behaviors not tolerated in class. Follow-through over the course of the year, when situations arise, will reinforce this message.

4.7 Identify at least two different kinds of background knowledge teachers must have in order to effectively teach about sexuality. (Hint: Recall the different kinds of professional knowledge discussed in Chapter 1.)

4.7

Professional knowledge about teachers' rights and responsibilities allows teachers to understand their proper role in the process and what they can and cannot do. Content knowledge provides accurate information that teachers can share with students. Pedagogical content knowledge allows teachers to present this information in effective ways.

4.8 Identify two specific ways in which alcohol or other drug use interferes with learning.
4.8

Alcohol and drug use can directly interfere with learning if taken during the day. The aftereffects can also interfere with learning the next day. Indirectly alcohol and drug use can interfere with homework and can encourage an antischool or antilearning bias in students.

4.9 Why might student concerns about safety and violence peak at the eighth-grade level? What implications does this have for middle schools? for middle school teachers?
4.9

Several factors might contribute here. One is the students themselves. They are changing rapidly, and this may make them feel uneasy and unsure of themselves. In addition, self-control mechanisms might not be well developed. The unstructured nature of middle schools, compared to elementary self-contained classrooms, may also contribute to student unease. Middle schools and middle school teachers can respond by making student safety and security a top priority.

4.10 Parents consistently rate discipline and safety among their top concerns about schools (Rose & Gallup, 2003). Given what you've read in this section, are these concerns justified? Defend your position with information taken from this section.
4.10

Are these concerns justified? Yes and no. Statistically speaking schools are relatively safe places. But from the parents' perspective the safety of their sons and daughters is a number one priority. When the parents send their sons and daughters off to school in the morning, parents want to feel assured that they are sending them to a safe place to learn. This is why this issue is such a priority for parents.

4.11 Why is the role of the teacher so important in identifying potential suicide victims?
4.11

The teacher's role is crucial for several reasons. First, because they see students daily, they may be in the best position to observe telltale signs of suicide. Also, because they are trained as professionals, they know what signs to look for. Finally, they may be the last line of defense to prevent this from happening.

4.12 Is child abuse easier to detect at the elementary or secondary level? Why?
4.12

Probably at the elementary level because teachers work with the same group of students all day and because students at this age are not as adept at hiding things from adults.

4.13 Explain how these characteristics of effective schools could contribute to resiliency in students place at-risk.
4.13

A safe, orderly school with caring teachers provides a nurturant environment for resilience to occur. Cooperation, community, and student responsibility send positive messages about personal and emotional growth. Demanding teachers and academic focus communicate that learning is important. Finally, parental involvement creates a cohesive team.

4.14 Which of these characteristics of effective instruction would be most effective in promoting student resilience? Why?

Though all are important for encouraging resilience, we conjecture that the affective ones like high expectations and emphasis on student responsibility might be the most powerful because they communicate to the student, "You can learn, and I'm here to help you."

Reflect on This: Questions and Feedback
(These can also be found on the Companion Website: www.prenhall.com/kauchak .)

Reflect on This (One): Reporting Child Abuse

1. You promised that you wouldn't tell anyone about your conversation with Janine. Should you keep or break the promise?

You broke the law by promising not to tell; the law in all 50 states and the District of Columbia requires teachers to report child abuse.

2. Who could you talk to about this problem? How much information should you reveal in the conversation?

You could talk to a school counselor, school psychologist, or your principal. All have had advanced training in dealing with this problem. You should share with them everything that you know.

3. What would you do in this situation?

Again, this is a personal decision, but you should realize that your options are constrained by the law and professional ethics.

Reflect on This (Two): Involving Students

1. What were the advantages and disadvantages of using the textbook originally?

Research suggests that texts provide a "crutch" for beginning teachers, giving them needed help in their initial planning and teaching efforts. In addition, the text probably aligns with the school's total language arts curriculum and may also align with mandated state or district tests. The obvious disadvantage is that it isn't motivating to students.

2. Why are you having such difficulties in involving the students in writing? What could you have done differently?

Because of an emphasis on skills in prior classes, students probably haven't had much experience with writing. In addition, the teacher just dumped the first assignment on students without any help or assistance.

3. Why did you encounter problems in involving students in small-group work?

Again, students might not have had experience in working with small groups or in critiquing each other's work. In addition, research suggests that teachers should give students small, doable tasks, monitor them, and hold them accountable.

4. What would you do now?

First, don't give up. Second, the suggestions in the previous feedback offer several starting points.

Video Perspectives: Questions and Feedback

Action, Reaction, and Zero Tolerance

1. What are the major goals of zero tolerance policies?

Zero tolerance policies in schools have two major goals: to make schools safer and change student behavior.

2. What are the advantages and disadvantages of zero tolerance policies?

The major advantages of zero tolerance policies are that they clearly outline rules for acceptable and unacceptable behavior and clearly define consequences for violating these rules. The major disadvantages are that there isn't clear research evidence that these policies work and their misapplication not only causes individual students problems, but also makes students doubtful about the validity of other rules.

3. What could schools do to minimize the negative effects of zero tolerance policies?

In implementing zero tolerance policies, schools should make a special effort to clearly explain the reasons for specific rules. In addition, administrators should use sound judgment and flexibility in applying these rules.

Video Discussion Questions and Feedback

1. Theodore Sizer is the Director of the Coalition for Effective Schools, which attempts to reform high schools. A major challenge facing high school reform is helping students placed at risk develop resiliency. From Dr. Sizer's perspective what is the most important thing that schools can do to develop resiliency in students? How do these suggestions compare to information in this chapter?

Dr. Sizer believes the most important part of making students resilient is to develop self-confidence of their own intellectual power or ability to learn. This approach emphasizes the cognitive dimension of learning; the text also emphasized affective strategies like caring and high expectations.

Self-Assessment Questions
(Note: Students have access to these questions and their feedback on the text's Companion Website.)

1. In the U.S. the **least** likely family pattern is
   a.   a single-parent family.
   b.   a blended family with children from previous marriages.
   c.   children living with grandparents or other relatives.
   d.   a two-parent family with two children and the mother staying at home.

2. Which of the following is **NOT** true of U.S. families?
   a.   Families headed by married couples make up over half of all households.
   b.   The majority of women with children are in the workforce.
   c.   The poverty rate for teenage families is roughly comparable to that of the general population.
   d.   Most teenage births occur out of wedlock.

3. Which of the following is **NOT** included as a factor in socioeconomic status (SES)?
   a.   Occupation
   b.   Marital status
   c.   Income
   d.   Education level

4. Which of the following is **NOT** true of poverty in the U.S.?
   a.   Poverty is more common in large urban areas.
   b.   Poverty is more common among minorities.
   c.   Poverty is more common among families headed by single mothers.
   d.   Poverty is more common among children.

5. Which of the following is **NOT** true of teenagers' sexual behaviors?
   a.   The majority of teenagers 15 to 19 years old report being sexually active.
   b.   The majority of sexually active teenagers use condoms.
   c.   The U.S. has the highest teenage birthrate among developing countries.
   d.   The teenage birthrate has declined recently.

6. Which of the following is **NOT** true about school violence and crime?
   a.   Student concerns about school safety are highest at the middle school level.
   b.   The most common form of school crime is theft.
   c.   Violence is most common in schools located in urban areas.
   d.   School violence and crime are most often connected to gangs.

7. Which of the following is **NOT** true of zero tolerance programs in schools?
   a.   They tend to be implemented differentially in different schools in the same district.
   b.   They tend to affect minorities to a disproportionate degree.
   c.   They often result in expulsion from school.
   d.   They are effective in differentiating between major and minor offenses.

8. Which of the following is **NOT** true of teenage suicide?
   a.   Boys are more likely than girls to attempt suicide.
   b.   The teenage suicide rate has doubled in the last 30 years.
   c.   Boys are more likely than girls to succeed at suicide.
   d.   A relatively small percentage of teenagers attempt suicide.

9. Which of the following school approaches to children placed at-risk has been found to be most effective?
   a.   Zero tolerance programs that address school crime and violence
   b.   Drug and alcohol programs that stress mental as well as physical health
   c.   Active involvement of community resources in redesigning schools
   d.   Security efforts that make schools safe havens for children

10. Which of the following most accurately describes the difference between low- and high-impact teachers for students placed at-risk?
   a.   High-impact teachers have better classroom management strategies.
   b.   Low-impact teachers use more indirect methods of instruction.
   c.   Low-impact teachers place too much emphasis on motivation.
   d.   High-impact teachers are more interactive in their teaching.

Self-Assessment Feedback

1. d   A two-parent family with two children and the mother staying at home is typical of only 6 percent of U.S. households.
2. c   Sixty percent of teenage families live in poverty as compared to 14 percent of the total population.
3. b   Marital status is not a factor in SES.
4. a   Poverty is more common in small towns and suburban areas.

5. b   Only 27 perent of sexually active females and 47 percent of sexually active males use condoms.

6. d   The actual percentage of students who belong to gangs is actually quite small.

7. d   One of the major criticisms of zero tolerance programs is that they often don't effectively differentiate between major and minor offenses.

8. a   Girls are three times more likely than boys to attempt suicide.

9. c   The most promising approach in this area is community involvement in which parents and other members of the community collaborate with school personnel in redesigning schools.

10. d   High-impact teachers are more personal, maintain high expectations, are more interactive in their teaching, and emphasize success and mastery of content.

PRAXIS Practice: Questions and Feedback

1. What characteristics of an effective school for students placed at-risk did Kari encounter?

The school where Kari taught displayed a number of characteristics for effective schools for students placed at-risk. Teachers' presence in the hallways contributed to a safe and orderly climate. In addition, greeting students encouraged a sense of community. Parental involvement was encouraged by having students accompanying them and acting as translators. A sense of community was also promoted by a student advisory period during which students got to know their teachers and fellow students.

2. What characteristics of an effective teacher for students placed at-risk did Kari display?

Effective teachers for students placed at-risk care about their students and have high expectations for their learning. Kari had high expectations for her students; she wanted them not only to learn grammar and punctuation but also how to write. In addition, she demonstrated caring by defining her students' learning as more than just having them pass some mandated tests. While helping students to do well on required tests is important, caring teachers also have other more important goals related to their students' long-term development and learning.

3. What aspects of Kari's instruction were effective for students placed at-risk?

Kari's instruction exhibited several characteristics of effective teaching for students placed at-risk. She emphasized student responsibility. Her teaching was interactive; she used group work and teacher questioning to involve students. She also assessed frequently, using the information she gained to adjust her instruction. Finally, she provided structure and support through her initial classroom assignment and the examples she used to model good writing.

Useful Web Site Addresses

Web Links for Chapter Terms

at-risk students
http://www.ed.gov/offices/OERI/At-Risk/index.html
http://www.ed.gov/pubs/EdReformStudies/EdReforms/chap1a.html
http://www.nwrel.org/comm/topics/atrisk.html
http://www.teach-nology.com/edleadership/at_risk/

diversity
http://www.crede.ucsc.edu/research/research.html

latchkey children
http://www.vachss.com/help_text/latchkey_kids.html

poverty
http://www.census.gov/hhes/www/poverty.html
http://www.census.gov

resilient students
http://www.ed.gov/pubs/Resiliency/intro.html

socioeconomic status (SES)
http://www.findarticles.com/cf_dls/m0961/2002_Annual/83789651/p1/article.jhtml
http://ideas.repec.org/p/nbr/nberwo/6943.html

zero tolerance program
http://nces.ed.gov/pubs2004/crime03/
http://www.ed.gov/databases/ERIC_Digests/ed451579.html
http://www.edweek.org/ew/newstory.cfm?slug=20scotus.h21

Web Links for "Teaching in an Era of Reform: The Zero Tolerance Issue"

ABA Recommends Dropping Zero Tolerance in Schools
http://www.cnn.com/2001/fyi/teachers.ednews/02/21/zero.tolerance.ap/

Center for the Study and Prevention of Violence: http://www.Colorado.EDU/cspv/

Interpretations of Zero Tolerance Vary: http://www.edweek.org/ew/newstory.cfm?slug=30zero.h21

School Policies on Sexual Harassment in This Era of Zero Tolerance
http://www.wcwonline.org/zerotol/main.html

Supreme Court Declines to Accept Zero Tolerance Case
http://www.edweek.org/ew/newstory.cfm?slug=20scotus.h21

Zero Tolerance Is Schools' First Line of Defense: http://www.manhattan-institute.org/html/_newsday-zero_tolerance.htm

Zero Tolerance Policies: http://www.ed.gov/databases/ERIC_Digests/ed451579.html

Zero Tolerance Policies Lack Flexibility: http://www.usatoday.com/educate/ednews3.htm

Zero Tolerance School Safety and Discipline Policies: http://www.schoolsecurity.org/trends/zero_tolerance.html

Zero Tolerance: What Parents Should Know: http://www.spannj.org/BridgeArchives/zero_tolerance.htm

Additional Chapter Web Sites

Child Abuse and Neglect

End Child Abuse: http://www.childabuse.org/
How to Report Suspected Child Abuse and Neglect
http://www.acf.dhhs.gov/programs/cb/publications/rpt_abu.htm
Mandatory Reporting of Child Abuse and Neglect: http://www.smith-lawfirm.com/mandatory_reporting.htm
National Clearinghouse on Child Abuse and Neglect Information: http://nccanch.acf.hhs.gov/
National Data Archive on Child Abuse and Neglect: http://www.ndacan.cornell.edu/
Prevent Child Abuse America: http://www.preventchildabuse.org/
Preparing Teachers for Conflict Resolution in the Schools
http://www.ericfacility.net/databases/ERIC_Digests/ed387456.html

Hate Crimes

ACLU Statement on Hate Crimes Act: http://archive.aclu.org/congress/l051199a.html
Bigotry, Prejudice and Homophobia—Safe Schools Coalition
http://www.safeschoolscoalition.org/RG-bigotry_prejudice_homophobia.html
National Center for Hate Crime Prevention: http://www.edc.org/HHD/hatecrime/id1.htm
National PTA Resources on Helping Children Cope with Tragedy
http://www.pta.org/parentinvolvement/tragedy/violence.asp
Police Notebook: Hate Crimes: http://www.ou.edu/oupd/hate.htm
Preventing Youth Hate Crimes: http://www.usdoj.gov/kidspage/hate.pdf
Protecting Students from Harassment and Hate Crimes: A Guide for Schools
http://www.ed.gov/offices/OCR/archives/Harassment/index.html

Homelessness

Facts About Homelessness: http://www.nationalhomeless.org/facts.html
McKinney-Vento 2001: Educating Children and Youth in Homeless Situations: Law, Policy, and Practice
http://www.nationalhomeless.org/reauthorization.html
National Center for Homeless Education: http://www.serve.org/nche/
National Coalition for the Homeless: http://www.nationalhomeless.org/
National Law Center on Homelessness and Poverty: http://www.nlchp.org/
Personal Experiences of Homelessness: http://www.nationalhomeless.org/experiences/index.html

Chapter 5
Education in the United States:
Its Historical Roots

Overview

This chapter, which describes the history of education in the United States, focuses on changing conceptions of teachers and teaching. Using changes in aims of education as a frame of reference, the chapter analyzes the evolving role of education in the United States. The *Decision Making: Defining Yourself as a Professional* section in this chapter asks the reader to project current trends into the future.

Chapter Goals

This chapter examines

- How European roots influenced American education
- Issues involved in the role of religion in American education
- Historical roots of free public education for all students
- How schools historically responded to different minority groups
- The role of the federal government in education

Chapter Outline

I. The Colonial Period (1607–1775)
    A. Differences in Colonies
        1. The Southern Colonies
        2. The Middle Colonies
        3. The New England Colonies
    B. European Crosscurrents
    C. The Colonial Legacy
    D. Video Perspectives: God and Evolution in Kansas Classrooms
II. The Early National Period (1775–1820)
    A. Redefining American Education: Religion and the Schools
    B. Educational Governance: Whose Responsibility?
    C. The Legacy of the Early National Period
III. The Common School Movement: The Rise of State Support for Public Education (1820–1865)
    A. The Common School Movement: Making Education Available to All
        1. The Contributions of Horace Mann
        2. Expansion of the Common School Movement
        3. Issues of Quality and Quantity in Teacher Education
    B. The Legacy of the Common School Movement
IV. The Evolution of the American High School
    A. Historical Roots of the Comprehensive High School
    B. Redefining the High School
    C. Junior High and Middle Schools
    D. American Secondary Schools: Future Directions
V. The Progressive Era
VI. Searching for Equality: The Education of Cultural Minorities
    A. Native American Education
    B. African American Education: Up from Slavery to . . .
        1. Proposed Solutions to the Problem

        2. The Courts Examine "Separate But Equal"
    C. Hispanic Education
    D. The Asian American Educational Experience
    E. The Search for Equality: Where Are We Now?
VII. The Modern Era: Schools as Instruments for National Purpose and Social Change
    A. The Cold War: Enlisting America's Schools
    B. The War on Poverty and the Great Society–Compensatory Education Programs
        1. Head Start
        2. Title I
        3. Putting Compensatory Education Programs into Perspective
    C. Exploring Diversity: The Federal Government's Role in Pursuing Equality
        1. The Civil Rights Movement
        2. Equity for Women
        3. Putting Federal Efforts into Perspective
    D. Teaching in an Era of Reform: The Federal Government Issue
        1. Setting Standards
        2. Testing
        3. Financial Incentives
VIII. Decision Making: Defining Yourself as a Professional

Transparencies

T 5.1 (Table 5.1) Changes in Educational Thought in Europe
T 5.2 (Table 5.2) A Summary of Historical Periods in American Education
T 5.3 (Figure 5.1) The Evolution of the American High School
T 5.4 (Table 5.3) Major Provisions of the Goals 2000 Act

Teaching Suggestions

I. The Colonial Period

The purpose of this section is to help students understand how education in the colonial period continues to influence education today.

- *Transparency 5.1* **"Changes in Educational Thought in Europe" describes the contributions of four European educational philosophers. Ask students to analyze what these thinkers had in common and how they differed from prevalent colonial thinking. Also, ask which views are still valued today.**

- **Point out that religion in the schools continues to be a flashpoint in U.S. education and the topic will be revisited in Chapter 9 (Law) and Chapter 10 (Curriculum).**

- **We've found that religion in the public schools is a topic that interests students, and most have strong opinions about it. Organize a debate around the pros and cons of religion in the schools. In the discussion help students differentiate between what is personally desired and what is legal at the present time.**

- *Going into Schools #1* **asks students to interview a teacher about recent historical trends in schools. Lead a discussion comparing different interview perspectives.**

- *Journal Starter #1* **asks students to reflect on their own views about religion in the schools and** think about how this could influence them as teachers.

II. The Early National Period

The purpose of this section is to help students understand the historical antecedents of present-day controversies over religion and the role of the federal government in education.

- Help students understand the historical origins of the First Amendment by reminding them of the reasons many colonists came to America–to escape the established religion of the Church of England.

- Point out that the Tenth Amendment laid the foundation for our present governance system, which they'll study in Chapter 8.

- Lead a discussion on the pros and cons of a centralized federal education system by having students brainstorm these as you write them on the board. Point out that most other countries have a centralized system. Ask why we don't.

- *Reflect on This* in this section asks students to wrestle with a teacher's obligation to meet or address externally imposed standards. Use this opportunity to help students understand how these issues will affect them as teachers.

III. The Common School Movement: The Rise of State Support for Public Education

The purpose of this section is to help students understand how the common school movement laid the foundation for today's public schools.

- *Transparency 5.2* summarizes the significant developments of this and the previous two periods and describes controversial issues that still remain.

- *Increasing Understanding 5.3* asks students to analyze recent immigration trends. To personalize this, ask students to describe their own immigrant roots, and list their countries of origin and dates of immigration. Put this information on a timeline, and discuss patterns and trends as a class.

- Point out that some one-room school houses still exist today. (This might also make an interesting topic for a more in-depth student investigation.) There is increased current interest in multiage classrooms and cross-age tutoring.

IV. The Evolution of the American High School

The purpose of this section is to help students understand how historical events influenced the development of U.S. secondary education.

- *Transparency 5.3* contains a timeline of the significant historical events in the evolution of the American high school. Ask students to extend and update the information to the present time.

- To personalize the information on the junior high and middle schools, ask students which they attended, and ask them to describe their own experiences in them, including both strengths and weaknesses of the schools as they perceived them.

- *Going into Schools #4* asks students to interview a middle school or junior high teacher about ways the schools attempt to meet the needs of developing adolescents. Have students report their findings back to the whole class.

V. The Progressive Era

The purpose of this section is to help students understand the historical roots of the progressive movement in U.S. education.

- Encourage students to make cross-chapter links with Chapter 6 (Philosophy), Chapter 10 (Curriculum), and Chapter 11 (Instruction). Point out that progressive ideas are still prevalent in many current reform efforts like the NCTM standards and constructivist learning theories.

VI. Searching for Equality: The Education of Cultural Minorities

The purpose of this section is to help students understand how U.S. schools have attempted to deal with students of color.

- To help students understand similarities and differences in approaches to schooling cultural minorities, draw a matrix on the board or overhead with different minority groups on the side and with major issues/approaches and problems on the top. Small groups could be assigned responsibility for different boxes or cells, and you could collate the total information into a handout for the class to discuss and analyze.

- Ask how language played a role in the success or failure of different cultural minority groups in the U.S. educational system. Refer students back to the information on ELL instruction in Chapter 3.

- The *Reflect on This* feature in this section asks students to think about the curricular and instructional issues involved in teaching cultural minorities.

VII. The Modern Era: Schools as Instruments for National Purpose and Social Change

The purpose of this section is to encourage students to think about schools as instruments of political and social change.

- Ask students to identify both advantages and disadvantages of viewing schools as instruments of national purpose. Write these on the board, and ask students whether this is a positive trend.

- Ask students to apply the concept of separate but equal to education for women and students with exceptionalities. Ask why separate but equal works in some instances but not in others.

- *Transparency 5.4* contains a summary of the Goals 2000 initiative. Ask whether these goals are still viable and valuable today.

- Organize a debate around the increased federal role in U.S. education. The *You Take a Position* assignment in the *Teaching in an Era of Reform* could serve as an informational base for this discussion. Ask students to identify strengths and weaknesses of each position.

- *Journal Starter #2* asks students to think about their own views on the proper role of the federal government in education.

Journal Starters

1.Encourage students to think about their own beliefs about the proper role of religion in education: What is the proper role of religion in the schools? What are the pros and cons of greater emphasis on religion in the schools? What religions did you encounter as you were growing up? How did they influence your development? What religions are you likely to encounter in your teaching? How will this influence your teaching?

2.Encourage students to think more deeply about the federal government's role in education: How big a role should the federal government play in education? Would education in the U.S. be improved by a comprehensive federal educational system? Have you ever benefitted from the federal government's role in education? How? How much variability in education is there within your state? How much is there within your region of the country? Are these regional differences helpful or damaging to education?

Increasing Understanding: Questions and Feedback

5.1 From a student perspective what advantages and disadvantages were there in instruction in native languages? From a national perspective what advantages and disadvantages were there in instruction in the native language?
5.1
From students' perspective, instruction in their own native language was easier, but this didn't provide access to other students and their languages. From a national perspective, instruction in their native language, while easier for the students, failed to produce a common language that could unify all colonies. The same issues arise today in the debate over bilingual education.

5.2 How would these philosophers have reacted to the New England schools? What changes would they have recommended?
5.2
They probably would have been aghast at many of the practices and would have recommended kinder, more child-centered practices.

5.3 Nationally, where are most recent immigrants to the U.S. from? What about your specific region of the country? What implications does this have for the schools and the teachers in them?
5.3
Nationally the most recent immigrants to the U.S. are from Mexico, Central and South America, followed by Southeast Asia and Asia. Regional trends vary. The arrival of these immigrants poses opportunities for ELL teachers. For example, in the Southwest large numbers of teachers who speak Spanish are needed.

5.4 How would you answer citizens without children who question the need for or legality of taxes for schools? How is this tax purpose similar to or different from using taxes to support a police or fire department or a mail system?
5.4
Schools benefit everyone, not just parents. Well-educated citizens are less likely to break the law and go to jail and are more productive members of the workforce. In many ways all of these services serve the national good. This is why it is illegal in some states for policemen, firemen, and teachers to strike, because lawmakers feel these services are essential for the public good.

5.5 Explain how the Committee of Ten membership and faculty psychology influenced decisions about the curriculum for non-college-bound students. How might the inclusion of parents on the committee, especially immigrant parents, have changed the nature of the recommendations?
5.5
Since the members were all college oriented, their recommendations were slanted in favor of a college-prep curriculum. Emphasis on faculty psychology resulted in an emphasis on memorizing static information. The inclusion of parents, especially immigrant ones, would probably have resulted in a more applied curriculum that

would have helped students cope with second-language learning and the demands of working in this new country.

5.6 Would progressive ideas be more compatible with a junior high or a middle school? Why?
5.6
Progressive ideas would be more compatible with a middle school because these schools are more student centered.

5.7 How would progressive educators react to the Indian boarding schools?   What adaptations might they suggest?
5.7
Progressive educators would abhor the Indian boarding schools because the focus of these schools was on assimilation and the learning of preestablished content.   Instead they would recommend emphasizing a curriculum based on students' interests and needs.

5.8 Why wasn't bilingual education a major issue with Native American education? with African American education?
5.8
Bilingual education wasn't a major issue for Native American education for several reasons.   First, there were so many different languages spoken by the different tribes that the languages were often only spoken and not written, and there were few teachers who could speak these languages.   All of these considerations made bilingual education logistically unfeasible.   With African American education the students already spoke English.

5.9 Describe a "melting pot" approach to teaching American history. Describe a multiflavored salad approach.
5.9
A "melting pot" approach would teach important dates and names, emphasizing mainstream commonalities.   A "multiflavored" approach would emphasize the unique contributions and challenges different groups encountered in our history.

5.10 Why were educational efforts during the Cold War focused on science, math, and foreign languages?
5.10
Educational efforts were focused on these areas because they were most important to the country's strategic defense.

5.11 How was the War on Poverty similar to other educational efforts aimed at minorities? Different?
5.11
Other efforts were focused on specific minority groups.   The War on Poverty focused on a lack of money, a problem that cut across all ethnic and cultural lines.   The War on Poverty was similar to earlier efforts in that it attempted to help underserved groups benefit from our country's educational system.

5.12 How does the concept of separate but equal relate to education for women and students with exceptionalities?
5.12
From figures on participation and funding, it appears that women still are at a disadvantage in some respects educationally.   (Other data, which you encountered in Chapter 3, suggest that the picture is more complex, with boys also encountering difficulties and problems in the educational system.) One goal for special education is to make the education of students with exceptionalities both integrated and equal, because research shows that separate results in unequal.

Reflect on This: Questions and Feedback
(These can also be found on the Companion Website: www.prenhall.com/kauchak .)

Reflect on This (One): Challenges of Standardized Testing

1. Who should be responsible for determining what content is best for the students in a class? How much should standardized tests and state district guidelines influence what a teacher does in the classroom?

This question cuts to the heart of teacher professionalism and autonomy. Are teachers just hired to implement a standard curriculum, or can they, on the basis of their professional judgment, alter the curriculum to best meet their students' needs? We'll return to the question of academic freedom again in Chapter 9, which discusses educational legal issues. For now we'll say that a teacher can adapt the curriculum to meet student needs but that the teacher needs to be able to professionally explain and defend these changes.

2. Do all students need the same curriculum? How much latitude should teachers have in adapting the curriculum to student needs?

The answers to these questions are similar to those with the first question. Not all children need the same curriculum; that's why teachers are trained professionals. The issue of teacher latitude in adapting the curriculum is likely to become more controversial in this era of increased attention to testing and reform.

3. What limitations do beginning teachers have in terms of professional decision making?

Beginning teachers have basically the same rights as experienced teachers with two exceptions. First, most beginning teachers are hired on a probationary basis, so tenure protections may be lacking (see Chapter 9). Second, they may not yet have established a positive professional reputation in their schools with parents and administrators. This reputation gives teachers more latitude in their classrooms.

4. What would you do in this situation?

This is a personal decision, of course. But our guess is that students will be faced with a decision similar to this in their first few years of teaching. They should be ready!

Reflect on This (Two): Involving All Students

1. What are the advantages and disadvantages of trying to call on all students during lessons?

A major advantage is that learning and motivation increase because all students are involved and feel part of a learning community. Disadvantages include students not wanting to participate and the pace of the lesson slowing down.

2. What should a teacher do if a student doesn't know the answer? What should a teacher do if the student doesn't want to participate?

Research suggests that prompting the student has both motivational and learning benefits. It communicates that all can learn and the teacher is there to assist in the process. If the student doesn't want to participate, teacher sensitivity is required. Short term the teacher might let the student "pass." Long term the teacher might talk to the student to discover the reasons behind the reticence. In addition, the teacher can purposefully give the student easier, open-ended questions with which the student can succeed.

3. What responsibilities does a teacher have in attempting to actively involve all students–girls, underachievers, cultural minorities–in lessons? Do these efforts have any negative consequences for more verbally aggressive students?

Within the general framework of being sensitive to individual and cultural differences, teachers have a responsibility to involve all students in learning activities. To do otherwise shortchanges girls, underachievers, and cultural minorities. Doing so does not have negative consequences for more verbally aggressive students. It teaches them to be patient and share classroom time and resources.

4. What would you do if you were the student teacher described in this case?

The answer to this question will, of course, vary. One possible suggestion is to use more small-group work that provides more opportunities for all to participate. Another is to purposefully design easier, open-ended questions that ensure success. A third possibility is to talk to students individually about this problem.

Video Perspectives: Questions and Feedback
God and Evolution in Kansas Classrooms

1. What are some reasons that religion is such a hotly debated topic in American education?

One major reason is historical; from colonial times there has been an ongoing tradition of religion influencing our schools. In addition, religion plays a central role in many Americans' lives, as do families and children. When these two areas overlap, controversy is probably inevitable.

2. What areas of the curriculum are most likely to encounter problems with religious issues?

Virtually all areas of the curriculum have overlap with religious topics and concerns. The humanities, including literature and art, continually deal with the meaning of life. The social sciences, including history and anthropology, attempt to explain the human condition. Even the sciences, especially biology, deal with human origins. Areas like math and grammar seem relatively safe.

3. What are the advantages and disadvantages of including religion in our schools?

A definite advantage is that integrating religion would link school to many homes and allow the teaching of values. However, the inclusion of religious advocacy is forbidden by the U.S. Constitution. In addition, the diversity of the U.S. in terms of differing religions makes the inclusion of any one religion impractical and counterproductive.

Self-Assessment Questions
(Note: Students have access to these questions and their feedback on the text's Companion Website.)

1. The historical significance of the Old Deluder Satan Act was that it
   a. required towns to provide education for children.
   b. encouraged religious instruction in public schools.
   c. set aside land for schools in every township.
   d. set up a system of schools for the ministry.

2. Which amendment to the Constitution established the principle of the separation of church and state?
   a. First
   b. Fourth
   c. Fifth
   d. Tenth

3. The Tenth Amendment to the Constitution is important because it
   a. clearly separated church and state.
   b. said areas of law not assigned to the federal government would be the responsibility of states.
   c. established common schools, which were the foundation of our public education system.

     d.   gave the federal government the right to support schools through taxes.

4. Common schools were founded on the belief that
     a.   students needed to have a moral education.
     b.   democracy required a well-educated citizenry.
     c.   all students needed to read and write English.
     d.   students needed to develop practical job skills in school.

5. Normal schools were important because they
     a.   established free public schools for all children.
     b.   provided access to education for immigrant children.
     c.   created a vehicle for upward mobility for minority children.
     d.   provided training for future teachers.

6. The Cardinal Principles of Secondary Education differed from the recommendations of the Committee of Ten in that the principles were more
     a.   academic.
     b.   rigorous.
     c.   applied.
     d.   explicit.

7. The progressive education movement believed that schools should
     a.   assist immigrants in the assimilation process.
     b.   teach basic skills to prepare children for life.
     c.   stress academics to help prepare students for college.
     d.   make connections between subjects and students' lives.

8. W.E.B. Dubois differed from Booker T. Washington in that he believed that
     a.   social activism was more important than cooperation.
     b.   applied courses were more valuable than academic ones.
     c.   high schools were important for African American success.
     d.   all African Americans should learn to read and write.

9. Historically which minority group fared the best in U.S. schools?
     a.   African Americans
     b.   Asian Americans
     c.   Hispanics
     d.   Native Americans

10. The Supreme Court case, *Brown v. the Board of Education of Topeka*, is important because it
     a.   established universal free education for all children.
     b.   outlawed the practice of racial discrimination.
     c.   banned the practice of separate but equal in schools.
     d.   eliminated discrimination through bilingual education programs.

Self-Assessment Feedback
1. a   The Old Deluder Satan Act became one of the foundations for our public education system because it required towns of over 50 people to establish a school for their children.
2. a   The First Amendment to the Constitution establishes separation of church and state.
3. b   This was important because it passed responsibility to the states.
4. b   Horace Mann, the major figure in the founding of the common schools, believed that an educated citizenry was crucial to a democracy.

5. d   Normal schools provided postsecondary education for women who were going to be teachers.
6. c   The Cardinal Principles placed much more emphasis on applied goals like vocational education, personal health, and civic education.
7. d   Progressive educators believed that schools should be microcosms of society, teaching students about the world through hands-on activities.
8. a   W.E.B. Dubois believed that social activism and actively fighting against segregation were more important than cooperation and accommodation.
9. b   On standardized test scores Asian American students generally perform the highest.
10. c   This important Supreme Court decision basically said that separate but equal, a central tenet of segregation policies, was illegal.

PRAXIS Practice: Questions and Feedback

1. Analyze Dave's comments in terms of the history of the middle school/junior high movement. Where would Dave's teaching more clearly fit?

Dave's teaching more clearly fits in a traditional junior high school, with its emphasis on academics and preparation for high school.

2. In which type of earlier school–Latin grammar school, academy, or English high school–would Dave's teaching fit the best? least?

Dave's teaching is most compatible with the Latin grammar school, with its emphasis on college preparation. It would be at odds with the academy because of its emphasis on practical subjects. It would also be at odds with the early English high school because it attempted to meet the needs of boys not planning to attend college.

3. Which report, the Committee of Ten or the Cardinal Principles of Secondary Education, would Dave agree with more? Why?

The report of the Committee of Ten strongly emphasized strong academic preparation for all students, even those not planning to go on to college. The Cardinal Principles of Secondary Education, by contrast, emphasized applied goals in basic skill areas as well as life skills such as civic education and effective use of leisure time.

4. What evidence of progressive education is there at Westmont Middle School?

Westmont's emphasis on problem-based learning contained elements of progressive education. In addition, if the team meetings focused on the needs of students, these too would be aligned with progressive education.

Useful Web Site Addresses

Web Links for Chapter Terms

academies
http://www.rootsweb.com/~txrober2/Edu3.htm

assimilation
http://www.ccsf.edu/Resources/Tolerance/sfor/assim02.html
http://www.prospect.org/print/V9/36/aleinikoff-t.html

character education

http://www.character.org/
http://www.ethicsusa.com/
http://www.charactercounts.org/
http://www.cde.ca.gov/character/

common school movement
http://i2i.org/Publications/Op-Eds/Education/op971015.htm
http://www.weac.org/GreatSchools/Issuepapers/commonschool.htm

compensatory education
http://www.ed.gov/pubs/EdReformStudies/EdReforms/chap7a.html
http://www.kerrlaw.com/SpEdTopics/compensatory.htm

comprehensive high school
http://www.nccte.org/publications/ncrve/mds-13xx/mds-1316.pdf

English classical school
http://www.mun.ca/rels/restmov/texts/tcampbell/etc/ECSOMA.HTM
http://cepa.newschool.edu/het/schools/ricardian.htm

Head Start
http://www.nhsa.org/
http://www.acf.dhhs.gov/programs/opa/facts/headst.htm
http://www.acf.hhs.gov/programs/hsb/
http://www.ehsnrc.org/
http://www.headstartinfo.org/
http://www.childrensdefense.org/head-start.htm

junior high schools: http://www.mala.bc.ca/homeroom/Content/Topics/Programs/2001/JNRHI/

Latin grammar school: http://personal.pitnet.net/primarysources/grammar.html

magnet schools: http://www.magnet.edu/

middle schools: http://www.nmsa.org/

normal schools
http://www.rootsweb.com/~mahampde/wn/toc.html
http://www.co.centre.pa.us/sketches/s12.htm

one-room schools: http://www.lib.cmich.edu/clarke/schoolsintro.htm

Old Deluder Satan Act: http://historyeducationinfo.com/edu1.htm

progressive education: http://www.albany.edu/~dkw42/s2_dewey_progr.html

separate but equal: http://www.law.umkc.edu/faculty/projects/ftrials/conlaw/sepbutequal.htm

Title I
http://www.pta.org/ptawashington/issues/titleone.asp
http://www.futureofchildren.org/usr_doc/vol5no3APPc.pdf

vouchers
http://abcnews.go.com/sections/us/DailyNews/scotus_vouchers020627.html
http://www.aft.org/research/vouchers/index.htm
http://www.nea.org/issues/vouchers/

War on Poverty
http://www.fordham.edu/halsall/mod/1964johnson-warpoverty.html
http://www.lexisnexis.com/academic/2upa/Aph/JohnsonPoverty.asp

Web Links for "Teaching in an Era of Reform: The Federal Government Issue"

AACTE Education Policy Clearinghouse: http://www.edpolicy.org/

      Testing Research: http://www.edpolicy.org/research/testing/index.php

      Teacher Quality: http://www.edpolicy.org/research/teacherq/index.php

      NCLB Research: http://www.edpolicy.org/research/nclb/index.php

Federal Role in Education: http://www.ed.gov/about/overview/fed/role.html?src=ln

Improving Student Achievement: http://www.rand.org/publications/MR/MR924/

NAEP Reading and Math Assessments in Urban Districts
http://nces.ed.gov/commissioner/remarks2003/12_17_2003.asp

National Assessment of Educational Progress: http://www.mredcopac.org/arti0018.htm

National Center for Educational Statistics: http://nces.ed.gov/pubsearch/

Nation's Report Card: http://nces.ed.gov/nationsreportcard/

No Child Left Behind: http://www.ed.gov/nclb/landing.jhtml

Web Links for "Exploring Diversity: The Federal Government's Role in Pursuing Equality"

1997 PBS Interview on Government Role in Education
http://www.pbs.org/newshour/@capitol/forum/september97/ff5_9-17.html

Main Street Republicans Support OERI: http://www.aera.net/gov/archive/n0200-01.htm

No Child Left Behind: http://www.ed.gov/nclb/landing.jhtml

Quality, Affordability and Access: Americans Speak on Higher Education
http://www.ets.org/aboutets/americaspeaks/2003find.html

White House Initiatives: http://www.ed.gov/about/inits/list/index.html?src=ln

Additional Chapter Web Links

Education in the United States

Blackwell History of Education Museum: http://www.cedu.niu.edu/blackwell/
History of American Education Web Project: http://www.nd.edu/~rbarger/www7/index.html
History of Education in the United States: http://www.indiana.edu/~eric_rec/ieo/bibs/histedus.html
History of Education on the Internet: http://library.gcsu.edu/~sc/magepages/magelink.html
History of Education Review: http://www.soe.jcu.edu.au/her/
History of Education: Selected Moments of the 20th Century
http://fcis.oise.utoronto.ca/~daniel_schugurensky/assignment1/index.html
Lessons of a Century: http://www.edweek.org/sreports/century.htm
The Center for Dewey Studies: http://www.siu.edu/~deweyctr/index2.html

Equality and Education

The Education and Employment of Women: http://www.indiana.edu/~letrs/vwwp/butler/educ.html#Text
Equality and Education: http://www.equaleducation.com/
Realizing Gender Equality in Higher Education: The Need to Integrate Work/Family Issues
http://www.ed.gov/databases/ERIC_Digests/ed340273.html
No Child Left Behind: Achieving Equality Through High Standards and Accountability
http://www.nochildleftbehind.gov/index.html

Chapter 6
Educational Philosophy:
The Intellectual Foundations of American Education

Overview

Chapter 6 describes the influence of different philosophical movements on schools and schooling. Classical philosophies–such as idealism, realism, pragmatism, and existentialism–together with their educational counterparts–perennialism, essentialism, progressivism, and postmodernism–are discussed in terms of their effects on past and current educational practices. The final section of the chapter helps developing teachers develop their own evolving philosophy of teaching.

Chapter Goals

This chapter examines

- What is philosophy?
- Philosophies and their influence on teacher professionalism
- Traditional philosophies and their influence on the process of learning to teach
- Prominent philosophies of education and their implications for education
- How to begin to form your philosophy of education

Chapter Outline

I.   Philosophy and Philosophy of Education
    A.   Philosophy and Teacher Professionalism
    B.   The Relationship Between Philosophy and Theory
II.   Branches of Philosophy
    A.   Epistemology
    B.   Metaphysics
    C.   Axiology
    D.   Logic
III.   Traditional Schools of Philosophy
    A.   Idealism
    B.   Realism
    C.   Pragmatism
    D.   Existentialism
    E.   Teacher Decision Making: Applying the Traditional Philosophies
IV.   Exploring Diversity: Philosophy and Cultural Minorities
V.   Philosophies of Education
    A.   Perennialism
    B.   Essentialism
    C.   Progressivism
    D.   Postmodernism
VI.   Decision Making: Defining Yourself as a Professional
    A.   The Role of Beliefs in a Philosophy of Education
    B.   Examining Your Beliefs
    C.   Forming a Philosophy

Transparencies

T 6.1 (Figure 6.1) Philosophy and Professionalism
T 6.2 (Table 6.1) The Traditional Schools of Philosophy
T 6.3 (Table 6.2) Classroom Applications of the Educational Philosophies
T 6.4 (Table 6.3) An Analysis of Allie's Philosophy of Education

Teaching Suggestions

I. Philosophy and Philosophy of Education

The purpose of this section is to introduce the idea of philosophy, differentiate philosophy from theory, and convince the student that philosophy plays an important role in a teacher's life.

■   **To help students differentiate between theories and philosophies, first have them brainstorm different theories (for example, theory of evolution, behavioral learning theory) and philosophies. Then create a 2 x 2 matrix with theories and philosophies on the side and similarities and differences on the top. As a class activity have the class fill in the empty cells.**

II. Branches of Philosophy

The purpose of this section of the chapter is to introduce students to the traditional branches of philosophy.

■   **To help students understand the focus of each of these branches, provide an example of a key question addressed by each branch.**

III. Traditional Schools of Philosophy

The purpose of this section of the chapter is to introduce students to four traditional schools of philosophy and encourage them to connect these to their thoughts about teaching.

■   **To encourage students to think more deeply about the topics, ask students which is most important to teachers–epistemology, metaphysics, axiology, or logic? Which is least important to teachers? Why?**

■   **To help students connect these philosophies to their teaching, ask them to rank order the philosophies in terms of their appeal to them. Also, ask how their teaching level (K–12) or content area influences this ranking.**

■   **To help students analyze these philosophies more deeply, write them on the board, and ask students which are most similar? which are most different? Why?**

■   ***Transparency 6.2* "The Traditional Schools of Philosophy" analyzes each in terms of metaphysics, epistemology, axiology, and educational implications. Focus on educational implications, and ask students in small groups what a classroom would look like with each philosophy.**

■   ***Reflect on This* in this section examines issues related to Native American education and alternate philosophies.**

IV. Exploring Diversity: Philosophy and Cultural Minorities

The purpose of this section of the chapter is to explore how culture influences philosophy.

- To encourage students to think about how cultural differences influence philosophies, discuss the current emphasis on individual achievement in our grading system. Ask what teachers could do to de-emphasize competition in classrooms.

- Emphasize the dangers of stereotyping students. Ask students for ways that teachers could minimize the tendency to stereotype.

V. Philosophies of Education

This section examines four educational philosophies. The purpose of this section is to help students understand how these different philosophies influence teaching and learning.

- *Increasing Understanding 6.8* asks students to analyze the philosophies of Allie and Brad, the teachers in the chapter's opening case, in terms of pragmatism.

- *Increasing Understanding 6.11* asks students to relate essentialism to high-stakes testing. Ask if high-stakes testing could be justified under any of the educational philosophies.

- Ask students how perennialism and essentialism are similar? How are they different? Which seems more valuable today?

- Progressivism grew out of pragmatism. Ask how they are similar. How are they different?

- *Increasing Understanding 6.12* asks students to connect postmodernism to the traditional philosophies in the previous section. Point out that postmodernism is not only the most recent but also the most controversial.

- *Reflect on This* in this section asks students to apply the educational philosophies to a problem in teaching American history.

- *Teaching in an Era of Reform* focuses on the "essential knowledge" debate. This might serve as a focal point for a class debate after students have researched the topic.

- *Transparency 6.3* "Classroom Applications of the Educational Philosophies" analyzes each philosophy in terms of critical dimensions of classroom life.

- Ask students to determine your philosophy of education in terms of this class. Have them document their analyses with information from the syllabus, class comments, and activities. When they are done, share your philosophy with them.

- *Journal Starter #1* asks students to reflect on their previous educational experiences and analyze them through philosophical lenses.

VI. Decision Making: Defining Yourself as a Professional

The purpose of this section is to encourage students to begin work on their own personal philosophy of education.

- *Portfolio Activity 6.2* asks students to assess their own developing philosophy of education. To illustrate the range of views in the class, write each educational philosophy on the board or overhead with a line next to it for scores, ranging from 5 (the lower score) to 20 (the highest).

Ask students to put their score for each philosophy on the line with their initials. Discuss similarities and differences, and ask students to explain their philosophies.

- ■ *Going into Schools #1* asks students to interview a teacher about his or her philosophy of education. After students have completed the assignment, group students by their teacher's philosophy, have them share the information they collected and then report back to the whole class.

- ■ *Going into Schools #2* asks students to analyze a teacher's classroom and decide which type of philosophy it reflects. Compare students' observations and conclusions with *Transparency 6.3* "Classroom Applications of the Educational Philosophies."

- ■ *Transparency 6.4* analyzes Allie's philosophy of education. Ask students to do the same with Brad's. (Students are asked to do this in *Increasing Understanding 6.15*.)

- ■ *Classroom Windows* video asks students to view two video clips of secondary social studies teachers. One is very teacher-centered, using lectures to present content, while the other is more interactive, using questioning to stimulate thinking. The questions in this feature ask students to analyze the teachers in terms of both traditional and educational philosophies.

- ■ *Journal Starter #2* asks students to analyze different philosophies in terms of their own developing philosophies of teaching and education.

Journal Starters

1. Encourage students to think about their prior educational experiences in terms of educational philosophies: Think about your educational experiences in K–12 education. Was there any one particular philosophy or philosophies that undergirded your educational experiences? What evidence do you have for this? Think about a particular teacher that was influential in your life. What kind of philosophy do you think guided his or her teaching? Why do you think so? What implications does this have for you as a future teacher?

2. Encourage students to think about their developing philosophies of teaching: Which educational philosophy is most appealing to you now? What elements of it are appealing to you? How will these elements influence you as a teacher? What elements of other philosophies would you like to incorporate in your teaching? Which philosophy is least compatible with your developing views on teaching? Why? What implications does this have for you as a teacher?

Increasing Understanding: Questions and Feedback

6.1
Figure 6.1 emphasizes knowledge, decision making, and reflection. Explain how autonomy is also illustrated in Allie's and Brad's conversation.
6.1
Allie's and Brad's autonomy was illustrated in the freedom they had to approach their instruction in ways that were consistent with their personal philosophies. For example, they each set their own goals and the aspects of instruction and learning that they would emphasize. Allie, for instance, chose to give a lot of quizzes, grounded in the belief that students basically want to learn but that they aren't initially intrinsically motivated to do so. She believed that their intrinsic motivation followed from their increased understanding of a topic. She had the autonomy that allowed her to approach her instruction in ways that were consistent with her philosophy. Similarly, Brad believed less in the value of frequent quizzes and essential knowledge, but he also had the autonomy to approach his instruction in ways that were consistent with his educational philosophy.

6.2

We said that philosophy guides practice. Does theory also guide practice? Explain.

6.2

Yes, theory also guides practice. For example, "People tend to imitate behavior they observe in others" was described as a principle of social cognitive theory. Teachers applying this principle will then behave in ways they would like to have their students imitate.

6.3

A woman is shopping for a new car. In making her decision, she places primary emphasis on cars' mileage ratings, their repair records, and evaluations from organizations such as the American Automobile Association. Is her "way of knowing" primarily the scientific method, intuition, or authority? Explain.

6.3

The woman's way of knowing is primarily the scientific method. She is using evidence–mileage ratings, repair records, and external evaluations–as a basis for making her decision.

6.4

With respect to epistemology, are Allie's and Brad's views quite similar or are they quite different? Explain, citing evidence taken directly from the case study to support your position.

6.4

Allie's and Brad's views with respect to epistemology are quite different. Allie tends to base her views on evidence, such as "Now, I was reading in one of my journals awhile back, and the authors were talking about the link between achievement and self-esteem, and it really made sense." Brad, in contrast, tends to rely more on intuition, as indicated by his comment, "So, reality is what we perceive it to be, and there's no objective source out there to decide which view is the 'right one.'"

6.5

Character educators see learners as unsocialized and in need of moral discipline. In contrast, moral educators see learners as undeveloped, needing stimulation to construct more mature moral views. Are these contrasting positions more closely related to metaphysics or to epistemology? Explain.

6.5

These contrasting positions are more closely related to metaphysics (what we know) than epistemology (how we know). For instance, for character educators reality is that learners are unsocialized, but for moral educators reality is that learners are undeveloped.

6.6

You're being asked to respond to margin questions, such as this one. We have concluded that questions such as these will increase your understanding of this book. Identify a major premise and a minor premise on which this conclusion could be based.

6.6

A major premise could be "Students understand more of the content they study when they are periodically asked to apply their understanding to a new situation," and a minor premise would be "Students are asked to apply their understanding to new situations in the margin questions."

6.7

Would idealists support the scientific method, or would they be critical of it? Explain. To which of the four branches of philosophy is this question most closely related? Explain.

6.7

Idealists would support the emphasis on logic and clear thinking that is emphasized in the scientific method. However, since the physical world is constantly changing, according to Idealists, they would be skeptical of relying on observations of the physical world as a basis for making decisions about reality. The question is most closely related to epistemology, since the scientific method is one way of "knowing."

6.8

Based on the conversation in our opening case study, would Allie's or Brad's views be more closely related to pragmatism? Cite evidence from the case to support your contention.

6.8

Brad's views would be more closely related to pragmatism. For example, Brad commented, "The person who really succeeds is the one who continues to learn and is able to adapt to changes in the world by solving the large and small problems he or she encounters." This comment is closely related to pragmatism's emphasis on practical problem solving.

6.9

Think about Allie's philosophical position in the case study at the beginning of this chapter. In what way or ways are her views consistent with perennialism? In what way or ways are they inconsistent with the views of perennialists? Explain.

6.9

Allie's views are consistent with perennialism in her emphasis on knowledge and clear thinking. They are not consistent in her emphasis on practicality. Her comment "Now, there's real, practical stuff out there that they need to know" illustrates this position. Perennialists are less concerned with information that is practical because, in their view, practicality changes too rapidly.

6.10

Would perennialists favor or would they be opposed to vocational education? Explain.

6.10

Perennialists are opposed to vocational education. Perennialists believe in a rigorous intellectual curriculum for all students. For perennialists education is preparation for future life, and the extent to which students find their studies relevant isn't crucial in the perennialist view.

6.11

High-stakes testing, in which students are required to pass standardized tests before they're allowed to graduate from high school, for example, is being emphasized today. Would essentialists react negatively or positively to this trend? Explain.

6.11

Essentialists react positively to this trend. Essentialists believe that a critical core of information exists that all people should possess. High-stakes tests measure the extent to which people actually do possess this information.

6.12

Of the traditional philosophies—idealism, realism, pragmatism, and existentialism—which would be most acceptable to postmodernists? Explain.

6.12

Existentialism would probably be most acceptable to postmodernists. Existentialists believe individuals create their own existence in their own unique way, so the focus is on the individual. Postmodernists believe that certain individuals—particularly white males of European descent—have been historically favored. These two views, while not identical, are more closely related than the views of postmodernism and the other traditional philosophies.

6.13

Throughout this text you've been asked to respond to margin questions such as this one. The fact that these questions exist and the types of questions being asked best reflect which of the educational philosophies? Explain.

6.13

These questions best reflect essentialism. The questions are based on the belief that a core of knowledge exists that all readers of this book should understand, and the questions are placed in the margins to help readers acquire that understanding. These are views grounded in essentialism.

6.14

Throughout this book we've provided references for the information we've presented. What does this imply about our epistemological beliefs? What does this imply about our axiological beliefs? Explain in each case.

6.14

Including references implies a belief that conclusions should be based on evidence. The conclusions are part of the text, and the sources that are cited are the evidence for the conclusions. It is an epistemology consistent with the scientific method. Providing evidence–in the form of citations–is based on the belief that academic ethics require that authors provide evidence for the conclusions they make and give credit to the people who provide the evidence.

6.15

Look again at Brad's thinking, as indicated by his conversation with Allie. Based on this information, describe what you believe is his philosophy of education. Explain how the philosophy is based on his beliefs.

6.15

Based on his conversation with Allie, we would describe his philosophy of education as follows: In Brad's view school should be preparation for life after students leave the classroom, and the way they best prepare for life is to practice life skills, which are the abilities to make decisions and solve real-world problems, not learn isolated facts. For Brad important knowledge is the knowledge people need to make decisions and solve problems. These views are based on the belief that the only way people learn to make decisions and solve problems is to practice both. These views are also based on the belief that reality is uncertain, so reality depends on the situation people are in at the time. In this regard Brad's views are closely aligned with pragmatism.

Reflect on This: Questions and Feedback
(These can also be found on the Companion Website: www.prenhall.com/kauchak .)

Reflect on This (One): How Alternative Philosophies Affect Teaching

1. To what extent are you responsible for encouraging all students to be in school and to be there on time?

Because as a professional you understand the important connections between time spent on learning and the amount learned, you are responsible for strongly encouraging all students to be in school and to be there on time. You can't force students to attend, but even tacitly endorsing students missing school or coming to school late would be unprofessional. However, you still need to communicate to these students that you care about them and want them to succeed in your classroom.

2. What could you do to maintain the momentum of your lesson yet accommodate the needs of your Native American students?

One effective strategy for maintaining lesson momentum is to ask a number of open-ended questions (questions for which a variety of answers are acceptable). For instance, suppose you're doing a lesson on plants and you have displayed a cactus and a broad-leafed plant. You might ask, "How are the two plants similar?" "How are the two plants different?" or "What do you notice about either one of the plants?" Questions such as these can significantly increase the participation of students who are reluctant to respond. Another effective strategy is to provide more wait time after questions are asked to provide students more time to respond. Another way to accommodate the needs of your Native American students is to downplay the competitive aspects of your class by using more cooperative learning activities that encourage students to work with each other in completing tasks and answering questions.

3. Should you continue to call on all the students, even though some of them prefer to not be called on at all?

Yes, we believe that you should call on students even though they're initially reluctant to respond. We believe that all students, including cultural minorities, fundamentally want to learn and be successful. If students are able to answer successfully and are not put in competitive situations, much of their reluctance to respond will disappear. The use of open-ended questions as we discussed in Item 2 would be an effective strategy for encouraging students to respond.

4. What would you do in this situation?

We would make every effort to call on all the students as equally as possible, and we would use open-ended questions and increased wait time as tools to promote participation.

Reflect on This (Two): Educational Philosophy in the Classroom

1. With which educational philosophy are your goals most closely aligned? With which are they least aligned?

Because of your emphasis on problem solving, critical thinking , and informed decision making, your goals are most aligned with progressivism. These goals are least aligned with perennialism and essentialism because these emphasize content over student problem solving.

2. Using one of these educational philosophies, how might you respond to students when they ask, "Why do we have to learn this stuff?"

This is a difficult question to answer to students' satisfaction. The most effective way to accommodate this issue is to actively involve students in motivating learning activities and help them be as successful as possible in these activities. The combination of motivating activities and success will result in their being less inclined to ask why they have to learn the information. Success can be promoted in two important ways. First, you can create the best quality examples or representations possible to illustrate the content you're teaching, and second, you can design your learning activities to actively involve students as much as possible. To see these suggestions implemented in a real-world classroom, look at the Classroom Windows video episode that accompanies this chapter. As you look at the episode, pay particular attention to the way Judy Holmquist, the teacher, represents the content for her students and how she involves them in the learning activity.

3. Should you "force" students to be involved if they're reluctant to participate? How might you involve reluctant students in lessons?

Yes, you should "force" students to be involved. We, of course, don't literally mean "force"; we mean encourage, and students can be encouraged by using effective representations of content, such as Judy's in the video episode, and open-ended questions as tools. The techniques described in the feedback for Reflect on This (I) are effective. These techniques include using open-ended questions and calling on all the students as equally as possible.

4. How would you handle the situation just described?

We would do what we've suggested in the feedback to questions 1, 2, and 3.

Classroom Windows: Questions and Feedback
Examining Philosophies of Teaching

1. Which of the traditional philosophies is most nearly reflected in Judy's teaching? Why do you think so?

Of the traditional philosophies Judy's teaching most nearly reflects pragmatism. Pragmatism emphasizes direct experiences and problem solving, and Judy's students were directly involved in gathering the information that appeared on her matrix, and they were involved in a form of problem solving as they searched for patterns and relationships in the information.

2. Which of the traditional philosophies is most nearly reflected in Bob's teaching? Explain why you think so.

Of the traditional philosophies Bob's teaching most nearly reflects realism. An understanding of our world is an important goal for realists, and an understanding of the causes of the Vietnam War helps us understand our world. Also, his focus was on information, as opposed to practical problem solving, which would be more nearly aligned with pragmatism.

3. Which of the educational philosophies is most nearly reflected in Judy's teaching? Explain why you think so.

Of the educational philosophies Judy's teaching most nearly reflects progressivism. Her lesson was learner-centered, her students collaborated in the activity, and she guided their learning with her questioning. These are all characteristics of progressivism.

4. Which of the educational philosophies is most nearly reflected in Bob's teaching? Explain why you think so.

Of the educational philosophies Bob's teaching most nearly reflects essentialism. Essentialism is grounded in the belief that important knowledge exists that all people should understand. Understanding the causes and outcomes of the Vietnam War would be viewed by essentialists as important to understanding today's world as an American citizen.

5. Which teacher, Judy or Bob, most clearly reflects your own personal philosophy of education? Explain.

The answer to this question depends on the individual. Our personal philosophies are more nearly aligned with Judy's than with Bob's. This is based on the belief that students need to be active participants in lessons in order to learn as much as possible. We also believe that essential knowledge exists that all teachers should know. In that regard our thinking is also guided by essentialism.

Self-Assessment Questions
(Note: Students have access to these questions and their feedback on the text's Companion Website.)

1. Sharon Horn has her second graders working on activities in which they determine what kinds of solutions will conduct electricity by connecting a battery and a flashlight bulb to electrodes placed in different liquids–such as fresh water, salt water, soft drinks, and oil–and seeing when the bulb lights up. "They love these activities, and this is the only way they get to where they really understand the ideas," Sharon contends. Sharon's approach to science is most strongly grounded in
    a.   perennialism.
    b.   essentialism.
    c.   progressivism.
    d.   postmodernism.

2. Joan Bray, an English teacher, has her students read *Beowulf* because "it's a classic piece of literature, and it deals with the struggle between good and evil, an idea that has existed forever." She continues, "Because the world changes so rapidly, the only thing we can really rely on is the ideas that we carry with us." The traditional school of philosophy on which Joan is most strongly basing her decision is
    a.   idealism.
    b.   realism.
    c.   pragmatism.
    d.   existentialism.

3. The educational philosophy on which Joan is most strongly basing her decision is
    a. perennialism.
    b. essentialism.
    c. progressivism.
    d. postmodernism.

4. "I don't care whether we were there to hear it or not," Jeffrey asserts. "When a tree falls in the woods, it makes a noise; now that's real." Jeffrey's assertion most closely relates to
    a. epistemology.
    b. ontology.
    c. axiology.
    d. logic.

5. An architect argues, "Simplicity is elegance. A building should have clean, smooth lines, and everything should be in symmetry." Which of the following most closely relates to the architect's comment?
    a. Philosophy of education
    b. Normative philosophy
    c. Epistemology
    d. Logic

6. "I know it if I see it," a person contends. "We can never be sure if something is true unless we're there to see it with our own eyes." These statements most reflect
    a. epistemology.
    b. ontology.
    c. axiology.
    d. logic.

7. "Schools should teach values, such as honesty, responsibility, and courtesy." This assertion is most closely related to
    a. epistemology.
    b. ontology.
    c. axiology.
    d. logic.

8. "Presidents come from populous states," Leroy says. "What makes you say that?" Andrea asks. "Roosevelt came from New York, Lyndon Johnson came from Texas, and Reagan came from California, and they're all states with a big population," Leroy responds. Leroy's comments can best be described as the result of
    a. epistemology.
    b. ontology.
    c. deductive reasoning.
    d. inductive reasoning.

9. Of the following which will be the most important factor influencing your personal philosophy of education?
    a. Your personal and professional beliefs
    b. Your pedagogical content knowledge
    c. Your personal axiology
    d. Your personal epistemology

10. Of the following which is the most important reason for having a well-defined philosophy of education?
   a.   A well-defined philosophy increases your professional autonomy.
   b.   A well-defined philosophy is required by teachers' codes of ethics.
   c.   A well-defined philosophy is part of teacher accountability.
   d.   A well-defined philosophy guides your decisions about professional practice.

Self-Assessment Feedback

1.   c   Learner-centered instruction that involves hands-on activities and emphasizes learner motivation is consistent with progressivism.
2.   a   Focusing on classic literature and the belief that "the only thing we can really rely on is the ideas that we carry with us" is consistent with idealism.
3.   a   Perennialism is grounded in idealism and shares many of the same beliefs.
4.   b   Ontology examines questions of reality and what is real.
5.   b   Normative philosophy describes the way things should be.
6.   a   The statement "We can never be sure if something is true unless we're there to see it with our own eyes examines" the question of "how we know," which is a question of epistemology.
7.   c   Axiology deals with values, morals, and ethics.
8.   d   Leroy made a general statement that was based on specific cases.
9.   a   Any philosophy is grounded in beliefs.
10. d   The purpose of a philosophy of education is to help you make professional decisions in ill-defined situations.

PRAXIS Practice: Questions and Feedback

1. Which educational philosophy is best reflected in Greg's comments? Explain.

Perennialism is the educational philosophy best illustrated by Greg's comments. Perennialism is grounded, in part, in idealism, and its proponents believe that a good education consists of examining enduring works in which time-honored issues are represented. Greg's desire to have his students study classics, such as Moby Dick *and* Les Miserables *reflects this belief.*

2. Which educational philosophy is best illustrated in Jaclyn's views? Explain.

Jaclyn's view best illustrates postmodernism. Postmodernists believe that many of the institutions in our society, including schools, are used by those in power to control and marginalize those who lack power. Clearly teachers have power over students. The fact that Jaclyn didn't want to put herself in the role of an authority figure is evidence of her desire to avoid putting herself into a position of power.

3. Which educational philosophy is best illustrated in Justin's position? Explain.

Progressivism is the educational philosophy best illustrated by Justin's comments. His emphasis on having the students conduct their own real-world and practical research demonstrates this view.

4. Which educational philosophy is best represented by Edna's comments? Explain.

Edna's view best illustrates essentialism. She believes that the students need math skills and the ability to think critically. These abilities are important for all people in all walks of life, a position taken by essentialists.

Useful Web Site Addresses

Web Links for Chapter Concepts

Preparing to Write a Personal Philosophy of Education: http://www.uwsp.edu/education/dkennedy/philos.htm

Existentialist: http://www.philosophypages.com/dy/e9.htm#exism

Sartre: Existential Life: http://www.philosophypages.com/hy/7e.htm#free

German Idealism: http://www.utm.edu/research/iep/g/germidea.htm

The Pragmatism Archive: http://www.pragmatism.org/archive/index.htm

Pragmatism in American Thought: http://www.thoemmes.com/american/pragmatism/pragmatism.htm

Web Links for "Teaching in an Era of Reform: The Essential Knowledge Issue"

Biographies of Philosophers: http://www.blupete.com/Literature/Biographies/Philosophy/BiosPhil.htm

Dictionary of Philosophical Terms and Names: http://www.philosophypages.com/dy/

The Encyclopedia of Philosophy of Education: http://www.vusst.hr/ENCYCLOPAEDIA/main.htm

Educational Theory: http://www.ed.uiuc.edu/EPS/Educational-Theory/default.asp

The Internet Encyclopedia of Philosophy: http://www.utm.edu/research/iep/

Overview of Educational Philosophies: http://jan.ucc.nau.edu/~jde7/ese502/assessment/lesson.html

Philosophy of Liberal Education: http://www.ditext.com/libed/libed.html

Philosophy of Education Journal: http://www.ed.uiuc.edu/EPS/PES-yearbook/

Web Links for "Exploring Diversity: Philosophy and Cultural Minorities"

Educational Philosophy in Black Perspective
http://tiger.coe.missouri.edu/~ray/EducationalPhilosophyBlackPerspective.html

American Indians in Higher Education: The Community College Experience
http://www.ed.gov/databases/ERIC_Digests/ed351047.html

Center for Research on Education, Diversity & Excellence: http://www.crede.ucsc.edu/

USC Center for Multilingual Multicultural Research: http://www.usc.edu/dept/education/CMMR/

Chapter 7
The Organization of American Schools

Overview

School aims, which were introduced in Chapters 5 and 6, are used to analyze different school organizational patterns. Developmental needs of learners and schools' responses to these needs are considered for the preschool, primary, middle, and high school levels. Schools are also analyzed in terms of research on effective schools.

Chapter Goals

This chapter examines

- What is a school?
- The organization of typical schools
- The structure of elementary schools and why they're organized the way they are
- The structure of high schools, junior highs, and middle schools and why they're organized the way they are
- The characteristics of effective schools

Chapter Outline

I.   What Is a School?
II. The Organization of Schools
    A.   Personnel
        1.   Administrators and Support Staff
        2.   Curriculum Specialists
    B.   The Physical Plant
    C.   Ccurriculum Organization
        1.   School Organization and the Curriculum
        2.   Developmental Characteristics of Students
        3.   Economics and Politics
III. Early Childhood Programs
IV. Elementary Schools
V.   High Schools, Junior Highs, and Middle Schools
    A.   The Comprehensive High School–Criticisms of the Comprehensive High School
    B.   Junior High and Middle Schools
VI. What Is an Effective School?
    A.   Research on Effective Schools
        1.   School and Class Size
            a.   School Size
            b.   Class Size
        2.   School Mission and Leadership
        3.   Safe and Orderly Environment
        4.   Parental Involvement–Through Technology
        5.   Academic Focus
        6.   High Collective Efficacy
        7.   Interactive Instruction
        8.   Frequent Monitoring of Student Progress
    B.   Taxpayers Perceptions of Effective Schools

1. Order and School Safety
2. Qualifications of Teachers
3. Student Scores on Standardized Tests

VII. Decision Making: Defining Yourself as a Professional

Transparencies

T 7.1 (Table 7.1) Common Ways to Organize Schools

T 7.2 (Table 7.2) Schedules for Two Elementary Teachers

T 7.3 (Figure 7.1) Characteristics of Effective Schools

T 7.4 (Table 7.3) National Parent–Teacher Association Standards for Parent/Family Involvement Programs

T 7.5 (Figure 7.2) Achievement Gains in High-Collective-Efficacy Schools Compared to Low-Collective-Efficacy Schools

T 7.6 (Table 7.4) Correlation Between Taking Advanced High School Math Courses and Graduating from College

Teaching Suggestions

I. What Is a School?

The purpose of this section of the chapter is to introduce students to the idea of a school as a multi-faceted institution.

■ **To help students understand that schools are part of a larger organizational structure, use one of the local elementary schools as a focal point, and trace the flow of students from there to a middle school and then a high school and then beyond.**

■ **To help students understand the relationship between social institutions and goals, first have students rank order the goals for schools listed in the text. Ask if there are others not listed. Then compare this list with goals for other social institutions like churches or chambers of commerce.**

II. The Organization of Schools

The purpose of this section is to provide students with some common organizational concepts that they can use to analyze schools at all levels.

■ **Locate a state school directory (hard copy or online) published by your state office of education or use the local school district and schools as a frame of reference. Most directories are organized by district and have the names and administrators for each school. Find several schools that differ in terms of organizational structure, and share these with your class. Ask them to explain possible reasons for these differences.**

■ **_Going into Schools #1_ asks students to visit several schools and describe the organizational structure in each. Ask students to share their findings in class.**

■ **_Transparency 7.1_ "Common Ways to Organize Schools" lists the most common K–12 organizational structures in the U.S. Have students compare these to local organizational patterns or those they encountered as students.**

III. Early Childhood Programs

The purpose of this section is to help students understand the growing importance of early childhood programs in education.

- The Web site for the National Association for the Education of Young Children (http://www.naeyc.org) contains valuable background information for this section.

- Ask students who are considering teaching at this level to research curricular and instructional issues and report back to the class.

- A current debate in this area contrasts developmentally appropriate curricula with those designed to prepare students for academic subjects. Using an early-childhood methods text as a reference, compare and contrast these.

- Grade retention, which students will encounter later in the chapter, is most common at the kindergarten level. Discuss the pros and cons of this practice at this and other levels.

IV. Elementary Schools

The purpose of this section of the chapter is to help students understand how elementary schools are commonly organized.

- *Transparency 7.2* "Schedules for Two Elementary Teachers" provides a detailed description of two teachers' schedules. Ask students how they are similar. How are they different? Which do students prefer? Why? How would they change either?

- *Increasing Understanding 7.5* asks students to analyze these two teachers' schedules in terms of the educational philosophies studied in Chapter 6.

- Encourage students to think about the challenges and rewards of teaching in an elementary classroom by referring back to the reasons in Chapter 1 that people go into teaching. Ask which of these reasons are most achievable in elementary schools. Which are least achievable?

V. High Schools, Junior High Schools, and Middle Schools

The purpose of this section of the chapter is to help students think about the goals of secondary education and the organizational strengths and weaknesses of different kinds of secondary schools.

- Ask students if a "shopping mall" is an accurate metaphor for their high school experience. Ask what are the strengths and weaknesses of this view of high schools. Ask if students can suggest alternate metaphors (e.g., cafeteria, museum, hospital).

- Ask students to analyze the middle school adaptations and judge which could be implemented readily at the high school level. Ask if this is desirable.

- *Teaching in an Era of Reform* focuses on grade retention. After students research the topic this, might be good for a classroom discussion or debate

- Again, encourage students to think about the challenges and rewards of teaching in a secondary classroom by referring back to the reasons in Chapter 1 that people go into teaching. Ask which of these reasons are most achievable in secondary schools. Which are least achievable?

- *Journal Starter #1* asks students to analyze their K–12 experiences in terms of their own experiences in schools. If they have children, they can do the same assignment using their children as the focal point.

VI. What Is an Effective School?

The purpose of this section of the chapter is to provide students with some conceptual tools to begin thinking about effective schools and schooling.

- Display *Transparency 7.3* **"Characteristics of Effective Schools." Ask which of these characteristics teachers can directly influence. How?**

- **The article on Creekland Middle School (Jacobson, 2000a) provides a look at creative ways to minimize the negative effects of large school sizes.**

- **The *Classroom Windows* Video "Within School Coordination: A Grade-Level Meeting" shows teachers discussing issues related to the classrooms and grade level. Share with students and ask what other issues might be discussed at meetings like this.**

- *Going into Schools #2* **and** *#3* **ask students to analyze a local school in terms of the criteria for effective schools. Have students share their findings in small groups and then with the whole class.**

- *Transparency 7.5* **"Achievement Gains in High-Collective-Efficacy Schools Compared to Low-Collective-Efficacy Schools" presents convincing evidence on the power of collective efficacy to influence student learning. Ask students to note differences for low-SES students.**

- *Reflect on This* **asks students to analyze a middle school in terms of general characteristics of both an effective school and an effective middle school.**

- *Transparency 7.6* **"Correlation Between Taking Advanced High School Math Courses and Graduating from College" compares the educational experiences of different ethnic groups. Ask how these findings relate to tracking. What might be other possible explanations?**

- *Journal Starter #2* **asks students to analyze their high school experiences in terms of the literature on effective schools. (We chose this level primarily because students can remember these experiences best. If they are older and have children, encourage them to do this assignment on their children's school or schools.)**

Journal Starters

1. Reflect on your own experiences in K–12 schools: How were the schools organized? How did this organization affect your life as a student? Did you attend a preschool or kindergarten? Was this a positive experience? Did you attend a middle school or junior high? Analyze your experience here in terms of chapter content. How large was your high school? Did it have tracks? What track were you in? Did you have friends in other tracks? What suggestions do you have to improve the organization of the schools you attended?

2. Analyze your high school experience in terms of the research on effective schools: How large was your school? How did the size influence you as a student? How big were the classes? Did the school have a clear academic focus? How did you know? What other foci contributed to or detracted from this focus? Were parents involved? How? Were the teachers positive? Did they teach interactively? What suggestions do you have to improve this school?

Increasing Understanding: Questions and Feedback

7.1

Would a family be considered a social institution? Why?

7.1

A family is a social institution. While the structure of the traditional family has changed, families still have established structures and rules, and one of a family's goals is to nurture the well-being of the children in the family.

7.2

What is the most likely reason that school policies are so rigid with respect to administering any form of medication?

7.2

School leaders are very concerned with student drug use, and zero-tolerance policies for drug use exist in many schools. In addition, legal issues are involved. As a result, schools establish policies that only specified health professionals may administer any form of a drug.

7.3

Strong efforts are being made in many areas to eliminate the use of temporaries. Identify at least two reasons that this would be the case.

7.3

Temporaries isolate teachers and students from their colleagues and peers. Also, temporaries may not have as much instructional support, such as Internet hookups, as classrooms in main buildings.

7.4

In Chapter 5 we learned that organizing elementary schools into grade levels occurred during the common school movement, which began about 1830. What was the rationale at that time for organizing elementary schools this way?

7.4

Organizing elementary schools into grade levels improved school quality in three ways. First, it reduced congested conditions, and second, it reduced the amount of overlap in the curricula often found in one-room schools. Third, grade differentiation resulted in more age-appropriate instruction and allowed content to be taught in greater depth for older students.

7.5

In both Sharon's and Susie's schedules, shown in Table 7.2, reading, language arts, and math are strongly emphasized. On which of the educational philosophies that you studied in Chapter 6 is this emphasis most likely based?

7.5

This emphasis is most likely based on essentialism. Essentialism emphasizes basic skills, and reading, language arts, and math are basic skill areas.

7.6

Think again about your study of Chapter 5. Identify three reasons the educational leaders decided that all students–college bound and non-college bound–should take the same curriculum.

7.6

First, the people making the decision were college professors and administrators, so they had a bias favoring a college-preparatory curriculum. Second, faculty psychology, a view of learning that emphasizes mental discipline and exercising powers of the mind, guided the thinking of the leaders. Third, large numbers of non-English-speaking immigrants and a growing lower class threatened to create divisions in American society. The leaders felt that a different curriculum for college- and non-college-bound students might create a class-based system of education and damage national unity.

7.7
Are middle schools more like elementary or high schools? Why?
7.7

Middle schools are more like high schools than like elementary schools. For instance, middle school schedules are organized in much the same way as high school schedules, and students have a different teacher for each course they take. The goal of middle schools is to help early adolescents make the transition from elementary school to high school, which is one of the reasons for organizing them like high schools.

7.8
Explain why size more strongly influences low-SES students than it does high-SES students. Think about the characteristics of students placed at-risk as discussed in Chapter 4.
7.8

Low-SES students, who are more likely to be placed at-risk, need more structure, support, and personal attention than do high-SES students. The likelihood of being able to provide this structure, support, and attention is greater in a smaller than in a larger school.

7.9
Earlier we saw that a disproportionate number of low-SES students tend to be enrolled in large schools. Is the involvement of low-SES parents likely to be greater than the involvement of high-SES parents? Explain. (Hint: Think about the influence of SES on learning which was discussed in Chapter 4.)
7.9

Low-SES parents are less likely to be involved in their children's education than are high-SES parents. Low-SES parents often struggle to make ends meet, so they have less flexibility than do high-SES parents, and low-SES parents are often less aware of the importance of parental involvement in children's education.

7.10
Do high-SES students need interactive instruction more than low-SES students, or vice versa? Explain, using the information from Figure 7.2 as the basis for your answer.
7.10

Although interactive instruction is important for all students, it is more important for low-SES than for high-SES children. High-SES children often have a richer background of school-related experiences, which equips them to better accommodate instruction that isn't interactive.

7.11
Look again at the characteristics of effective schools and effective teachers for students placed at-risk. (See pp. 149–151 in Chapter 4.) Those characteristics are very similar to the characteristics of effective schools we've discussed here. Explain why this is the case.
7.11

Effective schools and effective instruction for students placed at-risk aren't fundamentally different from effective schools and effective instruction for all students. For students placed at-risk the characteristics that make a school or teacher effective are even more important than they are for students not placed at-risk.

Reflect on This: Questions and Feedback
(These can also be found on the Companion Website: www.prenhall.com/kauchak .)

Working to Change the School Organization

1. To what extent is Henderson consistent with the characteristics of middle schools?

Wanting to create teams in which a history, English, math, and science teacher all have the same group of students and a common planning period is consistent with the characteristics of middle schools, as are the efforts to move away from lecture and toward more student involvement and integration of topics from different content areas.

2. In what area or areas is Henderson inconsistent with the characteristics of middle schools?

Henderson's emphasis on athletics, honor roll, and preparing students for competition is not consistent with middle school characteristics, because these efforts emphasize developmental differences that exist in early adolescence.

3. Based on the information presented, is Henderson likely to be a relatively effective or ineffective school? How do you know?

The vision that all students can learn and "all we have to do is believe it, and we can make it happen," as expressed by the school principal, is an essential characteristic of an effective school. Also, the effort to make instruction more interactive is another important characteristic of an effective school.

4. Would you accept a job at Henderson? Why?

If the school is able to maintain its vision, we would accept a job there.

Classroom Windows: Questions and Feedback

Within-School Coordination: A Grade-Level Meeting

1. At what time of the day did the meeting appear to be conducted? Why do you suppose it was conducted at this time?

The meeting appeared to be conducted before school. Teachers are reasonably well rested in the morning, and meetings tend to focus on issues that influence but don't directly relate to teaching and learning, such as student placement, scheduling, communication with parents, and coordination of programs. Because meetings occur before students and parents arrive, teachers are often better able to focus on topics such as these.

2. On what topics did the meeting focus? Why do you suppose the teachers focused on these topics?

As suggested in the answer to Item 1, the meeting tended to focus on topics and issues that weren't directly related to teaching and learning. This is common in grade-level meetings in elementary schools and in department meetings in middle and high schools.

3. What topics were conspicuously absent in the meeting's discussions? Why do you suppose this was the case?

The teachers didn't discuss topics or issues related to teaching and learning, especially those that occurred in individual teachers' classrooms. Instead, the teachers tended to focus on topics that were more schoolwide or gradewide.

4. How effective was the interaction in the meeting? Provide a rationale for your assessment of the effectiveness of the interaction.

The interaction in the meeting was quite effective. The teachers remained focused on the topics they intended to discuss, and each of the teachers appeared to feel comfortable offering opinions.

Video Discussions Questions and Feedback

1. Dr. Urie Triesman is a professor of mathematics at the University of Texas at Austin and director of the Charles A. Dana Center for Math and Science Education. His work focuses on school reform and ways that schools can be helped to improve. He believes principals are essential to effective schools. What does Dr. Triesman believe is the single most important thing that principals can do within a school to promote learning? Do you agree with him?

Dr. Triesman believes the single most important thing a principal can do is maintain a focus on students and learning.

2. Theodore Sizer is the Director of the Coalition for Effective Schools which attempts to reform high schools. From his perspective what are some arguments against grouping students together by age? How practical do you think the alternatives are?

Dr. Sizer argues that age is a poor way to group students. Instead students should be grouped together based on background knowledge and readiness to learn a new idea. This requires teachers to know what their students know and be able to regroup them readily on different topics.

3. Dr. John Goodlad is professor emeritus and codirector of the Center for Renewal at the University of Washington and president of the Independent Institute for Educational Inquiry. How does Dr. Goodlad believe that students suffer psychologically from grade retention? What alternatives are there to grade retention? Which of these do you think are most effective?

Dr. Goodlad emphasizes the social stigma of retention; other students know the student has been held back. Alternatives to grade retention include summer school programs and interventions that focus on specific problem areas.

Self-Assessment Questions
(Note: Students have access to these questions and their feedback on the text's Companion Website.)

1. "Social institutions designed to promote the intellectual growth and development of young people" best describe which of the following?
    a.   City governments
    b.   State governments
    c.   Churches
    d.   Schools

2. Which of the following is the best definition of *school district*?
    a.   An administrative unit within a geographical area that is responsible for education within its borders
    b.   A social institution designed to promote the intellectual growth and development of young people
    c.   The administrative unit responsible for the day-to-day operation of a school
    d.   A range of educational programs for young children, including infant intervention and enrichment programs, nursery schools, public and private pre-kindergartens and kindergartens, and federally funded Project Head Start

3. Which of the following best describes *school principals*?
    a.   Administrators given the responsibility for educating students within a certain geographic area
    b.   People given the ultimate responsibility for the operation of individual schools
    c.   People who have direct responsibility for student learning in individual classrooms
    d.   People specifically responsible for maintaining the order and safety of a school

4. You're a high school math teacher. Which of the following is *not* likely to be one of your duties?
   a.   Teach your math classes as effectively as possible
   b.   Monitor students as they move through hallways and attend assemblies in auditoriums
   c.   Contribute to the governance of the school
   d.   Attend football games and other sporting events

5. Which of the following best describes the school *curriculum*?
   a.   The belief that all students, regardless of ability, can master the topics they study
   b.   Training for teachers that helps them grow and develop as professionals
   c.   The facts, concepts, and other information students learn in school
   d.   The ideas that the school principal promotes that provide the vision for the school

6. Which of the following is the best description of *development*?
   a.   The ability to make, defend, and assess conclusions based on evidence
   b.   The facts, concepts, and principles students learn as they move from one grade to another
   c.   Changes in the way students think and relate to their peers, caused by maturation and experience
   d.   The ability to look at a controversial situation from both sides of the issue

Jack Gant is a teacher at Matthew Gilbert school. He is responsible for scheduling classes, collecting student records such as grades from teachers, and maintaining communication with district-level administrators and parents. Marianne Barnes also works at Matthew Gilbert. Her duties at the school include scheduling and coordinating the statewide assessment tests that all the students are required to take and providing a variety of information about course offerings and future options for students.

7. Based on your understanding of school organization, which of the following is Jack most likely to be?
   a.   A department head in the school
   b.   The school principal
   c.   A vice principal in the school
   d.   A guidance counselor at the school

8. Based on your understanding of school organization, which of the following is Marianne most likely to be?
   a.   The school principal
   b.   A vice principal at the school
   c.   An assistant principal at the school
   d.   A guidance counselor at the school

9. You're a first-year teacher, and one of your students comes to you complaining of a headache. Of the following which is your most acceptable course of action?
   a.   Give her two Tylenol tablets, and tell her to go and get a glass of water.
   b.   Send her to the school nurse.
   c.   Call one of the school's assistant principals and ask his or her advice.
   d.   Call the student's mother.

10. Based on research examining the collective efficacy of schools, which of the following statements is most accurate?
   a.   High-SES students will achieve higher levels than low-SES students at both high- and low-collective-efficacy schools, but the achievement gap between high- and low-SES students will be greater at high- than at low-collective-efficacy schools.
   b.   High-SES students will achieve higher levels than low-SES students at both high- and low-collective-efficacy schools, but the achievement gap between high- and low-SES students will be greater at low- than at high-collective-efficacy schools.

c. High- and low-SES students will achieve at approximately the same levels at high- and low-collective-efficacy schools, but high-SES students will achieve more at high-collective-efficacy schools than at low-collective-efficacy schools.

d. High- and low-SES students will achieve at approximately the same levels at high- and low-collective-efficacy schools, but low-SES students will achieve more at high-collective-efficacy schools than at low-collective-efficacy schools.

Self-Assessment Feedback

1. d   Schools are social institutions designed to promote the intellectual growth and development of young people.

2. a   School districts are administrative units given the responsibility for education within a geographical area.

3. b   School principals are the people given the ultimate responsibility for the operation of individual schools.

4. d   Attending football games and other sporting events will not be part of your professional duties.

5. c   The school curriculum is what students learn in schools.

6. c   Changes in the way students think and relate to their peers is a common description of development.

7. c   Vice principals are commonly responsible for scheduling, collecting records, and maintaining communication.

8. d   Guidance counselors coordinate statewide assessment tests and provide information about future options for students.

9. b   Teachers are forbidden by law from administering any form of medication to students.

10. b   High-SES students score higher than low-SES students at both high- and low-collective-efficacy schools, but the gap between them is greater at low-collective-efficacy schools.

PRAXIS Practice: Questions and Feedback

1. Identify at least five characteristics of an effective school that were illustrated in the case study. Take evidence directly from the case study to illustrate your description in each case.

The following characteristics of an effective school were illustrated in the case study:

School mission and leadership
Donna demonstrated that the school's mission was at the forefront of her teaching when she asked, "What are we in school for?" and the students immediately answered, "Learning!" indicating that it was continually emphasized. Donna also said, "And Mrs. Garnett commented on that again in our last assembly," which indicated that the principal set the tone for the emphasis on learning as a school mission.

Parental involvement
Donna required her students to take their tests home, have their parents sign them, and then put them in their notebooks. She also commented, "I want to be sure your parents know what we've been studying," and she also encouraged them to contact her by e-mail or phone.

Academic focus
Academic focus was demonstrated in at least four ways. First, Donna had high expectations as demonstrated by student comments such as, "Yeah, you don't dare come without it" (in reference to homework) and "Boy, Mrs. Barber, you had my whole family on the ropes last night. I had both my Mom and Dad helping me find examples of the elements you assigned us," and Donna's response, "That's great. I know it was a tough assignment, but it makes you think." Second, Donna maximized her time available for instruction. She started her instruction at 12:47 and

continued to 1:38, so of the available 55 minutes she used 51 for instruction. Third, her instruction remained focused on the content throughout, and finally, she focused on learning as a school mission.

High collective efficacy

High collective efficacy was demonstrated in Donna's comments, such as "In our last assembly when she [the school principal] emphasized that all of you can understand what you're studying and you can all be successful if you're willing to work" and "All the teachers in our school feel the same way."

Interactive instruction

Donna developed her entire lesson with demonstrations and question and answer.

Frequent monitoring of student progress

Frequent monitoring of progress was demonstrated in the comment "You know how Mrs. Barber is constantly saying that she wants to find out how well we understand this stuff" and in Donna's homework assignment, which is a form of assessment.

2. Identify one characteristic of Lincoln Middle School that is not consistent with an effective school.

Based on research examining school size, Lincoln Middle School is larger than an effective school should be.

3. Identify one characteristic of an effective school for which direct evidence doesn't exist in the case study.

Direct evidence indicating that the school environment is safe and orderly doesn't exist. Based on the students' responses in Donna's lesson, we would conclude that the environment is both safe and orderly, because we have no evidence to the contrary, but we don't have direct evidence for it.

Useful Web Site Addresses

Web Links for Chapter Terms

administrators
http://www.aasa.org/
http://www.education-world.com/a_admin/

advanced placement classes
http://www.collegeboard.com/student/testing/ap/about.html

curriculum: http://www.ascd.org/

early childhood education
http://www.ncrel.org/sdrs/areas/stw_esys/5erly_ch.htm
http://ecrp.uiuc.edu/v2n1/drummond.html
http://www.naeyc.org

effective school
http://www.effectiveschools.com/
http://www.mes.org/
http://www.education-world.com/a_issues/issues168.shtml

grade retention: http://www.educationworld.com/a_issues/issues021.shtml

high-collective-efficacy schools
http://www-personal.umich.edu/~rgoddard/AERA%202001%20CE%20TE%20Paper.pdf

looping: http://www.educationworld.com/a_issues/issues055.shtml

middle schools
http://www.educationworld.com/a_admin/admin208.shtml
http://www.nmsa.org/

principal
http://www.nassp.org/
http://www.naesp.org/

school district: http://www.nsba.org/site/index.asp

Web Links for "Teaching in an Era of Reform: The Grade Retention Issue"

Can Schools Stop Promoting Failure?: http://www.educationworld.com/a_issues/issues021.shtml

National Association of School Psychologists Position Statement on Student Grade Retention and Social Promotion
http://www.nasponline.org/information/pospaper_graderetent.html

Promotion and Retention Policies: http://www.ed.gov/offices/OERI/At-Risk/cds1rp06.html

Social Promotion: http://www.edweek.org/context/topics/issuespage.cfm?id=110

Social Promotion and Grade Retention: http://wwwcsteep.bc.edu/CTESTWEB/retention/retention.html

Taking Responsibility for Ending Social Promotion: A Guide for Educators and State and Local Leaders
http://www.ed.gov/pubs/socialpromotion/index.html

Where We Stand: Two Wrong Solutions: http://www.aft.org/stand/previous/1997/1097.html

Web Links for "Exploring Diversity: School Organization and the Achievement of Cultural Minorities"

Achievement Gap: http://www.edweek.org/context/topics/issuespage.cfm?id=61

An Analysis of the Research on Ability Grouping: Historical and Contemporary Perspectives
http://www.ucc.uconn.edu/~wwwgt/kulik.html

Beyond Social Promotion and Retention: http://www.ncrel.org/sdrs/areas/issues/students/atrisk/at800.htm

Class Size: http://www.edweek.org/context/topics/issuespage.cfm?id=44

Closing the Achievement Gap: http://www.ncrel.org/info/rc/sc/gapprint.htm

Consortium for Equity in Standards and Testing: http://wwwcsteep.bc.edu/ctest

Creating Sacred Places for Children: http://www.creatingsacredplaces.org/

Equity or Exclusion: http://www.ncscatfordham.org/binarydata/files/EQUITY_OR_EXCLUSION.pdf

Great Divide: http://www.edweek.org/sreports/qc03/templates/article.cfm?slug=17divide.h22

Indian Education Research: http://www.indianeduresearch.net/bibliogr.cfm?&cat=13

Language Learning and Academic Achievement: http://www.cal.org/crede/credeprg.htm#PROG1

NASP on Ability Grouping: http://www.nasponline.org/information/pospaper_ag.html

Panel Asks for Action on Hispanic Achievement Gap: http://www.edweek.org/ew/ewstory.cfm?slug=31hispanic.h22

The Role of Culture in Minority School Achievement
http://www.ksbe.edu/services/pase/pdf/journal/Hana%20Hou/2003HanaHou14.pdf

School/Community Partnerships to Support Language-Minority Student Success
http://www.crede.ucsc.edu/research/llaa/rb5.shtml

Students in Big-City Schools Trail Peers on NAEP Scores:
http://www.edweek.org/ew/ewstory.cfm?slug=43naepurban.h22

Teacher Quality: http://www.edweek.org/context/topics/issuespage.cfm?id=50

Tracking: http://www.edweek.org/context/topics/issuespage.cfm?id=26

Chapter 8
Governance and Finance:
Regulating and Funding Schools

Overview

Chapter 8 describes the uniquely American configuration of school governance and finance. Constitutional law is used as a framework to analyze the interconnected forces influencing both the governance and the finance of American education. Recent innovations such as charter schools and school choice are used to illustrate and analyze governance and finance issues.

Chapter Goals

This chapter examines

- How schools are regulated and run
- How the governance of schools affects teachers
- How schools are funded
- How different ways of funding schools result in inequalities in education
- How school choice reforms like vouchers and charters affect education as well as teachers' lives

Chapter Outline

I.   Governance: How Are Schools Regulated and Run?
    A.   Governance: A Legal Overview
    B.   State Governance Structures
        1.   State Boards of Education
        2.   State Office of Education
    C.   School Districts
        1.   Local School Boards
            a.   Functions of School Boards
            b.   Membership and Selection of School Boards
        2.   The Superintendent
        3.   The District Office
        4.   The School Principal
II.   School Finance: How Are Schools Funded?
    A.   School Funding Sources
        1.   Local Funding
        2.   State Revenue Sources
        3.   Federal Funding for Education
    B.   Educational Revenues: Where Do They Go?
III. Emerging Issues in School Governance and Finance
    A.   Savage Inequalities: The Struggle for Funding Equity
    B.   Site-Based Decision Making
    C.   School Choice
        1.   Charter Schools
            a.   Teacher Involvement in Charter Schools
            b.   Issues of Quality in Charter Schools
        2.   Video Perspectives: Home Room: One Last Chance
        3.   Vouchers–Public Reactions to School Choice

Transparencies

T 8.1 (Figure 8.1) State Administrative Organizational Structures
T 8.2 (Figure 8.2) Functions of Local School Boards
T 8.3 (Table 8.1) Profile of School Principals
T 8.4 (Figure 8.3) Revenues from Local, State, and Federal Sources
T 8.5 (Table 8.2) State-by-State Spending per Student
T 8.6 (Figure 8.4) Educational Expenditures on Different District Programs

Teaching Suggestions

I. Governance: How Are Schools Regulated and Run?

The purpose of this section of the chapter is to help students understand how governance issues will influence their lives as teachers.

- **Display *Transparency 8.1* "State Administrative Organizational Structures." Check your state's office of education Web site to determine the organizational structure in your state. Compare your state's organizational structure with the one in *Transparency 8.1*, and ask students to discuss differences.**

- ***Portfolio Activity 8.3* asks students to visit your state's Web site to check on the administrative structure as well as licensure requirements in the state. Use this assignment to encourage students to check out other information on this Web site.**

- **Find out how many school districts there are in your state. Share this with students, and ask them to compare that number with national figures. Discuss the advantages and disadvantages of large and small school districts.**

- **Locate information about the local school district(s) in your area. Share this information with students, and compare it with information in the text.**

- ***Increasing Understanding 8.2* asks students to analyze advantages and disadvantages of large and small districts from a beginning teacher's perspective.**

- **Display *Transparency 8.2* "Functions of Local School Boards." Ask students how each of these functions could affect them as teachers.**

- ***Discussion Questions #1* and *#2* ask students to think about the composition of school boards.**

- **Have students attend a local school board meeting and share their reactions with the class.**

- ***Transparency 8.3* "Profile of School Principals" contains demographic information about principals at different levels. Some questions you might ask include these: Why are there more female principals at the lower levels? Why are there more minorities at the lower levels? Why does pay differ at these different levels?**

- *Going into Schools #2* asks students to interview a teacher about the principal at the school. Ask students to share their findings in class. The results of this interview should make a lively discussion topic.

- *Journal Starter #1* asks students to think about the school governance structures they encountered and how those structures influenced them as students.

II. School Finance: How Are Schools Funded?

The purpose of this section of the chapter is to help students understand how school finance can influence their lives as teachers.

- *Transparency 8.4* "Revenues from Local, State, and Federal Sources" provides a historical look at funding from these three sources.

- *Increasing Understanding 8.7* asks students to discuss the pros and cons of "sin taxes."

- *Transparency 8.5* "State-by-State Spending per Student" allows students to compare their state's funding with that of neighboring states and the nation at large. Remind students that these figures don't reflect a state's commitment to education.

- Transparency 8.6 "Educational Expenditures on Different District Programs" shows where district funds go. Ask how these percentages might change in urban and rural districts.

- *Reflect on This* presents students with a case study involving different types of school districts and encourages students to consider how district-to-district differences can influence their lives as teachers.

- *Journal Starter #2* asks students to reflect on their own experiences in schools and how school finance may have influenced those experiences.

III. Emerging Issues in School Governance and Finance

The purpose of this section of the chapter is to introduce students to major reform issues in the areas of school governance and finance and encourage students to think about how these reforms will influence them as teachers.

- *Discussion Question #4* asks whether districts across a state and across the nation should be funded equally.

- A major way that differences in districts' funding play out is in teacher salaries. Locate the salary schedules for several local districts, and share these with your class, linking them to funding differences.

- A recent article in *Education Week* (*20*[24], February 28, 2001, p. 1) discusses recent concern about the large number of charter schools that close.

- *Teaching in an Era of Reform* focuses on the privatization movement in education. Use students' increased background knowledge in a discussion or debate on this topic.

Journal Starters

1. Think about how governance structures affected you as a student and how they will influence you as a teacher. In what kind of district did you go to school? Was it large or small? Did you know who the superintendent was? Did you know the principals in the schools you were attending? What types of interactions did you have with them? What kinds of interactions did the principals have with teachers? with parents? What suggestions do you have to make these governance structures more effective?

2. Think about school finance and how it influenced your life as a student. Was your district adequately funded? How did the funding compare with that of neighboring districts? Were the school facilities well maintained? Did you have labs for your science classes? Were there enough textbooks to go around? Were they recent? Were extracurricular activities adequately funded? If the school district obtained additional funding, where would you recommend it be spent?

Increasing Understanding: Questions and Feedback

8.1
What do the arrows pointing downward in Figure 8.1 suggest about the line of authority in school governance? Who will teachers most directly answer to?
8.1
The arrows suggest that the line of authority is top down. Teachers will directly answer to principals, the on-site representative of authority.

8.2
From a beginning teacher's perspective what might be some advantages and disadvantages of starting in a large district? a small district?
8.2
One advantage to a large district is a large central support staff with experts in areas like math, reading, and technology. A disadvantage is the large bureaucracy that often makes it difficult to get things done quickly. A small district will lack these resources, but the possibility of getting things done quickly and the likelihood of early advancement and promotion are greater.

8.3
From a teacher's perspective which of the school board functions is likely to be most important? least? Explain.
8.3
Probably the most important is budget because it affects teachers' wallets. Except in extreme cases the maintenance of school buildings and buses is least important; they are usually done automatically.

8.4
Offer at least one reason that the percentage of male administrators is higher in high schools than in middle or elementary schools. (Hint: Think back to your study of the teaching force in Chapter 2.) Offer at least one reason that the percentage of female administrators is not higher than 55 percent at the elementary level.
8.4
More male administrators at the secondary level can be explained by the larger number of male teachers at that level. The dearth of female administrators at the elementary level could result from negative gender stereotyping or the false belief that females can't be effective leaders.

8.5
What is the most likely reason the board member said to Carla, "I'm sorry, but I'm not sure exactly what 'manipulatives' are"? Think about the makeup of school boards in answering this question.

8.5
School board members are typically lay citizens with no educational training or background.

8.6
Explain why the federal government's share of funding is much less than the local and state shares.
8.6
This reflects the historical trend toward local control and away from national or federal control of education.

8.7
Liquor and tobacco taxes are often called "sin taxes" because they target commodities that either pose health risks or are viewed as socially unacceptable by a portion of the population. What are the advantages and disadvantages of "sin taxes"?
8.7
The advantage of sin taxes is that they discourage unhealthy lifestyles. The disadvantage is that there isn't a link between the sin tax and a person's income or the person's use of the schools.

8.8
Would state offices of education and local school boards prefer categorical or block grants? Why?
8.8
They prefer block grants because they give the most freedom to use the funds as educators see fit.

8.9
Explain how percentages in Figure 8.4 would be different for a new and growing school district as compared to a stable rural school district.
8.9
The percentage for new buildings would be greater for growing or expanding districts.

8.10
Explain why the California and Texas court cases ended up in different court systems.
8.10
Since education funding is a legal responsibility of the states, the wording of their state constitutions is important.

8.11
Explain why teachers in large urban districts might feel stronger than those in a suburban district about teacher input into educational decisions.
8.11
Urban districts tend to be larger, making it more difficult to solicit and use teachers' ideas.

Reflect on This: Questions and Feedback
(These can also be found on the Companion Website: www.prenhall.com/kauchak .)

The Importance of Pay

1. How important is pay in the selection of a first job? What other financial considerations besides pay would influence you?

Other considerations besides pay might include benefits such as medical and dental coverage, as well as retirement benefits. In addition, teachers should consider cost of living, which is heavily influenced by housing costs as well as travel expenses to and from work.

2. Many people go into teaching because they want to make a difference and make the world a better place. Some

of the toughest schools are also those where teachers can make the most difference. How important is this dimension of a job?

Personal goals are very important in satisfaction with a teaching position. Before taking their first job, beginning teachers should think long and hard about why they are going into teaching and what they expect to get out of it.

3. Job satisfaction is often closely connected to opportunities for professional growth. Teachers need to grow and develop if they are to remain happy in their jobs. How important are opportunities for professional growth in a first job?

Mentoring, support, and opportunities for personal growth not only are important for job satisfaction, but may be essential for survival. Beginning teachers who receive mentoring help are considerably more likely to remain in teaching. They should be sure to check on professional growth opportunities before signing their first contracts.

4. Which job would you take? Why?

This is a personal decision based on individual values and goals. One bit of advice is not to forget about personal lifestyle when making this decision. Would you personally be happier living in an urban, rural, or suburban setting? The answer to this question may strongly affect satisfaction with a first job.

Video Perspectives: Questions and Feedback

Home Room: One Last Chance

1. How is this charter school different from ones that you've read about?

The biggest difference is that it is a residential facility. Although other charter schools target inner-city African American students, this is the only one that has a residential program.

2. Why aren't there more charter schools like this across the country?

Cost is probably the major factor. A residential school is probably at least four or five times more expensive than a regular school. In addition, many parents might not want their children living away from home at a young age

3. What positive features of this school could be transported to other schools?

Probably the most beneficial aspects of this school are its emphasis on academics and positive expectations for student success. The curriculum clearly identifies essential knowledge, called Gates, and expects each student to master the content.

Video Discussion Questions and Feedback

1. Theodore Sizer is the Director of the Coalition for Effective Schools which attempts to reform high schools. Dr. Sizer believes that parental choice and involvement are central to school reform effects. In Dr. Sizer's opinion what are some arguments in favor of school choice? Which of these arguments are most persuasive? Do you believe school choice will improve education?

Dr. Sizer believes that school choice is important because it provides alternatives and gives students and parents a choice, which is a democratic principle. Choice, he believes, is essential to democracy. Another argument for choice is that both teachers and students will be more positive about schools that they can choose.

Self-Assessment Questions
(Note: Students have access to these questions and their feedback on the text's Companion Website.)

1. Control of schools was made the legal responsibility of the individual states by the
    a.   First Amendment to the Constitution.
    b.   Fourth Amendment to the Constitution.
    c.   Tenth Amendment to the Constitution.
    d.   Fourteenth Amendment to the Constitution.

2. In terms of school district numbers the historical trend in the U.S. has been
    a.   more districts with increased specialization.
    b.   fewer districts with larger size.
    c.   the same number of districts with greater interdistrict cooperation.
    d.   more districts with increased cooperation.

3. Which of the following is **NOT** a major function of local school boards?
    a.   Governance of finances
    b.   Responsibility for personnel
    c.   Oversight of curriculum
    d.   Day-to-day administration

4. The chief state officer in the state office of education has a role similar to what position in local districts?
    a.   Superintendent
    b.   Principal
    c.   Curriculum coordinator
    d.   Head of personnel

5. Recently local school boards' number one concern has been
    a.   school safety and violence.
    b.   student uniforms and dress.
    c.   drug policies.
    d.   student achievement.

6. Historically, financial support for schools has come primarily from
    a.   income taxes.
    b.   real estate taxes.
    c.   tuition.
    d.   alcohol and tobacco taxes.

7. Which of the following is **NOT** a typical characteristic of local school board members?
    a.   Wealthy
    b.   Male
    c.   Minority
    d.   Professional worker

8. From a teacher's perspective the most powerful influence on instruction is the:
    a.   state superintendent.
    b.   district superintendent.
    c.   district instructional coordinator.
    d.   school principal.

9. Which of the following is **NOT** a major source of state funding for education?
   a. Sales tax
   b. Income tax
   c. Sin taxes
   d. Real estate taxes

10. State tax-credit plans are a variation on
    a. site-based management.
    b. charter schools.
    c. vouchers.
    d. funding equalization programs.

Self-Assessment Feedback

1. c   The Tenth Amendment to the Constitution clearly assigned legal responsibility to the 50 individual states.
2. b   The historical trend has been consolidation into fewer and larger districts.
3. d   The district superintendent is responsible for the day-to-day administration of the school district.
4. a   The chief state officer's role is similar to that of a district superintendent, who is responsible for the day-to-day administration of the school district.
5. d   Spurred by recent reform efforts, school boards have increasingly focused on student achievement.
6. b   Historically, financial support for schools has come from real estate taxes.
7. c   Minorities have tended to be underrepresented on local school boards.
8. d   The school principal exerts the strongest influence on a school's instructional climate.
9. d   State real estate taxes are not typically a major source of revenues for states, though they are for districts.
10. c   Tax-credit plans are variations on vouchers and are an alternate way to provide choice to parents.

PRAXIS Practice: Questions and Feedback

1. How would you respond to Tom and Andrea's comments about who actually determines teachers' salaries?

Both state legislators and school board members influence teachers' salaries; nationally they contribute about the same percentage(around 45%) to educational budgets. State legislators do so through sales taxes, income taxes, and taxes on things like liquor, tobacco, oil and mining and corporate incomes. Local school boards also influence teachers' salaries by income primarily generated through property taxes.

2. How accurate was Tom's comment that principals' salaries "beat" teachers' salaries? (You may want to refer to Table 1.2 in Chapter 1, which describes teachers' salaries across the nation.)

In 2001–2002 at the elementary level, the average principal's salary was $73,114, while the average teacher's salary was $43,250. That's about a $30,000 difference. However, teachers' salaries are for nine months whereas principals' are for eleven months. A recent survey revealed only a $17,000 differential between elementary teachers and principals when salaries were equated on a 180-day year (Carr, 2003).

3. Is the experience of Tom and Andrea's superintendent unusual? What factors lead to superintendents' short tenures?

The experience of Tom and Andrea's superintendent is not unusual, especially if they teach in an urban district. The average tenure for all superintendents is about 5.6 years, but this is shortened to 2.8 years for superintendents in urban districts.

Useful Web Site Addresses

Web Links for Chapter Terms

school choice
http://www.edweek.org/context/topics/issuespage.cfm?id=30#archives
http://www.heritage.org/schools/welcome.html
http://www.edexcellence.net/library/bolick.html

charter schools
http://www.publicagenda.org/specials/vouchers/voucherhome.htm
http://www.uscharterschools.org/pub/uscs_docs/home.htm

curriculum
http://www.educationworld.com/preservice/learning/curr_standards.shtml
http://www.ascd.org/

home schooling: http://www.educationworld.com/a_curr/curr060.shtml

local school boards
http://www.nsba.org/site/index.asp
http://www.asbj.com/

school district: http://www.nsba.org/site/index.asp

school principal
http://www.nassp.org/
http://www.naesp.org/

site-based decision making
http://www.educationworld.com/a_admin/admin176.shtml
http://www.ncrel.org/sdrs/areas/issues/envrnmnt/go/go100.htm

state tax-credit plans: http://www.schoolchoices.org/roo/taxcredits.htm

state board of education: http://www.nsba.org/site/index.asp

virtual schools
http://www.educationworld.com/a_curr/curr119.shtml
http://www.educationworld.com/a_tech/tech052.shtml
http://www.educationworld.com/a_tech/tech052a.shtml

vouchers
http://abcnews.go.com/sections/us/DailyNews/scotus_vouchers020627.html
http://www.theatlantic.com/issues/99jul/9907vouchers.htm
http://www.aft.org/research/vouchers/index.htm
http://www.nsba.org/novouchers/vsc_docs/Voucher_myths.pdf
http://www.nea.org/issues/vouchers/
http://www.au.org/vouchers.htm

Web Links for "Teaching in an Era of Reform: The Privatization Issue"

Comparison of Achievement Results for Students Attending Privately Managed and Traditional Schools in Six Cities
http://www.gao.gov/new.items/d0462.pdf

Is the Private Sector Qualified to Reform Schools?: http://www.edweek.org/ew/ewstory.cfm?slug=03hernandez.h22

Privatization of American Schools: http://www.edweek.org/context/topics/issuespage.cfm?id=15

Report Examines Privatized School's Scores: http://www.edweek.org/ew/ewstory.cfm?slug=11Private.h23

Reports Paint Opposite Pictures Of Edison Achievement
http://www.edweek.org/ew/ewstory.cfm?slug=25edison.h22

Web Links for "Exploring Diversity: School Choice and Cultural Minorities"

Choice: http://www.edweek.org/context/topics/issuespage.cfm?id=43

Looking for a Better Choice: Latinos Are Playing a Key Role in Promoting School Voucher Programs
http://www.hispaniconline.com/magazine/2003/dec/Features/school.html

NAACP No to School Choice: http://www.capitalresearch.org/news/news.asp?ID=151

Private School Vouchers: Myth vs. Facts: http://www.au.org/vouchers.htm

Rethinking Schools: False Choices–Vouchers, Public Schools and Our Children's Future
http://www.rethinkingschools.org/SpecPub/voucher.htm

School Choice: http://www.edweek.org/context/topics/issuespage.cfm?id=30#archives

School Choice 2000: What's Happening in the States: http://www.heritage.org/schools/welcome.html

School Choice: Answers to the Most Frequently Asked Legal Questions
http://www.edexcellence.net/library/bolick.html

School Choices: The Citizen's Guide to Education Reform: http://www.schoolchoices.org/

School Choice Programs: What's Happening in the States: http://www.heritage.org/schools/

School Choice Trade Offs: http://www.edweek.org/ew/newstory.cfm?slug=36godwin.h21

School Vouchers: Issues and Arguments: http://www.schoolchoices.org/roo/vouchers.htm

Studies Show School Choice Widens Inequality: Popular Among Parents, But Little Evidence That Children Learn More: http://www.gse.harvard.edu/news/features/schoolchoice07131995.html

Trends and Issues: School Choice (Public Voucher Plans)
http://eric.uoregon.edu/trends_issues/choice/public_vouchers.html

The Truth About Education Vouchers: New Information on School Choice
http://www.edreform.com/school_choice/truth.htm

U.S. Department of Education: What Really Matters in American Education?
http://www.ed.gov/Speeches/09-1997/

Additional Chapter Web Links

Governance in Education

American Association of School Administrators: http://www.aasa.org/
American Federation of Teachers: http://www.aft.org/
Links to State Education Associations: http://www.ccsso.org/seamenu.html
National Association of Elementary School Principals: http://www.naesp.org/
National Association of Secondary School Principals: http://www.nassp.org/
National Association of State Boards of Education: http://www.nasbe.org/
National Education Association: http://www.nea.org/
National School Boards Association: http://www.nsba.org/site/index.asp

Site-Based Management

Behind the Numbers: When States Spend More: http://www.prospect.org/archives/36/36rothfs.html
School-Based Management, What Is It?: http://www.ed.gov/pubs/OR/ConsumerGuides/baseman.html
School-Based Budgeting/Site-Based Management: http://www.bctf.bc.ca/ResearchReports/96ei04/
Site-Based Decision Making: http://fnopress.com/sbm/sbmtoc.html
Site-Based Management: Boon or Boondoggle?: http://www.education-world.com/a_admin/admin176.shtml
Transferring Decision Making to Local Schools: Site-Based Management:
http://www.ncrel.org/sdrs/areas/issues/envrnmnt/go/go100.htm
The National School Boards Association: http://www.nsba.org
The American Association of School Administrators: http://www.aasa.org
The Council of Chief State School Officers: http://www.ccsso.org
About Charter Schools: http://edreform.com/charters.htm
United States Charter Schools: http://www.uscharterschools.org/

Chapter 9
School Law:
Ethical and Legal Influences on Teaching

Overview

The chapter begins by examining how ethics and law influence professional decision making. The U.S. legal system is described as an overlapping and interconnected web of federal, state, and local influences. The concepts of rights and responsibilities are then used to frame legal issues for both teachers and students.

Chapter Goals

This chapter examines

- Legal and ethical aspects of teaching
- The organization of the U. S. legal system
- Teachers' professional rights and responsibilities
- Issues related to religion and the schools
- Students' rights and responsibilities

Chapter Outline

I. Law, Ethics, and Teacher Professionalism
    A. The Law and Its Limitations
    B. Ethical Dimensions of Teaching
II. The American Legal System
    A. Federal Influences–Federal Laws
    B. State and Local Influences
    C. The Overlapping Legal System
III. Teachers' Rights and Responsibilities
    A. Teacher Employment and the Law
        1.   Licensure
        2.   Contracts
        3.   Tenure
        4.   Dismissal–Reduction in Force
    B. Academic Freedom
    C. Copyright Laws
    D. Teacher Liability–Child Abuse
    F. Teachers' Private Lives–Teachers with AIDS
    G. Teaching in an Era of Reform: The Teacher Tenure Issue
IV. Religion and the Law
    A. Prayer in Schools
    B. Religious Clubs and Organizations
    C. Religion and the Curriculum
    D. Teaching About Religion in the Schools
V. Students' Rights and Responsibilities
    A. Students' Freedom of Speech
    B. Permissible Search and Seizure
    C. Student Records and Privacy

D. Corporal Punishment
E. Student Rights in Disciplinary Action
F. Students with AIDS
G. Exploring Diversity: Affirmative Action
H. Video Perspectives: Affirmative Action
VI. Decision Making: Defining Yourself as a Professional

Transparencies

T 9.1 (Figure 9.1) Teachers' Rights and Responsibilities
T 9.2 (Figure 9.2) Students' Rights and Responsibilities

Teaching Suggestions

I. Law, Ethics, and Teacher Professionalism

The purpose of this section of the chapter is to help students understand differences between legal and ethical issues and how both influence professional decision making.

■   To help students differentiate between legal and ethical issues, have students analyze the opening cases with Jason Taylor and Sash Brown in terms of this dichotomy.

■   *Going into Schools #3* asks students to interview a teacher about professional ethics.

■   *Increasing Understanding 9.2* analyzes ethical dimensions in terms of the two limitations of laws, their being general and reactive.

■   Refer students back to the NEA Code of Ethics found in Chapter 1. Point out that the AFT has a similar code.

■   *Portfolio Activity 9.2* asks students to relate ethics and law.

II. The American Legal System

The purpose of this section of the chapter is to provide an overview of the complex U.S. legal system.

■   To make the general questions raised at the beginning of this section more specific, relate them to later court cases described in this chapter, and pose these as cases or problems to consider.

■   The First, Fourth, and Fourteenth Amendments to the Constitution are important enough to teachers that students should analyze and understand them. All teachers should know their basic focus.

■   Later in the chapter the text argues that good teachers not only know and follow the law but also use it to teach their students about the U.S. legal system. Emphasize this point throughout the chapter. *Going into Schools #5* asks your students to interview secondary students about their knowledge of legal issues.

■   *Journal Starter #1* asks students to reflect on their own personal encounters with the U.S. legal system.

III. Teachers' Rights and Responsibilities

The purpose of this section of the chapter is to help prospective teachers understand their basic legal rights and responsibilities.

- *Transparency 9.1* "Teachers' Rights and Responsibilities" provides an overview of the issues in this section of the chapter.

- Contact your state office of education, and obtain information about both licensure requirements and the professional practices board that examines special situations like teacher felony convictions. Share this information with your class. *Going into Schools #1* also addresses these issues.

- Contact a local school district, and ask them to send their Policies and Procedures manual. In it you'll find information on issues like tenure, dismissal, and reduction in force.

- The Fischer et al. (2003) book contains a number of additional cases on academic freedom. Present these to the class to analyze and debate.

- Contact a local chapter of either the NEA or the AFT, and either have them speak to your class or send materials on student memberships, legal issues, and liability insurance.

- *Discussion Question #5* asks students about the legal issues surrounding the private lives of teachers.

- *Reflect on This* provides a realistic case study of a teacher facing a liability issue. Encourage students to connect to the legal issues being discussed.

- Use the topic of sex education (discussed in Chapter 10) to explore the issue of academic freedom further.

IV. Religion and the Law

The purpose of this section of the chapter is to help students understand legal issues surrounding religion in the schools.

- Using a Saturday newspaper that advertises church services or a phone book, point out the religious diversity in your area and state. Remind students of this diversity as you discuss the issues in this section.

- Make sure that students understand the difference between advocating a particular religion and teaching about religion. Use the guidelines in the chapter to make this differentiation clear. *Increasing Understanding 9.9* asks students to differentiate between these two approaches.

- Link the topic of religion in the schools to character and moral education discussed in Chapter 10. *Discussion Question #2* addresses the issue of religion in the schools.

- *Journal Starter #2* asks students to reflect on their own personal position about the proper role of religion in their classroom.

V. Students' Rights and Responsibilities

The purpose of this section of the chapter is to help prospective teachers understand students' rights and responsibilities.

- *Transparency 9.2* "Students' Rights and Responsibilities" provides an overview of the topics in this section. Ask students to compare these with teachers' rights and responsibilities.

- In an interesting recent case of students' freedom of speech, a state of Washington court ruled in favor of a student suspended for mocking an assistant principal on a Web site (*Education Week, 20*[24], Feb. 28, 2001, p. 4). The fact that the Web site was operated off campus was central in the decision.

- *Increasing Understanding 9.10* analyzes students' freedom of speech more closely, using actual court cases.

- Recently the American Bar Association came out against zero tolerance policies, claiming they fail to consider each case on an individual basis (see *Education Week, 20*[24], Feb. 28, 2001, p. 3). Zero tolerance policies were discussed in Chapter 4.

- Find out what your state's policy is on corporal punishment. Discuss the pros and cons of this practice. The topic usually elicits a lively discussion among students. *Discussion Question #4* addresses this topic.

- *Going into Schools #2* asks students to examine a district's policy handbook of students' rights and responsibilities.

Journal Starters

1. Encourage students to think about their own relationship to the U.S. legal system: Have you had any personal encounters with the system? Did you feel that the system was protecting your rights? What role do lawyers play in this system? Do you feel the legal system is fair to all SES groups? Is the system fair to all ethnic groups? How was the U.S. legal system presented to you as a student? How were your rights and responsibilities as a student explained to you? What implications do your responses have for the way you'll teach about the U.S. legal system in your classes?

2. Encourage students to think about the role that religion should play in education: What are the most common religions in this geographic area? What other religious groups exist in the area? Do religious groups ever try to influence what goes on in public schools in terms of curriculum? To what extent does academic freedom influence teachers' ability to address religion in the classroom? What is the major difference between teaching about religion and advocating religion? Which is better, character or moral education? What role will religion play in your classroom?

Increasing Understanding: Questions and Feedback

9.1
Think back to your study of Chapter 6, which examined philosophical issues and education. How does this section relate to your study of that chapter? Explain specifically.
9.1
A major branch of philosophy is axiology, which examines values and ethics.

9.2
Earlier we said that laws are limited because they're *general* and *reactive*, that is, written in reaction to problems in

107

the past. Which of these two limitations also applies to professional codes of ethics?

9.2

Actually both limitations apply to professional codes of ethics. Codes are written in general terms and change in reaction to ethical problems and issues.

9.3

Which amendment is relevant to Jason's situation at the beginning of this chapter? Why?

9.3

Jason's dilemma involved freedom of speech, which is covered by the First Amendment to the Constitution. You'll read more about this issue later in the chapter under academic freedom.

9.4

One of the criteria used by the courts is the age of the students involved. How might this criterion influence the case involving taboo words; that is, would the verdict have been different if the class were in a middle school or an elementary school? Why?

9.4

Our guess is a definite yes. The courts consider educational value to students when considering the legality of controversial issues. The topic of taboo words and the taboo words themselves would be less appropriate for younger learners.

9.5

If a copyright violation were to occur and the problem went to the courts, would these be state or federal courts? Why?

9.5

The case would go to a federal court because copyright laws involve federal laws.

9.6

How might these two factors–age and special situations–have influenced the court's decision in the Oregon beach case?

9.6

The children were very young, and an ocean beach is a potentially dangerous setting for a field trip. Both are important issues in this case.

9.7

A teacher became involved in her city's gay rights movement, passing out leaflets at demonstrations and making speeches. Her school district warned her and then fired her for her activity. What legal issues would be involved here?

9.7

The fact that she passed out the leaflets would make notoriety an issue. However, this, in itself, would not be proof that the teacher is homosexual. In addition, homosexuality in and of itself is not a reason for dismissal. Finally, the teacher's right to pass out information is protected by the First Amendment to the Constitution, which guarantees free speech.

9.8

Which aspect of the First Amendment–establishment or free exercise–would relate to the case involving the portrait of Jesus Christ? Why?

9.8

Establishment would be an issue here. By displaying a portrait of Jesus Christ, the school is suggesting that Christianity is being endorsed by the school.

9.9

A biology teacher wants his students to know how the Bible is the basis of the theory of creationism. Would this be

legally permitted? Why? Under what circumstances wouldn't it?
9.9
It would be permitted because the teacher is not advocating or teaching the Bible, merely relating it to course content. However, there should be an educationally defensible reason for bringing the Bible into the classroom, and it should not be presented as religious truth or dogma.

9.10
How are the two cases involving students' freedom of speech similar? different?
9.10
Both involve freedom of speech, which is guaranteed by the First Amendment. However, the key distinction here is disruption and interference with a school's central mission, which is to educate youth.

9.11
You are a high school teacher and receive a letter from a prospective employer of one of your former students. The letter contains a form that asks you to provide, in addition to a letter of recommendation, information about the student's GPA. What are the legal aspects of this request?
9.11
Under the Buckley Amendment you cannot release parts of a student's record, like GPA, without the permission of the student or his or her parents. In addition, it would be a good idea to check with the student to see if he or she requested that you fill out the recommendation form.

9.12 How would these guidelines apply to the Pennsylvania principal who paddled a first grader?
9.12
The size of the principal and the fact that he used a paddle and did so four times could easily lead to the conclusion of the punishment being cruel and excessive. In addition, hitting the child four times suggests educating the child wasn't his first priority.

9.13
What amendment to the Constitution guarantees students due process? (Hint: Under what circumstances are teachers guaranteed due process?)
9.13
Due process–both for teachers and for students–is guaranteed by the Fourteenth Amendment.

Reflect on This: Questions and Feedback
(These can also be found on the Companion Website: www.prenhall.com/kauchak .)

Classroom Management

1. To what extent are you responsible for the actions of students like Damien?

Teachers are legally responsible for the actions of all students, including ones like Damien. Teachers act in loco parentis, *serving as guardians for the children under their care.*

2. If this problem developed into a liability suit, what factors would the courts consider in judging whether you were negligent?

The courts would consider several factors here. Perhaps the most important is the age and mental abilities of the students involved. Also the courts would want to know if the children were warned of dangers and whether the teacher took precautionary measures, anticipating possible dangerous situations.

3. In hindsight were there some things you could have done differently in terms of this science activity?

Definitely students should have been warned of the dangers of chemical substances. In addition, you might have monitored Damien more carefully. This last suggestion is a grey area, or judgment call, as the teacher is responsible for all the children in a class, not just one.

Video Perspectives: Questions and Feedback
Affirmative Action

1. What are the arguments for and against affirmative action policies in admissions?

Proponents of affirmative action contend that it is an effective mechanism for righting past wrongs and for recruiting a diverse student body. Opponents contend that it unfairly punishes nonminorities, in essence arguing that two wrongs don't make a right.

2. How is a point-based formula system different from a quota system?

Quota systems allocate a certain number of slots to minorities, disregarding qualifications, for the most part. Formula systems don't create quotas but instead allocate extra points for desired aspects of diversity such as race, gender, geographic origins, or socioeconomic status.

3. What might be some potential educational benefits of a diverse student body?

Having diversity in a student body exposes students to different opinions and perspectives. It also provides opportunities for students to learn about other cultures and to learn how to interact with different types of people.

Self-Assessment
(Note: Students have access to these questions and their feedback on the text's Companion Website.)

1. Which teacher right is **NOT** protected by tenure?
    a.   Notification of charges for dismissal
    b.   A continuing contract in a school district
    c.   Due process
    d.   Assignment to the same school and grade level

2. The Family Educational Rights and Privacy Act, known as the Buckley Amendment, ensures the right of:
    a.   teachers to see the files of students under their charge.
    b.   parents to see school files kept on their own children.
    c.   parents to see personnel files of their children's teachers.
    d.   teachers to see the files of students in the whole family.

3. Which statement about corporal punishment in the schools is **NOT** true?
    a.   It is prohibited in all states.
    b.   The Constitution does not prohibit it.
    c.   States can prohibit it.
    d.   Local districts can prohibit it.

4. Actions against nonminorities that attempt to correct for past discrimination against members of minority groups are known as
    a.   majority discrimination.
    b.   affirmative action.
    c.   de jure legal actions.

d.   de facto discrimination.

5. Which of the following is **NOT** a limitation of using laws as guides for professional behavior?
    a.   They are general, not specific.
    b.   They are reactive rather than proactive.
    c.   They apply only to teachers, not students.
    d.   They tell teachers only what they can rather than should do.

6. The First Amendment to the Constitution guarantees
    a.   freedom from cruel and unusual punishment.
    b.   the right of freedom of speech.
    c.   freedom from unreasonable searches and seizures.
    d.   due process in any legal proceeding.

7. The Fourth Amendment to the Constitution guarantees
    a.   freedom from cruel and unusual punishment.
    b.   the right of freedom of speech.
    c.   freedom from unreasonable searches and seizures.
    d.   due process in any legal proceeding.

8. The Fourteenth Amendment to the Constitution guarantees
    a.   freedom from cruel and unusual punishment.
    b.   the right of freedom of speech.
    c.   freedom from unreasonable searches and seizures.
    d.   due process in any legal proceeding.

9. In considering teachers' academic freedom, which of the following is **NOT** important to the courts?
    a.   The specific content area being taught
    b.   The teacher's goal in discussing a topic or using a method
    c.   The age of students involved
    d.   The relevance of the materials or content to the course

10. Courts, in attempting to determine negligence, consider all of the following **EXCEPT**
    a.   whether the teacher attempted to anticipate dangers.
    b.   the age and mental abilities of students.
    c.   whether students were warned or cautioned.
    d.   the experience of the teacher in similar situations.

Self-Assessment Feedback

1. d   Tenured teachers have a right to continued employment, due process, and notification of charges for dismissal, but they do not have a right to say where they will be teaching.
2. b   The Buckley Amendment ensures parents the right to see their children's educational records and files.
3. a   Corporal punishment in the schools is prohibited in most but not all states.
4. b   Affirmative action attempts to correct for past discrimination by taking actions that favor those groups that were previously adversely affected by discrimination.
5. c   Laws governing schools apply to both teachers and students.
6. b   The First Amendment to the Constitution guarantees the right of freedom of speech and is crucial to teachers' academic freedom.
7. c   The Fourth Amendment to the Constitution protects both students and teachers from unreasonable searches and seizures.

8. d   The Fourteenth Amendment to the Constitution guarantees due process for both teachers and students.
9. a   Academic freedom is not content area specific. However, the content or issue being contested must be relevant to the specific course under consideration.
10. d   The teacher's experience is irrelevant. The courts require that all teachers, regardless of experience, protect their students from danger.

PRAXIS Practice: Questions and Feedback

1. What professional legal issue were Janice and Kyle wrestling with, and what legal safeguards influence this issue?

They were wrestling with the issue of academic freedom, which is safeguarded by the First Amendment to the U.S. Constitution, which guarantees the right of free speech to all citizens.

2. How did the two teachers differ in terms of work experience, and how might this influence their curricular decisions?

Jan had 4 years of teaching experience, whereas Kyle was a first-year teacher. This suggests that Jan had tenure and Kyle didn't. However, this shouldn't affect academic freedom, which covers all teachers, regardless of tenure status.

3. Comment on Jan's statement "We can't talk about religion in school" from a legal perspective.

Teachers can talk about religion in school; they just need to be careful that neither they nor their students proselytize or actively advocate one religion over another.

4. From a professional ethics perspective, what advice do you have for Kyle about his discussion of local union controversies?

Ethically teachers should present both sides of an issue when discussing controversial topics. This shouldn't be difficult for Kyle to do if he plans ahead.

Useful Web Site Addresses

Web Links for Chapter Terms

academic freedom: http://www.unesco.org/iau/tfaf_statment.html

affirmative action: http://www.affirmativeaction.org/resources/index.html

Buckley Amendment: http://www.ed.gov/policy/gen/guid/fpco/ferpa/index.html

copyright laws: http://www.copyright.gov/title17/

establishment clause of the Constitution: http://caselaw.lp.findlaw.com/data/constitution/amendment01/02.html

fair use guidelines: http://www.uspto.gov/web/offices/dcom/olia/confu/

free exercise clause of the Constitution: http://caselaw.lp.findlaw.com/data/constitution/amendment01/05.html

in loco parentis: http://publications.naspa.org/cgi/viewcontent.cgi?article=1284&context=naspajournal

licensure
http://www.aft.org/edissues/teacherquality/tealic.htm
http://www.nea.org/esea/eseateach.html

professional ethics
http://www.phy.ilstu.edu/ptefiles/311content/ethics/neaethics.html
http://www.aft.org/history/histdocs/code.html

religion in schools: http://www.aclu.org/ReligiousLiberty/ReligiousLibertylist.cfm?c=139

reduction in force
http://www.nea.org/nr/nr990308.html
http://www.aft.org/research/models/contracts/teacher/cincinnati/270.htm

teaching contract
http://www.edweek.org/sreports/special_reports_article.cfm?slug=02Unions.htm
http://www.nea.org/neatoday/0401/spotlight.html
http://www.findarticles.com/cf_0/m2185/1_12/69974550/p1/article.jhtml

tenure: http://www.aft.org/research/reports/tenure/Laruep.htm

Web Links for "Teaching in An Era of Reform: The Teacher Tenure Issue"

Confronting a Tough Issue: Teacher Tenure: http://www.edweek.org/sreports/qc99/ac/mc/mc6-s1.htm

NEA Declares Class Size "The Most Urgent Issue Before Congress": http://www.nea.org/nr/nr990308.html

Sample Contracts: Reduction in Force Procedures
http://www.aft.org/research/models/contracts/teacher/cincinnati/270.htm

Teacher Tenure: http://www.ericfacility.net/databases/ERIC_Digests/ed282352.html

Teacher Tenure: NASBE: http://www.nasbe.org/Educational_Issues/Policy_Updates/5_3p.html

Tenure: http://www.nea.org/he/tenure.html

Tenured Teachers: The Good, The Bad, The Tenured: http://www.psparents.net/Teacher%20Tenure.htm

The Changing Face of Teacher Tenure: http://www.aft.org/research/reports/tenure/Laruep.htm

The Push Against Tenure: http://www.aft.org/stand/previous/1996/072896.html

Web Links for "Exploring Diversity: Affirmative Action"

Affirmative Action and People with Disabilities: http://www.dol.gov/odep/pubs/ek98/affirmat.htm

Affirmative Action Fact Sheet: http://www.dol.gov/esa/regs/compliance/ofccp/aa.htm

Affirmative Action Program Regulations: http://www.dol.gov/dol/topic/hiring/affirmativeact.htm

Affirmative Action Under Attack: http://www.washingtonpost.com/wp-srv/politics/special/affirm/affirm.htm

American Association for Affirmative Action: http://www.affirmativeaction.org/about.html

American Association for Affirmative Action Resources: http://www.affirmativeaction.org/resources/index.html

Ten Myths About Affirmative Action
http://www.understandingprejudice.org/readroom/articles/affirm.htm

The Real Affirmative Action Problem
http://www.businessweek.com/bwdaily/dnflash/may2003/nf20030530_3584_db045.htm

Additional Chapter Web Links

Educational Law

Education Law: http://www.priweb.com/internetlawlib/99.htm
Education Law: An Overview: http://www.law.cornell.edu/topics/education.html
ADA Homepage: http://www.usdoj.gov/crt/ada/adahom1.htm
American Association for Affirmative Action Resources
http://www.affirmativeaction.org/resources/index.html
Compilation of Education Laws: http://edworkforce.house.gov/publications/compindex.htm
Constitutional Topic: Due Process: http://www.usconstitution.net/consttop_duep.html
Court Rules Pupils' Grading Classmates' Work Violates Federal Ruling
http://www.education-world.com/a_jssues/issues126.shtml
Family Educational Rights and Privacy Act (FERPA)
http://www.ed.gov/policy/gen/guid/fpco/ferpa/index.html
http://www.epic.org/privacy/education/ferpa.html
Federal Laws Prohibiting Job Discrimination Questions and Answers
http://www.eeoc.gov/facts/qanda.html
First Amendment Law Materials: http://www.law.cornell.edu/topics/first_amendment.html
Legal Information Institute: http://www.law.cornell.edu/topics/topic1.html
Legal Requirements of Inclusion: http://www.uni.edu/coe/inclusion/legal/index.html
No Child Left Behind: http://www.nclb.gov/
Students' Rights: http://www.aclu.org:80/issues/student/hmes.html
Supreme Court Collection: http://supct.law.cornell.edu/supct/topiclist.html
U.S. Constitution: First Amendment: http://caselaw.lp.findlaw.com/data/constitution/amendment01/
Wright's Law: http://www.wrightslaw.com/

Copyright

Copyright and K–12: Who Pays in the Network Era?: http://www.ed.gov/Technology/Futures/rothman.html
Copyright Resources from the PBS Videoconference of 2.20.03
http://www.umsl.edu/services/cte/Movies/pbs_resources.html
TEACH Act: http://www.copyright.gov/title17/
TEACH Act: http://www.arl.org/info/frn/copy/TEACH.html
The TEACH Toolkit: http://www.lib.ncsu.edu/scc/legislative/teachkit/

Learners' Civil Rights

First Amendment Law Materials (Speech, Press, Religion, Assembly)
http://www.law.cornell.edu/topics/first_amendment.html
Internet Legal Resources on Special Education and Disabilities
http://aace.virginia.edu/go/specialed/resources/legal.html
Manual on School Uniforms: http://www.ed.gov/updates/uniforms.html
Students' Rights: http://www.aclu.org:80/issues/student/hmes.html

Chapter 10
The School Curriculum

Overview

The aims of education are used to frame the evolving American curriculum. The formal and informal curriculum are described in terms of different curricular emphases. Reform movements in education are placed within a historical context and used to analyze current curricular trends. Curriculum controversies are described in terms of ideological struggles over the control of American education. Specific examples such as textbooks, banned books, and under-represented minorities are used to illustrate these ideological conflicts.

Chapter Goals

This chapter examines

- The influence of philosophy on the curriculum
- States' and local districts' attempts to control the curriculum
- The relationship between textbooks and the curriculum
- The influence of professional organizations on the curriculum
- Controversies surrounding the curriculum

Chapter Outline

I. What Is Curriculum?
    A. The Relationship Between Curriculum and Instruction
    B. Parts of the Curriculum
        1. The Explicit Curriculum
            a. Curriculum in Elementary Schools
            b. Curriculum in Middle Schools
            c. Curriculum in Junior High and High Schools
            d. Integrated Curriculum
        2. The Implicit Curriculum
        3. The Null Curriculum
        4. Extracurriculum
II. Forces That Influence the Curriculum
    A. Curriculum and the Professional Teacher
    B. Philosophical Foundations: Sources of Curriculum
    C. Textbooks
    D. Standards and Standardized Testing
        1. Professional Organization Standards
        2. State and District Standards
            a. Curriculum Guides
            b. Standardized Testing
            c. Graduation Requirements
    E. The Federal Government
III. Controversies in Curriculum
    A. A National Curriculum
    B. Social Issues
        1. Sex Education
        2. Moral and Character Education–Service Learning

3. Creationism Versus Evolution
4. Censorship

IV. Decision Making: Defining Yourself as a Professional

Transparencies

T 10.1 (Table 10.1) Two Elementary Teachers' Schedules
T 10.2 (Figure 10.1) Forces Influencing Curriculum
T 10.3 (Table 10.2) Philosophical Foundations of Curriculum
T 10.4 (Table 10.4) The Federal Government's Influence on Curriculum
T 10.5 (Table 10.5) Examples of Changes in Emphasis in Mathematics

Teaching Suggestions

I. What Is Curriculum?

> **The purpose of this section of the chapter is to help students understand what curriculum is and how it will influence their lives as teachers.**

> ■ Use your own class to help students understand the differences between and the interrelationships among curriculum and instruction. Get them to do the same in their own content areas or levels. *Increasing Understanding 10.1* also deals with this issue.

> ■ *Transparency 10.1* contains the two elementary teachers' schedules we first encountered in Chapter 7. Emphasize that this is the explicit curriculum. Ask elementary education majors how they would adjust these to fit their own priorities and goals.

> ■ *Going into Schools #1* asks students to analyze a teacher's lesson plans in terms of the explicit and implicit curriculum.

> ■ Use your own syllabus to illustrate how the implicit curriculum is communicated to students. Obtain teachers' disclosure statements, and point out how they also reflect the implicit curriculum.

> ■ Ask students to share their extracurricular experiences in schools. Ask them how important they believe these experiences were for them? How important are they for the students they'll be teaching?

> ■ Although the results linking extracurricular participation to many desired school outcomes are impressive, caution students that most of this research is correlational. Encourage them to explain the correlations in two ways.

> ■ *Journal Starter #1* asks students to reflect back on their own experiences with curriculum and how it influenced them as students.

II. Forces That Influence the Curriculum

> **The purpose of this section of the chapter is to help students understand the forces that will influence them and their curricula as they become teachers.**

> ■ Use *Transparency 10.2* "Forces Influencing the Curriculum" to provide an overview of this section of the chapter. Point out that multiple forces can exert curricular pressures at any one

time.

- Emphasize the teacher's central and critical role in ultimately deciding on the curriculum in a classroom.

- *Transparency 10.3* "Philosophical Foundations of Curriculum" links three curricular foci–needs of individuals, needs of society, and academic disciplines–to the four educational philosophies discussed in Chapter 6. Ask students which focus is most important to them? Which is least important? Is this congruent with their developing philosophy of education?

- *Going into Schools #2* asks students to analyze a teacher's planning in terms of textbook resources.

- *Portfolio Activity 10.2* asks students to analyze a textbook in terms of their own philosophy of curriculum.

- *Going into Schools #3* asks students to interview a teacher about the various forces that influence curriculum.

- *Reflect on This* presents your students with a curriculum dilemma involving mandated curriculum focusing on basic skills that may run counter to the learning needs of students.

- *Portfolio Activity 10.3* asks students to analyze either a state or a district curriculum guide in terms of both organization and usefulness.

- *Transparency 10.4* "The Federal Government's Influence on Curriculum" contains a number of examples of legislative acts that have affected curriculum. Point out which are still having an influence on today's curriculum.

- This chapter's *Classroom Windows* video feature focuses on the same math classroom that introduced this chapter. Use the video to provide a concrete example of math reforms at the elementary level.

- *Transparency 10.5* "Examples of Changes in Emphasis in Mathematics" describes recent math curriculum reform efforts. Use this to analyze the video clip of a math lesson in *Classroom Windows*.

III. Controversies in Curriculum

The purpose of this section of the chapter is to help students understand current curricular controversies that will influence their lives as teachers.

- Ask students to discuss the pros and cons of a national curriculum. Refer students back to historical issues raised on this topic in Chapter 5.

- Connect the topic of sex education to academic freedom, discussed in Chapter 9. Ask students where they stand on the issue.

- Differentiate between character and moral education. Link to the religious controversies in Chapter 9. Ask students which approach makes the most sense to them.

- Ask students who have been involved in service learning to share their experiences with the class.

- Ask if any students have read any of the books targeted for censorship. Ask if they understand why these books were targeted. Emphasize the conflicts between parental choice and teacher autonomy and academic freedom in this issue.

- Bring into class several social studies or literature texts, and have the class examine them in terms of the contributions of women and minorities. Have the class note the date of publication in terms of their analysis.

- *Journal Starter #2* encourages students to think about these curricular controversies in terms of themselves as beginning teachers.

Journal Starters

1. Encourage students to think about the curriculum they encountered: When did you attend school? What was emphasized in the curriculum? How did you know this was important? What aspects of the implicit curriculum, like values and standards of behavior, were emphasized? How did the extracurriculum influence your growth and development as a student? Who participated with you in these activities? Based upon your experiences, what changes in the curriculum would you suggest for your students?

2. Encourage students to think about how curricular controversies will influence their lives as teachers: Which of the curricular controversies described in the text will have the biggest influence on your teaching? Which are most important to you personally? How do these curricular controversies relate to teacher autonomy and academic freedom? Should the curriculum be used to reinforce student values or to examine them? Which approach–character education or moral education–will be most valuable to you as a teacher? How will curriculum controversies affect you as a beginning teacher?

Increasing Understanding: Questions and Feedback

10.1
You show your students two short essays on the overhead projector. One effectively makes and defends an argument, and the other does not. Your purpose in doing so is to help your students learn to make and defend an argument in writing. Identify the curriculum decision and the instruction decision in what you did. Describe an alternative to your instructional decision (a different way of helping your students reach the goal).
10.1
Deciding that you want to help your students learn to make and defend an argument in writing is a curriculum decision. Displaying the two essays is an instructional decision. A common, but less desirable, instructional decision is to simply explain the characteristics of an effective essay that makes and defends an argument in writing.

10.2
How much time does each teacher devote to math? What do these allocations suggest about the relative importance of language arts compared to math?
10.2
Sharon spends 50 minutes a day on math, and Susie spends 75 minutes a day on math. For Sharon math is slightly less important than language arts; for Susie it's slightly more important.

10.3
Think again about block scheduling which you first studied in Chapter 2. (An example of this would be having classes meet for 90–100 minutes a day for half of the school year.) Identify at least two ways in which block scheduling might influence the curriculum.

10.3

A primary way in which block scheduling can influence the curriculum is in content coverage. Longer class periods allow teachers to cover topics in more depth, which can result in increased student learning. A second possible influence is in time for practice and feedback. Longer class periods give teachers more opportunities to work with students who are having difficulty with the topics they're studying.

10.4

Look again at Sharon's and Susie's schedules. What do the schedules indicate about each teacher's priorities? Explain.

10.4

The schedules indicate that language arts and math are high priorities for both teachers, and other areas such as science and social studies are relatively low priorities. The evidence for this conclusion is that a large portion of each day is devoted to language arts and math, but little time is devoted to science and social studies.

10.5

Explain why it is important for teachers to be aware that the implicit curriculum exists. Provide an example to illustrate your answer.

10.5

Students often learn about teachers' values and priorities through the implicit curriculum. For instance, if a teacher encourages and helps students who are struggling to understand a topic, students learn that struggles are all part of the learning process. On the other hand, if teachers are impatient with struggling students, they learn that struggling is undesirable, and those who don't struggle are favored.

10.6

A student participates in a high school jazz band. Under what conditions would this be part of the explicit curriculum? part of the extracurriculum? Explain your answer.

10.6

If jazz music is a course for which the student receives a grade, participating in the jazz band is part of the explicit curriculum. If it isn't a formal course, participating in the jazz band is part of the extracurriculum.

10.7

Teachers who feel strongly that basic skills are a crucial part of the curriculum are basing their decision most nearly on what educational philosophy? Explain.

10.7

Teachers who strongly emphasize basic skills are grounding their decisions in essentialism as a philosophy. Essentialists believe that a body of knowledge exists that all people should understand in order to function effectively in today's world, and basic skills are part of that core body of knowledge.

10.8

The emphasis on children's needs is most nearly based on which educational philosophy? Explain.

10.8

The emphasis on children's needs is most nearly based on progressivism. Chapter 6 explained that progressivism emphasizes curriculum that focuses on real-world problem solving and individual development.

10.9

How are educational philosophies reflected in textbooks? For example, what would you expect to see in a math textbook based on essentialism? a math textbook based on progressivism? Explain in each case.

10.9

Philosophy is reflected in textbooks by the topics the text covers and the way in which the topics are presented. For instance, a math textbook grounded in essentialism would provide for a great deal of practice in basic skills, whereas a textbook grounded in progressivism would more strongly emphasize real-world problem solving.

10.10

Look again at what is receiving increased emphasis in science. What educational philosophy is best reflected in this increased emphasis? Explain.

10.10

Essentialism and progressivism are both reflected in the increased emphasis. For instance, "studying fewer topics in depth" reflects essentialism, and "discussion and communication between teacher and students and students with each other" and "guiding students in active inquiry" reflect progressivism.

10.11

You are required by your principal to follow state curriculum guides. You find some factual errors in one of the sections. As a professional teacher, what should you do? Explain.

10.11

You should teach the information in a way that is conceptually correct, and you should then contact your grade-level chairperson or department head, who will then contact the district or state leadership to make them aware of the error. (It would also be perfectly acceptable for you to directly contact the district or state leadership.)

10.12

To what educational philosophy–perennialism, progressivism, essentialism, or postmodernism–is *A Nation at Risk* most closely related? Explain.

10.12

A Nation At Risk is most closely aligned with Essentialism. The book suggests that American students are leaving school without enough knowledge and skills to keep America competitive in today's global economy. This emphasis on knowledge and skills is consistent with the views of essentialists.

10.13

What principle is grounded in the First Amendment? What implications has this principle had for education?

10.13

The First Amendment provides the principle of the separation of church and state. This principle has had many implications for education, such as forbidding public money to be given to religious schools and the prevention of any religious beliefs being taught in public schools.

Reflect on This: Questions and Feedback

(These can also be found on the Companion Website: www.prenhall.com/kauchak .)

Teaching Basic Skills Using Personal Experiences

1. Why do you suppose the students so intensely dislike the book's exercises?

The most likely reason the kids so intensely dislike the exercises is that they don't see that exercises of this type have anything to do with their lives, and relevance for these kids is important for their motivation.

2. Is being able to write using correct grammar and spelling an important goal?

Writing using correct grammar and spelling is certainly an important goal. The question in this case is _how_ to best help the students acquire the skills, not _if_ the skills are important.

3. In one approach to learning to write, students master basic skills and then use the skills when they write. An alternative is to have students simply write and then develop the basic skills using the writing. Which is the better approach? Why do you think so?

This question is controversial. Some people advocate the first approach; others advocate the second. Our position is to adopt the approach that has the greater likelihood of working. Since the first approach doesn't seem to work with the students in this situation, the second seems more viable.

4. What would you do in the situation just described?

We would adopt the second approach in Question 3. Our rationale is strictly pragmatic; it's the approach that appears to have the greater likelihood of helping the students learn to write effectively.

Classroom Windows: Questions and Feedback

The Math Curriculum in Elementary Schools

1. You considered the implicit curriculum in Suzanne's classroom earlier in the chapter. Based on what you have sees in the video, describe the implicit curriculum in her classroom in more detail.

The following include some of the ideas that Suzanne's students are learning through the implicit curriculum: making mistakes is part of the learning process, being actively involved is valuable and important, acquiring math skills is practical and part of the real world, and teachers and students work together to promote learning.

2. Which of the educational philosophies is most nearly reflected in Suzanne's teaching? Explain why you think so.

Suzanne's teaching most nearly reflects progressivism. Her instruction was learner-centered and focused on real-world problems.

3. Consider the forces that influence the curriculum: philosophy, textbooks, the local district, the national government, and professional organizations. Then rate the influence you believe each had on Suzanne's curriculum. Use the following scale for your rating: 4 = very strong influence, 3 = strong influence, 2 = weak influence, 1 = no influence.

- Philosophy   1   2   3   4
- Textbooks   1   2   3   4
- Local district   1   2   3   4
- National government   1   2   3   4
- Professional organizations   1   2   3   4

Explain your rating in each case.

We recognize that assessing influences is highly subjective, but with that note of caution we would rate the influences on Suzanne's curriculum as follows:

Philosophy	*4*	*Suzanne described her beliefs about the importance of students being involved in their learning activities and math being practical. These beliefs were part of her personal philosophy of education.*
Textbooks	*2*	*While textbooks influence teachers in general and they also influenced Suzanne's teaching, they had a minor influence in the video episode.*
Local district	*3*	*The philosophy of Suzanne's district promoted student-centered learning.*
National government	*1*	*No evidence of national government influence was observable in the episode.*
Professional organizations	*3*	*The National Council of Teachers of Mathematics strongly endorses the kind of learning that was evident in the video episode.*

4. To what extent did Suzanne display professionalism in the episode you saw? Explain your analysis.

Suzanne demonstrated the characteristics of a professional. She displayed a great deal of professional knowledge, she was a licensed teacher, and she demonstrated high levels of autonomy and decision making.

Video Discussions: Questions and Feedback

1. Theodore Sizer is the Director of the Coalition for Effective Schools, which attempts to reform high schools. In his view what is the most important thing that schools can do to prepare students for college? Where in the curriculum would we find this emphasis, and how could teachers integrate it into their teaching?

Dr. Sizer recommends constantly challenging students by asking why, rather than having them memorize lots of information. This approach could be integrated into any area of the curriculum but often clashes in content areas that are full of facts that students are expected to memorize.

2. Dr. Sizer recommends a standard, focused curriculum for all students. How could a standard, focused curriculum be used to encourage student critical thinking? What are the advantages and disadvantages of this approach to curriculum?

Dr. Sizer recommends a very focused curriculum in which understanding is continually stressed. Teachers do this by constantly saying, "Explain that to me." An advantage to this approach is that it emphasizes depth of understanding over breadth or coverage. A disadvantage might be that some areas like art, music, and physical education might get neglected.

Self-Assessment Questions
(Note: Students have access to these questions and their feedback on the text's Companion Website.)

1. Which of the following best describes what students learn that is found in their textbooks?
    a. The explicit curriculum
    b. The implicit curriculum
    c. The integrated curriculum
    d. The extracurriculum

2. Which of the following best describes what students learn from the values teachers communicate through their interactions with students?
    a. The explicit curriculum
    b. The implicit curriculum
    c. The integrated curriculum
    d. The extracurriculum

3. Some students participate in extracurricular activities such as sports and clubs. Which of the following best describes the relationship between participation in extracurricular activities and academic achievement?
    a. There is no relationship between participation in extracurricular activities and achievement; the participation of high and low achievers is about the same.
    b. Students who participate in sports are higher achievers than those who don't participate, but students who participate in clubs are lower achievers than those who don't participate.
    c. Students who don't participate in extracurricular activities are higher achievers than students who do participate.
    d. Students who participate in extracurricular activities, in general, are higher achievers than those who don't participate.

4. Which of the following statements best describes the influence of the individual teacher on the curriculum?
   a. Since much of curriculum in mandated by states, individual teachers have little influence on the curriculum.
   b. The individual teacher influences curriculum more than any other source except the federal government.
   c. The individual teacher influences curriculum more than any other source except local districts.
   d. The individual teacher influences curriculum more than any other influence.

5. Which of the following best describes the influence of textbooks on the curriculum?
   a. Textbooks strongly influence curriculum decisions for both beginning teachers and veterans.
   b. Textbooks strongly influence curriculum decisions for beginning teachers but not for veteran teachers.
   c. Textbooks strongly influence curriculum decisions for veteran teachers but not for beginning teachers.
   d. Textbooks have little influence on curriculum decisions for either beginning teachers or veterans.

6. Testing is an important influence on curriculum. Of the following which is the most likely result of the impact of testing on the curriculum?
   a. Curriculum integration (such as the integration of math and science) in middle schools
   b. Most secondary teachers relying primarily on lecture as a teaching method, because lecture allows the greatest amount of content to be covered in the shortest amount of time
   c. Reading, writing, and math being emphasized in the elementary curriculum, and science and social studies being de-emphasized
   d. Hands-on learning activities being emphasized in all areas of the curriculum, particularly in the elementary curriculum

7. You plan to place a great deal of emphasis on writing with your students. Which of the following best describes your decision?
   a. It is an instructional decision, because the students will have to be taught how to write effectively.
   b. It is a curriculum decision, because curriculum describes *what* students will be taught.
   c. It is an administrative decision, because statewide assessment tests virtually always measure students' ability to write.
   d. It is a political decision, because our country's leaders believe that our students don't possess the basic skills necessary to function effectively in today's world.

8. You display two sample persuasive essays on the overhead, one that is well written and one that isn't, and in a discussion you help students understand the characteristics of an effective persuasive essay. Which of the following best describes your action?
   a. It is an instructional decision, because this is the way you plan to teach the students *how* to write effectively.
   b. It is a curriculum decision, because curriculum describes *what* students will be taught.
   c. It is an administrative decision, because statewide assessment tests virtually always measure students' ability to write.
   d. It is a political decision, because our country's leaders believe that our students don't possess the basic skills necessary to function effectively in today's world.

9. Which of the following best describes character education?
   a. Analysis of a variety of moral perspectives
   b. Development of moral reasoning
   c. Teacher as a problem poser and facilitator
   d. Transmission of moral values

10. Which of the following best describes moral education?
   a. Translation of moral values into moral behavior
   b. Using ethical dilemmas as a focus for problem solving
   c. Practicing and rewarding desirable values
   d. Teacher as a role model

Self-Assessment Feedback

1.   a   The content found in textbooks makes up part of the explicit curriculum.
2.   b   The implicit curriculum is communicated through teachers' values and the unspoken routines and procedures that occur in classrooms.
3.   d   Research indicates that students who participate in extracurricular activities are higher achievers than those who don't participate in these activities.
4.   d   The teacher is the strongest influence on curriculum.
5.   a   Textbooks strongly influence curriculum decisions for both beginning teachers and veterans.
6.   c   Teachers tend to teach content for which students will be held accountable. In today's elementary schools reading, writing, and math are the most frequently tested.
7.   b   Deciding to place a great deal of emphasis on writing is a curriculum decision. (*How* you plan to do so is an instructional decision.)
8.   a   Displaying the examples and involving the students in a discussion is an instructional decision, because it describes *how* you plan to reach your goal.
9.   d   Character education emphasizes the transmission of moral values and rewarding students for displaying those values.
10.   b   Moral education emphasizes moral reasoning, which could be accomplished by posing ethical dilemmas.

PRAXIS Practice: Questions and Feedback

1. Describe differences in David's explicit curriculum compared to Steve's. Explain how these differences relate to teacher autonomy.

Although the two teachers taught the same topic, the information they wanted the students to understand was quite different. David's curricular decisions emphasized cause-and-effect relationships in the information the students were studying (such as why Mercury is so hot on one side and so cold on the other). Steve's curricular decisions resulted in his emphasizing factual information about the planets, such as their names in order from the sun. These differences reflect the autonomy of the two teachers. Standards, for example, can specify general guidelines, but teachers must still make specific curriculum and instruction decisions such as these.

2. Describe differences in the implicit curriculum for these two teachers.

Important differences between the two teachers existed with respect to the implicit curriculum. For example, David's students learned that they played an active role in first acquiring information about the planets, and second, finding relationships in the information after it was organized. They also learned that thinking analytically about information is an integral part of schooling. Steve's students learned that sitting quietly and receiving information is the way that classes are conducted. They also learned that memorizing factual information is the way that learning occurs.

3. Describe differences between the two teachers with respect to the forces that influence teachers' curriculum decisions.

Based on the information we have in the case study, a clear philosophy was the strongest influence on David's curriculum decisions. "The kids need to be able to think about this kind of stuff" is evidence of this influence. In contrast, Steve's curriculum decisions were most strongly influenced by the textbook he was using. The fact that his first instructional move was to assign the chapter as reading suggests this influence. We don't have evidence in the case study for the influence of either standards or the federal government.

4. Explain how David's and Steve's curriculum decisions influenced their instruction.

Since David's curricular decisions emphasized thinking and relationships, his instruction focused on fostering interactions between him and his students and the students with each other. It isn't possible to emphasize thinking by simply presenting information. By comparison Steve's curricular decisions emphasized factual information, which is most efficiently delivered with a straightforward presentation.

Useful Web Site Addresses

Web Links for Chapter Terms

curriculum
http://www.funderstanding.com/curriculum.cfm
http://www.ascd.org/
http://www.scarbvts.demon.co.uk/edmods.htm

implicit, explicit, null curriculum
http://www.scarbvts.demon.co.uk/curric.htm/
http://www.teachersmind.com/eisner.htm
http://learningconference.com/ProposalSystem/Presentations/P000491

extracurriculum: http://www.mhhe.com/socscience/education/sadker/sg/07sum.htm

Web Links for "Teaching in An Era Of Reform: The Curriculum Reform Issue"

National Council of Teachers of Mathematics: http://www.nctm.org

NCTM Standards: http://standards.nctm.org

Ed Reforms Parallel NYSUT's Calls for Action
http://www.nysut.org/newyorkteacher/2003-2004/031022regents.html

Trying to Figure Out Why Math Is So Hard for Some
Theories Abound: Genetics, Gender, How It's Taught
http://www.washingtonpost.com/ac2/wp-dyn?pagename=article&node=&contentId=A26826-2003Dec1&notFound=true

Issues in Math Education: http://www.educationallycorrect.com/Issues/math.htm

Math Council Loses Hard-Earned Credibility: http://mathematicallycorrect.com/frankallen.htm

Mathematics Successful Transition Requires Curriculum Reform
http://clerccenter.gallaudet.edu/products/perspectives/may-jun98/math.html

Middle School Math Reform: http://www.naesp.org/ContentLoad.do?contentId=473

National Summit on Mathematics Education of Teachers
http://www7.nationalacademies.org/mseb/Zal%20Usiskin%20CBMS%20PDF%20FIle.pdf

New York City Math Wars: http://www.educationnews.org/nyc_math_warsnyc_honest_open_log.htm

The Politics of Curriculum Reform: How to Make a Silk Purse into a Sow's Ear
http://comnet.org/cpsr/essays/politics.htm

Weaving Gender Equity into Math Reform: http://www.terc.edu/wge/checklist.html

You Do the Math!: http://www.haaretz.com/hasen/pages/ShArt.jhtml?itemNo=267177

Web Links for "Exploring Diversity: Minorities and Women in the Curriculum"

About Women in World History Curriculum: http://www.womeninworldhistory.com/wiwhc.html

A Curriculum for Women: http://www.nald.ca/province/que/ywca/wfw3.htm

Annotated Bibliography of Multicultural Issues in Mathematics Education
http://jwilson.coe.uga.edu/DEPT/Multicultural/MEBib94.html

Consortium on Race, Gender, and Ethnicity: http://www.crge.umd.edu/

Critical Issue: Educating Teachers for Diversity: http://www.ncrel.org/skrs/areas/issues/educatrs/presrvce/pe300.htm

Fostering Intercultural Harmony in Schools: Research Findings: http://www.nwrel.org/scpd/sirs/8/topsyn7.html

Multicultural Education: http://www.eagle2.american.edu/~gb3107a/mult.htm

Multicultural Education in Elementary and Secondary Schools
http://www.ed.gov/databases/ERIC_Digests/ed327613.html

Multicultural Education and Ethnic Groups: Selected Resources
http://wwwlibrary.csustan.edu/lboyer/tmp/multicu.htm

Multicultural Education Paths: http://www.edchange.org/multicultural/sites1.html

Multicultural Pavilion: Teacher's Corner: http://curry.edschool.virginia.edu/go/multicultural/teachers.html

New Arguments for Diversifying the Curriculum: Advancing Students' Cognitive Development
http://www.diversityweb.org/Digest/Sm99/curriculum.html

The Use of Multicultural Curricula and Materials to Counter Racism in Children
http://www.findarticles.com/cf_dls/m0341/4_55/62521563/p2/article.jhtml?term=

We Hold These Truths to Be Self-Evident: Evidence of Democratic Principles in Our Schools
http://edweb.sdsu.edu/people/cmathison/truths/truths.html

Welcome to the American Indian Science and Engineering Society-Multicultural Education Reform Efforts
http://spot.colorado.edu/~aises/aises.html

What Is Culture?: http://www.wsu.edu:8001/vcwsu/commons/topics/culture/culture-index.html

Additional Chapter Web Links

Curriculum Development

Association for Supervision and Curriculum Development: http://www.ascd.org/
Character Education Partnership: http://www.character.org/
Civil Literacy and the Cyber-Pilot's License: http://ctl.stanford.edu/teach/NTLF/v9n5/viewpoint.htm
Curriculum and Education: http://www.scarbvts.demon.co.uk/edmods.htm
Curriculum Approaches and Definitions: http://www.coe.ufl.edu/courses/todd/curriculum.html
Designing Standards-Based Lessons: http://www.rmcdenver.com/useguide/lessons/design.htm?
Eisner on Curriculum: http://www.teachersmind.com/eisner.htm
Experiential Learning: http://www.scarbvts.demon.co.uk/explearn.htm
Guidelines for Appropriate Curriculum Content and Assessment in Programs Serving Children Ages 3 Through 8
http://www.naeyc.org/resources/position_statements/pscuras.htm
Hilda Taba: Inductive Thinking: http://ivc.uidaho.edu/mod/models/taba/index.html
Insiders and Outsiders, Understanding the Implicit Curriculum
http://learningconference.com/ProposalSystem/Presentations/P000491
Integrated Curriculum: http://www.nwrel.org/scpd/sirs/8/c016.html
Levels of Curriculum (formal, hidden, received): http://www.scarbvts.demon.co.uk/curric.htm/
Models of Teaching: http://ivc.uidaho.edu/mod/index.html
Moral Development and Moral Education: An Overview: http://tigger.uic.edu/~lnucci/MoralEd/overview.html
National Service-Learning Clearinghouse (NSLC): http://www.servicelearning.org/
Observing the Hidden Curriculum: http://www.coedu.usf.edu/edf200598/handouts/html/m111.htm

Professional Organizations

American Alliance for Health, Physical Education, Recreation and Dance: http://www.aahperd.org/
American Association of School Librarians: http://www.ala.org/
American Association of Teachers of French: http://aatf.utsa.edu/
American Association of Teachers of German: http://www.aatg.org/
The American Council of the Teaching of Foreign Language: http://www.actfl.org/
American Federation of Teachers: http://www.aft.org/
Association for the Advancement of Computing in Education: http://curry.edschool.virginia.edu/aace/site/
Association for Career and Technical Education: http://www. acteonline.org/
Association for Education Communications and Technology: http://www.aect.org
Association of American Geographers: http://www.aag.org/
Association of Physics Teachers: http://www.aapt.org/aaptgeneral/geneinfo.html
Center for Civic Education: http://www.civiced.org/
The Council for Exceptional Children: http://www.cec.sped.org
The International Reading Association: http://www.ira.org
International Society for Technology in Education: http://www.iste.org.
Music Educators National Association: http://www.menc.org/
Music Teachers National Association: http://www.mtna.org/
The National Art Education Association: http://www.naea-reston.org/
The National Association for the Education of Young Children: http://www.naeyc.org/
National Association of Biology Teachers: http://www.nabt.org/
National Board for Professional Teaching Standards: http://www.nbpts.org
The National Council for the Social Studies: http://www.ncss.org
The National Council of Teachers of Mathematics: http://www.nctm.org
The National Council of Teachers of English: http://www.ncte.org

The National Dance Association: http://www.aahperd.org/nda/nda-main.html
National Education Association: http://www.nea.org/
The National Science Teachers Association: http://www.nsta.org

Professionalism

American Federation of Teachers: http://www.aft.org/
American Society for Ethics in Education: http://www.edethics.org/
Center for Education Reform: http://edreform.com/
MCREL Standards: http://www.mcrel.org/topics/topics.asp?topicsid=14
National Education Association Code of Ethics for the Profession: http://www.nea.org/aboutnea/code.html
National Teachers Hall of Fame: http://www.nthf.org
National Assessment of Educational Progress: The Nation's Report Card
http://nces.ed.gov/nationsreportcard/site/home.asp
On the Commitment to Professionalism in Teaching: http://www.nbpts.org/standards/
Teaching as a Career : http://www.aft.org/career/index.html
What to Look for in a Teacher Preparation Program: http://www.ncate.org/future/lookfor.htm

Designing Standards-Based Lessons: http://www.rmcdenver.com/useguide/lessons/design.htm?

Developing Content Standards: Creating a Process for Change: http://www.ed.gov/pubs/CPRE/rb10stan.html

Evaluating State Curriculum Standards: http://www.nasbe.org/Policy_Updates.html

The Evergreen Project: Educational Standards by State: http://www.ajschools.com/teachers/find/standards.htm

Goals 2000: http://www.ed.gov/G2K/ProgRpt96/natgoals.html

Implementing Standards-Based Reform: http://www.nasbe.org/Policy_Updates.html

NASBE: http://www.nasbe.org/Policy_Updates.html

Parents Ask About Standards: http://www.rmcres.com/famed/askabout/english/standard.html
(in Spanish at http://www.rmcres.com/famed/askabout/spanish/estandares.html)
Frequently asked questions and their responses are located at this site.

Standards: What Are They?: http://www.ed.gov/pubs/IASA/newsletters/standards/

Chapter 11
Instruction in American Classrooms

Overview

A central role for teachers is to promote student development and learning. The chapter begins with an examination of the research on effective teaching and its implications for instruction. The chapter then takes a historical look at two views of learning–behaviorism and cognitive psychology. Implications of the cognitive revolution in teaching are described in terms of learner-centered instruction, learner self-regulation, social influences on learning, and changing views of assessment.

Chapter Goals

This chapter examines

- How effective teachers plan for instruction
- The kinds of personal characteristics effective teachers possess
- The instructional strategies effective teachers use
- How effective teachers manage their classrooms to create productive learning environments
- How effective teachers assess their students
- The theories of learning on which effective teachers base their instruction

Chapter Outline

I. Looking in Classrooms to Define Effective Teaching
    A. Planning and the Teacher as a Professional
        1. Objectives and Teacher Thinking
        2. Instructional Alignment and Teacher Thinking
    B. Personal Characteristics
        1. Personal Teaching Efficacy
        2. Caring
        3. Modeling and Enthusiasm
        4. Teacher Expectations
    C. Teaching Strategies
        1. Classroom Organization
        2. Communication–Communication and Knowledge of Content: Implications for Teachers
        3. Teacher Questioning
            a. Frequency
            b. Equitable Distribution
            c. Wait-time
            d. Prompting
            e. Appropriate Level of Difficulty
        4. Effective Presentation of Subject Matter
            a. Use of Examples
            b. High Levels of Interaction
        5. Effective Feedback
    D. Classroom Management
        1. Using Effective Instructional Strategies
        2. Preventing Problems Through Planning
            a. Preparing Rules and Procedures
            b. Communication with Parents

3. Intervening Effectively
4. Serious Management Problems: Violence and Aggression
E. Effective Assessment–Changing Views of Assessment: Alternative Assessment
II. Using Our Understanding of Learning to Define Effective Teaching
A. Behaviorism
B. Cognitive Views of Learning
C. Classroom Windows: Learning About Balance Beams in Fourth Grade
D. Teaching in an Era of Reform: The Teacher-Centered Versus Learner-Centered Issue
III. Decision Making: Defining Yourself as a Professional

Transparencies

T 11.1 (Figure 11.1) Dimensions on Which Effective and Less Effective Teachers Differ
T 11.2 (Figure 11.2) A Taxonomy of Learning, Teaching, and Assessing
T 11.3 (Table 11.1) Characteristics of Effective Organization
T 11.4 (Table 11.2) Obedience and Responsibility Models of Management
T 11.5 (Table 11.3) Examples of Classroom Rules
T 11.6 (Table 11.4) Comparison of Behaviorist and Cognitive Views of Learning

Teaching Suggestions

I. Looking in Classrooms to Define Effective Teaching

The purpose of this section of the chapter is to help students understand the teacher effectiveness research and how it can be used to guide instruction.

A. *Transparency 11.1* **"Dimensions on which Effective and Less Effective Teachers Differ" provides an overview of the content in this section.**

- **Connect the concept of caring back to our discussion of caring in Chapter 2. Ask why caring is so important in teaching. Ask students for examples of caring teachers they have had. How did students know these teachers cared?**

- **Connect the concept of modeling to legal issues concerning teachers' private lives in Chapter 9. Point out that modeling can focus on both cognitive and affective outcomes. Ask students for examples of each.**

- **See Good and Brophy (2003) for an in-depth description of the teacher-expectations research. Point out that this line of research began with *Pygmalion in the Classroom*, an experimental attempt to alter teachers' expectations.**

- **Analyze one of the *Classroom Windows* videos (the one in Chapter 10 would be good for this) in terms of teacher expectations. Did the teacher communicate both verbally and nonverbally that she expected all students to learn? How did she do this?**

- *Going into Schools #1* **asks students to interview a teacher about his or her questioning strategies. Encourage your students to analyze these in terms of teacher expectations.**

- **Analyze one of the *Classroom Windows* videos (Judy's lesson in Chapter 6 would be a good one for this) in terms of questioning strategies. Help students develop different observation instruments (e.g., frequency, wait-time, and equitable distribution) before viewing, and have** different groups of students observe for these different aspects and report back to the whole class.

■ Relate the quality of teaching examples to pedagogical content knowledge first described in Chapter 1. How is pedagogical content knowledge related to content knowledge? Ask students for additional effective examples that they have encountered in classrooms.

■ *Transparency 11.4* "The Obedience and Responsibility Models of Management" describes similarities and differences between these two approaches to management. Connect these models to behaviorist and cognitive approaches to learning discussed later in the chapter.

■ *Reflect on This* asks students to analyze a classroom that is having both management and motivation problems.

■ Use your own assessment system as a concrete frame of reference for the topic of assessment. Point out that many of the *Going into Schools* and *Portfolio* assignments in the text are performance assessments.

■ Chapter 1 discusses teaching portfolios in greater depth. Emphasize the proactive role that students play in constructing a portfolio.

■ *Journal Starter #1* asks students to reflect on effective teachers they have had.

II. Using Our Understanding of Learning to Define Effective Teaching

The purpose of this section of the chapter is to introduce students to behaviorist and cognitive views of learning and to illustrate how these influence instruction.

■ To concretely illustrate instructional differences between behavioral and cognitive perspectives on learning, show the *Classroom Windows* video from Chapter 6. This video juxtaposes a teacher-centered lecture with an interactive one that uses questioning to involve students in the lesson.

■ *Transparency 11.6* "Comparison of Behaviorist and Cognitive Views of Learning and Teaching" compares and contrasts these views of learning. Use this overhead to analyze the two lessons involving Kevin Langeman and Leslie Nelson in the text.

■ *Classroom Windows* contains a video of a fourth-grade teacher using learner-centered strategies to teach students about balance beams and balancing equations.

■ *Teaching in an Era of Reform* asks students to take a position on the advantages of teacher-versus learner-centered instruction. You can use this background knowledge in a discussion or debate or to analyze one of the *Classroom Windows* videos.

■ *Journal Starter #2* asks students to reflect on past teachers they've had that embraced either a behaviorist or a cognitive view of learning.

Journal Starters

1. Encourage students to think about their own personal experiences with effective teachers: Which teachers stand out in your own mind as effective teachers? What made them effective? How much of their effectiveness was related to personal characteristics? Did they plan thoroughly? How could you tell? What kinds of teaching

strategies did they use? How did they manage their classrooms? How did they assess learning? What implications does all this have for you as a teacher?

2. Encourage students to think more deeply about differences between behaviorist and cognitive approaches to teaching: Can you recall a teacher or teachers who used behaviorism in their teaching? What did they do that reflected this orientation to teaching? How did it make you feel? Was it effective? Can you recall a teacher or teachers who were more cognitive in their approach to teaching? What did they do that reflected this orientation to teaching? How did it make you feel? Was it effective? What implications do your responses have for you as a teacher?

Increasing Understanding: Questions and Feedback

11.1
Research indicates that when they plan, beginning teachers write much more on paper than do veterans (Neale, Pace, & Case, 1983). Does this suggest that beginning teachers plan more effectively than veteran teachers? Explain.
11.1
This doesn't suggest that beginning teachers plan more effectively than veterans. The key to effective planning is clear teacher thinking. For beginning teachers clarifying thinking often requires that the teachers write information on paper. For veterans clear thinking doesn't require as much information in writing.

11.2
Classify the objective "to know what the term *equivalent fraction* means" into one of the cells of the taxonomy.
11.2
Knowing what the term equivalent fraction *means would be best classified into the cell where "factual knowledge" intersects with "remember."*

11.3
Explain why low-efficacy teachers are likely to spend less time on learning activities than high-efficacy teachers.
11.3
Since high-efficacy teachers believe they're able to get all students–regardless of ability–to learn and low-efficacy teachers don't believe they're able to get all students to learn, low-efficacy teachers are likely to expend less effort in their teaching. In addition, low-efficacy teachers may have more problems with classroom management.

11.4
Identify the single most important indicator of caring that exists. Use this indicator to explain why you are likely to react badly when an instructor arrives 15 minutes late to an appointment.
11.4
Time is the most important indicator of caring that exists. Everyone has 24 hours a day, so choosing to allocate some of the 24 hours to another person indicates that the other person is important. Similarly, an instructor arriving late to an appointment communicates that you're not important enough for him or her to be sure to be on time. You understand what the late arrival communicates, and you resent it.

11.5
Does *thematic lessons* imply that teachers should avoid interjecting additional material into lessons? Explain.
11.5
No, thematic lessons *does not imply that teachers should avoid interjecting additional material into lessons. It does mean, however, that the teacher should be clear about how the additional material relates to the topic the students are studying.*

11.6

Suppose some students in a classroom are rarely called on. Explain what is likely to happen with these students.

11.6

Students who are rarely called on are likely to become less involved in lessons, and gradually they stop paying attention to what is going on. In time they begin to feel less welcome in the class and may even come to believe that they're not as bright as those who are called on more frequently.

11.7

Based on what you saw in the episode at the beginning of this section, does Shirley base her management on an obedience model or a responsibility model? Cite specific evidence from the episode to support your answer.

11.7

Shirley bases her management on a responsibility model. For example, in response to Sondra's protest, Shirley says, "When we talked about our rules at the beginning of the year, we agreed that it was important to listen when other people are talking." Agreeing on rules and providing rationales for them encourage students to accept responsibility for their own behavior.

11.8

A geography teacher assesses her students' understanding of longitude and latitude by having them identify the longitudes and latitudes of several cities around the world. Is this a traditional or an alternative assessment? Explain.

11.8

This is an alternative assessment. Being able to find the longitude and latitude of cities around the world is a real-life task, and directly measuring student performance through real-life tasks is characteristic of alternative assessment.

11.9

Give an example of the use of punishment in Jeff's interaction with his students. Explain why it is an example of punishment.

11.9

When Lonnie was asked to decide whether she *or* her *was correct in the sentence "Will Antonio and (she, her) run the concession stand?" Lonnie replied, "Her." Jeff then said, "Not quite, Lonnie. This one is a little tricky, but it's the nominative case." This is an example of punishment because Lonnie is less likely to say* her *in a similar situation in the future, which is a decrease in behavior.*

11.10

Reflection is the process of asking ourselves questions, such as What am I doing in my class? and Why am I doing that? If Jeff had been a reflective teacher, would he have conducted his lesson as he did? Explain.

11.10

If Jeff had carefully reflected on his teaching, he probably wouldn't have conducted his lesson as he did. His goal was for students to be able to use pronouns correctly in writing, as indicated by his comment, "This is important, because we want to be able to use good English when we write, and this is one area where people get mixed up. . . . So, when we're finished with our study here, you'll all be able to use pronouns correctly in your writing." However, his lesson focused on isolated sentences, so his lesson and his goal were not consistent with each other.

11.11

Assess Leslie's teaching using the effective teaching characteristics outlined in Figure 11.1.

11.11

Teacher planning, teaching strategies, and assessing learning are the three dimensions for which the most evidence exists. Leslie was well planned. She had her examples (actually, an example and a nonexample) prepared on transparencies and ready to be displayed. And she made arrangements to have a second overhead in her room, so she could display the two transparencies at the same time. She was well planned.

Leslie used effective teaching strategies. She was well organized, her language was clear, and she questioned effectively, particularly in the area of equitable distribution. She used high-quality examples, and she developed her lesson with high levels of interaction. She provided effective feedback during the course of the lesson.

134

Leslie's assessment was aligned with her learning objective and her learning activity.

We don't have direct evidence for her personal characteristics or classroom management. However, because her instructional strategies were effective, the likelihood of her having classroom management problems was significantly reduced.

Reflect on This: Questions and Feedback
(These can also be found on the Companion Website: www.prenhall.com/kauchak .)

Maintaining Order in the Classroom

1. Why do you suppose some of the students are disruptive?

The most likely reason the students are disruptive is that you're conducting the lesson by talking, and you're attempting to help the students understand the topic by explaining rather than questioning.

2. Why do you believe many of the students are inattentive?

The answer to this question is similar to the answer for Question 1. In addition to the fact that you're explaining instead of questioning, you've done little to capture and maintain their attention, such as displaying information on the overhead projector.

3. Are teachers responsible for making sure that students pay attention in class, or should paying attention be the responsibility of students?

Both are responsible. Students should learn that paying attention is important, and they're responsible for doing so. In addition, teachers must teach in ways that capture students' attention, such as presenting information visually as well as verbally.

4. What would you do in this situation?

We would create some vignettes that illustrate nationalism, *display the vignettes on the overhead, and guide the students in a discussion of the information on the overheads. The following are two possibilities:*

The students at Matthew Gilbert School are very loyal to their school. "They don't talk the way we do," they comment when other schools are mentioned. They also say things like, "We go to the same church, and we like to hang out together on the weekends." "We're *Gilbertites*," they say. "We don't want to be anybody else, and we don't want anyone telling us what to do."

Students at nearby Eugene Butler School feel the same way about their school. "We don't want someone coming in here and changing our school," they say. "We understand each other when we talk. The others are different than we are. They play funny music, and they don't do the things we do after school or on the weekends." "We're *Butlerans* and we don't want to be anything else."

Classroom Windows: Questions and Feedback
Learning About Balance Beams in Fourth Grade

1. Was Jenny's instruction based primarily on behaviorism or on cognitive views of learning? Explain your reasoning.

Jenny's instruction was based primarily on cognitive views of learning. The lesson focused on thinking and understanding, not on observable responses to specific and isolated questions.

135

2. To what extent did Jenny display the personal characteristics of effective teachers, the strategies of effective teachers, and effective classroom management? Cite specific evidence from the lesson to support your conclusions.

Jenny displayed many of the personal characteristics and teaching strategies as well as the classroom management of effective teachers. Her behavior suggested that she believed all the students could learn and she expected them to do so. She developed her lesson with questioning rather than explaining, she represented her topic effectively (with her balances), and the students were orderly and participated in the lesson.

3. Which of the educational philosophies (described in Chapter 6) was most nearly reflected in Jenny's teaching? Explain why you think so.

Jenny's instruction most nearly reflected progressivism. The lesson was student-centered and focused on a practical, real-world problem.

4. We examined explicit and implicit curricula in Chapter 10. Describe both the explicit and implicit curriculum implied in Jenny's lesson. Cite specific evidence from the lesson to support your conclusions.

The explicit curriculum in Jenny's lesson focused on the principle for making a balance beam balance. She wanted the students to understand that the number of tiles times the distance on one side of the fulcrum was equal to the number of tiles times the distance on the other side of the fulcrum. The implicit curriculum implied in the lesson was that students should learn to cooperate and solve problems in school and that school is a place where students are actively involved in learning.

5. To what extent did Jenny display professionalism in the episode you saw? Explain your analysis.

Jenny displayed the characteristics of a professional. She demonstrated the knowledge of content, pedagogical content knowledge, general pedagogical knowledge, and knowledge of learners and learning characteristic of a professional, and she demonstrated a great deal of autonomy in planning and conducting her lesson.

Self-Assessment Questions
(Note: Students have access to these questions and their feedback on the text's Companion Website.)

1. The body of knowledge describing differences in the behavior of teachers of high-achieving students compared to that of teachers of lower-achieving students is best described as
    a.   classroom management research.
    b.   social cognitive research.
    c.   behaviorist research.
    d.   teacher effectiveness research.

2. Which of the following best describes personal teaching efficacy?
    a.   Teachers' beliefs about their abilities to positively affect student learning
    b.   The efficiency with which teachers establish classroom rules and routines
    c.   Teachers behaving in ways they would like to have students imitate
    d.   Teachers' willingness and ability to invest time and energy in the development of young people

3. Which of the following is best illustrated when teachers are willing to spend time with students?
    a.   Personal teaching efficacy
    b.   Caring
    c.   Modeling
    d.   Logical consequences

4. Behaving in ways that you would like students to imitate best describes which of the following?
    a.   Logical consequences
    b.   Caring
    c.   Personal teaching efficacy
    d.   Modeling

5. Research indicates that teachers treat some students better than others by calling on them more often, giving them more time to answer, and prompting them more when the students were originally unable to answer. Which of the following best describes why teachers treat the students better?
    a.   They care more about the better-treated students.
    b.   They are better models for the better-treated students.
    c.   They have higher expectations for the better-treated students.
    d.   They are more enthusiastic about working with the better treated students.

6. The consistency among teachers' goals, learning activities, practice they provide for students, and assessment best describes which of the following?
    a.   Instructional alignment
    b.   Cognitive descriptions of instruction
    c.   Personal teaching efficacy
    d.   Teacher effectiveness research

7. Which of the following best illustrates a teacher's demonstration of wait-time?
    a.   A teacher asks, "What is the first thing we should do in this problem? . . . Jennifer."
    b.   A teacher says, "Wait a minute and watch carefully how I solve this problem."
    c.   A teacher says, "Wait for me after school, and I will help you with the ones you asked about."
    d.   A teacher asks, "How many of you are waiting to get your quizzes back?"

8. "Changes in observable behavior occurring as a result of experience" best describes which of the following?
    a.   Learning as an application of teacher effectiveness research
    b.   Learning from a cognitive point of view
    c.   Learners constructing understanding that makes sense to them
    d.   Learning from a behaviorist point of view

9. Which of the following descriptions most accurately explains the statement "Learners are active."
    a.   It is a basic principle on which cognitive learning theory is based.
    b.   It is one of the findings of the teacher effectiveness research.
    c.   It is an important belief of teachers with high personal teaching efficacy.
    d.   It is a rationale for instructional alignment.

10. A teacher identifying a goal, presenting students with information, and guiding students to the goal is best described as
    a.   modeling.
    b.   cognitive learning.
    c.   teacher effectiveness learning.
    d.   discovery learning.

Self-Assessment Feedback

1.   d   Teacher effectiveness research is the body of knowledge describing differences in the behavior of teachers of high-achieving students compared to that of teachers of lower-achieving students.
2.   a   Personal teaching efficacy is teachers' beliefs about their abilities to positively affect student learning.
3.   b   Caring is best illustrated when teachers are willing to spend time with students.

4.   d   Behaving in ways that you would like students to imitate best describes modeling.

5.   c   Teachers treat some students better than others by calling on them more often, giving them more time to answer, and prompting them more when the students were originally unable to answer because they have higher expectations for the favored students.

6.   a   The consistency among teachers' goals, learning activities, practice they provide for students, and assessment best describes instructional alignment.

7.   a   Wait-time is illustrated when a teacher asks students a question, pauses briefly to give the students a chance to think about their answers, and then selects a student to respond.

8.   d   "Changes in observable behavior occurring as a result of experience," best describes the definition of learning from a behaviorist point of view.

9.   a.   The statement "Learners are active" best describes a basic principle on which cognitive learning theory is based.

10.   d   Discovery learning best describes a teacher identifying a goal, presenting students with information, and guiding students to the goal.

PRAXIS Practice: Questions and Feedback

1. Was Diane's instruction aligned? Explain why or why not.

Diane's instruction was aligned. Her objective was for the students to understand comparative and superlative adjectives and to be able to use them in writing. Her learning activity focused on understanding, and her seatwork gave them practice in writing using comparative and superlative adjectives. Her quiz required them to know both. Each part of her instruction–her objectives, her learning activity, the practice, and the assessment–was consistent with each of the other parts.

2. Was Diane's instruction teacher-centered, or was it learner-centered? Explain.

Diane's instruction was learner-centered. She used high-quality examples, she guided the lesson with her questioning, students were involved throughout, and student thinking was emphasized. These are each characteristics of learner-centered instruction.

3. Assess Diane's questioning. Support your assessment with information taken directly from the case study.

Diane's questioning was consistent with the characteristics of effective questioning discussed in the chapter. She asked a great many questions (frequency), and she demonstrated equitable distribution. For example, in one sequence she called on a different student by name each time–Mary, Sheila, Kevin, Nicholas, Todd, and Vicki. She gave the students time to think (wait-time), and she adjusted her level of questions to be consistent with her objectives. Evidence of prompting didn't exist in the case study because the students were able to answer each of her questions.

4. Did Diane base her instruction primarily on behaviorism or on cognitive views of learning? Explain.

Diane's instruction was based on cognitive views of learning. She used real-world examples that contained all the information students needed to reach her objectives. She focused on the students' thinking and understanding, as opposed to simply reinforcing them for providing correct verbal statements, and she developed the lesson in such a way that the students were active throughout.

Useful Web Site Addresses

Web Links for Chapter Terms

alternative assessment
http://www.ncrel.org/sdrs/areas/issues/methods/assment/as800.htm
http://www.ericfacility.net/databases/ERIC_Digests/ed395500.html
http://www.enc.org/topics/assessment/altern/

assessment
http://www.aurbach.com/alt_assess.html
http://www.aahe.org/assessment/principl.htm
http://www.ncahigherlearningcommission.org/resources/assessment/Lopez_Levels_2000.pdf
http://pblmm.k12.ca.us/PBLGuide/AssessPBL.html

behaviorism
http://plato.stanford.edu/entries/behaviorism/
http://www.biozentrum.uni-wuerzburg.de/genetics/behavior/learning/behaviorism.html

caring: http://www.caringteachers.com/

classroom management
http://education.indiana.edu/cas/tt/v1i2/what.html
http://eric-web.tc.columbia.edu/digests/dig74.html
http://www.ncrel.org/sdrs/areas/issues/envrnmnt/drugfree/sa2lk9.htm
http://www.shpm.com/articles/child_behavior/behavman4.html
http://www.honorlevel.com/techniques.html
http://www.extension.umn.edu/distribution/familydevelopment/components/6961_03.html
http://ss.uno.edu/ss/homepages/cmanage.html
http://7-12educators.miningco.com/msub49.htm

classroom organization: http://teacher.scholastic.com/professional/futureteachers/classroom_organization.htm

cooperative learning
http://www.ed.gov/pubs/OR/ConsumerGuides/cooplear.html
http://www.sheridanc.on.ca/coop_learn/cooplrn.htm
http://www.educationworld.com/a_curr/curr287a.shtml

discovery learning
http://www.nwlink.com/~donclark/hrd/history/discovery.html
http://www.duq.edu/~tomei/ed711psy/c_bruner.htm

instructional alignment: http://www.starcenter.org/products/articles/howalign.html

instruction: http://www.funderstanding.com/instruction.cfm

learner-centered instruction
http://www.nicic.org/Downloads/PDF/TrainingResources/018534/018534.pdf
http://www.oid.ucla.edu/Webcast/Sianme/SIANME_990312.html

learning (behaviorist) : http://psychclassics.yorku.ca/Skinner/Theories/

learning (cognitive) : http://necsi.org/events/cxedk16/cxedk16_2.html

learning theories: http://tip.psychology.org/theories.html

modeling
http://cty.jhu.edu/teaching/strategies/analysis/modelling.htm
http://www.oise.utoronto.ca/~doncrest/hunter%20lesson%20design.htm

goals: http://www.wrightslaw.com/advoc/articles/plan_iep_goals.html

performance assessment
http://www.ascd.org/cms/index.cfm?TheViewID=916
http://www.ericfacility.net/databases/ERIC_Digests/ed423312.html

personal teaching efficacy
http://chiron.valdosta.edu/whuitt/col/teacher/tcheff.html
http://www.positivepractices.com/Efficacy/EfficacyLinks.html

portfolios
http://electronicportfolios.org/portfolios/bookmarks.html
http://www.ericfacility.net/ericdigests/ed385608.html
http://www.aurbach.com/ttp2.html

procedures: http://para.unl.edu/para/Organization/lesson5.html

prompt
http://www.nwrel.org/msec/science_inq/strategies.html
http://www.creativity-portal.com/howto/writing/writing.prompts.html

questioning frequency
http://www.nwrel.org/scpd/sirs/3/cu5.html
http://www.exploratorium.edu/IFI/resources/workshops/artofquestioning.html

responsibility model of management: http://www.brains.org/classroom_management.htm

rules
http://www.education-world.com/a_lesson/lesson274.shtml
http://www.responsiveclassroom.org/newsletter/15_2NL_1.asp

teacher-centered instruction
http://www.nctq.org/bulletin/v2n16.html
http://www.secondaryenglish.com/approaches.html

thematic lessons
http://www.todaysteacher.com/ThematicTeaching.htm
http://www.ssd.org/Education/jae/articles/jae199457022805.pdf

transition signals: http://www.foothill.net/~moorek/transitions.html

wait-time
http://www.ericfacility.net/databases/ERIC_Digests/ed370885.html
http://www.atozteacherstuff.com/articles/wait-think-time.shtml

withitness
http://www.cals.ncsu.edu/agexed/leap/aee535/Management.ppt

Web Links for "Teaching in an Era of Reform: The Teacher-Centered versus Learner-Centered Issue"

Enticing Education Schools to Focus On Teacher-Centered Instruction: http://www.nctq.org/bulletin/v2n16.html

An Experiment Using Teacher-Centered Instruction versus Student-Centered Instruction as a Means of Teaching American Government to High School Seniors: http://www.secondaryenglish.com/approaches.html

Designing Learner-Centered Instruction
http://www.nicic.org/Downloads/PDF/TrainingResources/018534/018534.pdf

Engines of Inquiry: Teaching, Technology, and Learner-Centered Approaches to Culture and History
http://www.georgetown.edu/crossroads/guide/engines.html

Learner-Centered Classrooms, Problem-Based Learning, and the Construction of Understanding and Meaning by Students: http://www.ncrel.org/sdrs/areas/issues/content/cntareas/science/sc3learn.htm

Learner-Centered Instruction: Are Students Prepared for It?
http://www.oid.ucla.edu/Webcast/Sianme/SIANME_990312.html

Learner-Centered Psychological Principles: A Framework for School Redesign and Reform
http://www.apa.org/ed/lcp.html

Learner-Centered Syllabi Workshop: http://www.cte.iastate.edu/tips/syllabi.html

Teacher-Centered to Learner-Centered Educational Model: http://fie.engrng.pitt.edu/fie98/papers/yeary.pdf

Web Links for "Exploring Diversity: The Achievement Gap and Effective Teaching"

Achievement Gap Widening, Study Reports: http://www.edweek.org/ew/vol-16/14race.h16

Bridging the Great Divide: Broadening Perspectives on Closing the Achievement Gaps
http://www.ncrel.org/policy/pubs/html/bridging/

Can Teacher Education Close the Achievement Gap?
http://www.educationnews.org/aera_symposium_can_teacher_educa.htm

Closing the Achievement Gap: State Strategies That Work
http://www.nasbe.org/Research_Projects/Achievement_Gap.html

Closing the Achievement Gap: No Child Left Behind: http://www.nclb.gov/next/closing/

Critical Behaviors and Strategies for Teaching Culturally Diverse Students:
http://www.ericfacility.net/ericdigests/ed435147.html

Education Reforms and Students At-Risk: A Review of the Current State of the Art
http://www.ed.gov/pubs/EdReformStudies/EdReforms/

Improving Teacher Quality: http://www.subnet.nga.org/educlear/achievement/quality/quality_problem.html

Instructional Strategies for Migrant Students: http://www.ericfacility.net/databases/ERIC_Digests/ed388491.html

Investigating Achievement Gap Differences and Staff Commitment to Continuous Learning in High-Performing Schools: http://www.ael.org/page.htm?index=519&pd=1

Kids At-Risk: Can Educators Help?: http://www.education-world.com/a_issues/issues109.shtml

Reflections and Success Stories: http://www.ncela.gwu.edu/success/

Success for All: A Summary of Evaluations: http://www.ericfacility.net/databases/ERIC_Digests/ed425250.html

Tools for Schools: School Reform Models Supported by the National Institute on the Education of At-Risk Students http://www.ed.gov/pubs/ToolsforSchools/

Why Ability Grouping Widens the Achievement Gap: http://educationright.tripod.com/id23.htm

The Achievement Gap: http://www.edweek.org/sreports/gap.htm

Chapter 12
Technology in American Schools

Overview

The chapter begins with a brief history and overview of technology and teaching. Different ways that technology can influence learning are described and linked to different teaching functions. Technology's value as a teacher-support tool is also discussed. The chapter concludes with an examination of issues for the future and a look at how technology will change teaching.

Chapter Goals

This chapter examines

- Different descriptions of instructional technology
- Uses of instructional technology
- Teacher-support applications of technology
- Instructional issues in the use of technology
- Access issues in the use of technology

Chapter Outline

I. What is Technology?–Contrasting Views of Technology
II. Using Technology in the Classroom
    A. Using Technology to Support Instruction
    B. Using Technology to Deliver Instruction
        1. Drill and Practice
        2. Tutorials
    C. Using Technology to Teach Problem Solving and Higher-Level Thinking Skills
        1. Simulations
        2. Problem Solving
        3. Databases and Spreadsheets
    D. Word Processing: Using Technology to Teach Writing
    E. Exploring Diversity: Employing Technology to Support Learners with Disabilities
        1. Adaptations to Computer Input Devices
        2. Adaptations to Output Devices
    F. Using the Internet as an Instructional Tool
        1. The Internet as a Communication Tool–Advantages and Disadvantages of Internet Communications
        2. Using the Internet in Problem-Based Learning
        3. Distance Education Technologies
III. Teacher-Support Applications
    A. Preparing Instructional Materials
    B. Classroom Assessment
        1. Planning and Constructing Tests
        2. Administering Tests
        3. Scoring and Interpreting Tests
        4. Maintaining Student Records
    C. Communicating with Parents
IV. Instructional Issues in the Use of Educational Technology
    A. Instructional Goals for the Use of Technology

143

    B.   Quality of Available Software

    C.   Curricular Issues

        1.   Alignment Problems

        2.   Time Constraints

    D.   Plagiarism and Cheating

    E.   Teaching in an Era of Reform: The Censorship Issue–Teachers and Internet Filtering

V.   Access Issues in the Use of Technology

    A.   Cost of Technology– Federal Support

    B.   Equity Issues in Access to Technology

        1.   Ethnicity and Technology Access

        2.   Income and Technology Access

        3.   Gender Divides

    C.   Equity Issues: Proposed Solution

VI.   Decision Making: Defining Yourself as a Professional

Transparencies

T 12.1 (Figure 12.1) Classroom Applications of Technology

T 12.2 (Table 12.1) Integrating Technology into Different Content Areas

T 12.3 (Table 12.2) Assessment Functions Supported by Computers

T 12.4 (Table 12.3) Ethnicity and Technology Access

T 12.5 (Table 12.4) Household Income and Technology Access

Teaching Suggestions

I. What Is Technology?

The purpose of this section of the chapter is to introduce two differing views of technology in education.

- **Share with your students your own views of technology–why you use what you do and what obstacles exist to greater technology usage.**

- ***Increasing Understanding 12.1* asks how teachers' and students' roles change in hardware and process views of technology usage.**

- ***Discussion Question #1* asks which view of technology–hardware or process–is more prevalent in the schools and why.**

- ***Journal Starter #1* asks students to reflect on their own personal histories with computers.**

- ***Portfolio Activity #1* asks students to evaluate their own knowledge of and proficiency with technology.**

II. Using Technology in the Classroom

The purpose of this section of the chapter is to provide an overview of the different ways that technology can be used to support learning in the classroom.

- ***Transparency 12.1* "Classroom Applications of Technology" provides an overview of the content in this section.**

- *Going into Schools #3* asks students to inventory the various kinds of technology available in a local school.

- *Transparency 12.2* "Integrating Technology into Different Content Areas" provides an overview of different ways to integrate technology into instruction. Ask students in different content areas to discuss the application in their areas.

- Check with the media lab in your building to see what simulation and problem-solving software is available for students to experiment with individually. Or take the class to the media lab, and set up stations that students can rotate through.

- Point out that the same issue of technology as a stand-alone system versus being integrated into instruction is also occurring in teacher education. Presently most programs have stand-alone courses, but there is a concerted push to integrate technology into various courses in teacher ed programs.

- *Classroom Observation Guide #1* asks students to observe and compare computer usage in two classrooms.

- *Reflect on This* asks students to react to a dilemma in which a parent complains about the overuse of technology in problem solving at the expense of content in the text.

- *Transparency 12.3* "Assessment Functions Supported by Computers" summarizes the different assessment tasks that computers can assist with.

- Share with students the assessment tools available with this text. Point out that though similar assessment packages will be available to them, the quality of the items is often questionable.

- Have a special educator come in to talk about applications of assistive technology in students' areas.

- To provide a concrete frame of reference, ask students how current distance-education technologies have advantages over older correspondence courses.

- The *Classroom Windows* video for this chapter contains a clip of a second-grade teacher, Suzanne Brush, using technology to supplement her lesson on graphing. (This lesson was the introductory case in Chapter 10.)

III. Teacher-Support Applications

The purpose of this section of the chapter is to help students understand different ways that technology can assist teachers beyond direct instructional assistance.

- Share with your class ways that you use technology to support your instruction. Contrast this with 5 or 10 years ago. Be honest in describing technology's advantages and disadvantages.

- Point out all the technology support tools that come with this text. Which ones do you think are most valuable? Which are least valuable? Why?

- Bring into class one of the commercial test-preparation programs, and show students the different ways it can assist teachers.

IV. Instructional Issues in the Use of Educational Technology

The purpose of this section of the chapter is to introduce students to major controversies in technology usage they'll encounter as professionals.

- *Classroom Observation Guide #2* asks students to compare computer usage in labs versus classrooms from a teacher's perspective.

- *Going into Schools #3* asks students to interview a teacher about a district's Internet filtering policy.

- *Going into Schools #4* asks students to interview a teacher about the technology support that exists in his or her district.

- *Discussion Question #4* asks students whether Internet filtering should occur at the local or national level. Point out that recent federal legislation already requires schools to filter out pornography.

V. Access Issues in the Use of Technology

The purpose of this section of the chapter is to encourage students to think about access issues and how they will affect their teaching.

- *Transparency 12.4* "Ethnicity and Technology Access" provides a breakdown of technology use by different ethnic groups. Ask students to explain these differences.

- *Transparency 12.5* "Household Income and Technology Access" describes different technology-use patterns for different incomes.

- *Increasing Understanding 12.12* asks students to predict whether more computers in the future will be found in labs or classrooms. Use this as a discussion starter.

- *Portfolio Activity 12.2* asks students to analyze a text series they'll be using in terms of the technology support offered with it.

- *Journal Starter #2* asks students to assess their own familiarity with various types of technology.

Journal Starters

1. Encourage students to think about their own personal histories with technology: What is your earliest memory of technology being used in the classroom? What kinds of technologies were common in your elementary school? in your high school? When did you first encounter a computer? When did you first learn to word process? When did you first own a computer? How do you primarily use computers? What do the answers to these questions suggest about your readiness to use technology in your teaching?

2. Encourage students to assess their own competence in the area of technology: Do you presently own a computer? How do you use it? Are you connected to the Internet at home? How do you use the Internet? Have you ever used databases or spreadsheets? Have you ever taken a course online? Have you ever used a computer to create graphics? Have you ever used tutorial software? Have you ever used a computer simulation? In general, how tech savvy are you, and how will this influence your effectiveness as a teacher?

Increasing Understanding: Questions and Feedback

12.1
Compare the teacher's role when using technology with a hardware view versus a process view. How do the teacher's and student's roles change? How might you incorporate these two views in your own classroom? What benefits would you expect to gain from either approach?
12.1
In a hardware view of technology, the teacher uses technology to disseminate information; the students' role is to acquire information. In a process view of technology, the teacher integrates technology into instruction, using it as a tool to involve students. In this perspective students learn to use technology as a powerful tool to analyze and organize information.

12.2
Based on the definition of *hypermedia*, identify one important difference between multimedia, a collection of different media forms, and hypermedia.
12.2
Hypermedia is self-contained; multimedia integrates several media types.

12.3
Was the HyperStudio™ stack that Lisa developed to teach her students to make change aimed at rote memorization tasks or a higher level? Explain.
12.3
It was aimed at a higher level because students were learning how to do something, not just memorize information.

12.4
Recall Lisa's program to teach her students how to make change. How might she adapt her work to make it more realistic by reformatting it into a simulation?
12.4
Simulations attempt to imitate the real world. Lisa might design the simulation so students are making change in situations similar to the one in the store they'll be working in later.

12.5
Based on the information in this section, explain why word processing can result in more positive attitudes toward writing.
12.5
Word processing with a computer can make the process easier, which is motivating. It can also make the product better, which can also be motivating.

12.6
How can assistive technology be combined with computer-based instruction? with technology as a learning tool? with technology as a communication tool?
12.6
Computer-based instruction could be used to help students with exceptionalities learn basic knowledge and skills. Technology could also be used to help develop students' learning skills by showing students how it could be used to organize and analyze information. Technology could also be used to help these students learn to write and to communicate with other students on the Internet.

12.7
What is one advantage of a chat room over a bulletin board? One disadvantage?
12.7
The major advantage is that a chat room is synchronous, allowing students to interact with each other at the same time. This can also be a disadvantage because it requires students to be on the computer at the same time.

12.8

"Flaming," or the process of sending emotional and often derogatory e-mails, has become a communication problem. Using the information in this section, explain why flaming has become more common.

12.8

Because students can't see the people they are communicating with, they don't get immediate feedback about the effects of their message on others. Becoming sensitive to the effects of our actions on others is a developmental task that students learn over time.

12.9

What kind of school computer configuration is most compatible with the goal of computer literacy? Why isn't this configuration compatible with other ISTE goals?

12.9

Computer labs are most compatible with computer literacy. The other ISTE goals require computers to be in the classroom, integrated into instruction.

12.10

What can teachers do to ensure a match between software and either district curricula or tests?

12.10

The first step is to become familiar with district curricula and tests. The second is to become knowledgeable about the strengths and weaknesses of the software. Reading about the software helps but is no substitute for actually trying it out.

12.11

Is the problem of Internet access more serious at some K–12 levels than others? in some content areas than others? Why?

12.11

Internet access is important at all levels but might be most crucial at upper levels, where students are using it to research topics and communicate with peers elsewhere. In a similar way it might be most essential in areas like science, health, and social studies where students use it to do their own research on topics.

12.12

In the future would you predict that more school computers will be found in labs or in classrooms? Why? How does your answer relate to process and hardware views of technology?

12.12

In the future as more students come to school with basic computer skills, more emphasis will be placed on integrating computers into the curriculum, which will require their integration into the classroom.

12.13   The major trend that we see in Table 12.4 is increased access to computers, both at school and at home, as income increases. Predict whether the access disparities between high- and low-income households will increase or decrease in the future.

12.13

As technology becomes cheaper, it should also become more accessible, making these disparities smaller.

Reflect on This: Questions and Feedback

(These can also be found on the Companion Website: www.prenhall.com/kauchak .)

1. How would you respond to this parent's question?

You might try explaining that research suggests that students learn better when they are involved in cooperative problem solving. Or you might invite her to observe the class while your students are working. A third alternative is to show her students' work products and explain to her how working in groups and producing these products are also helping students learn content.

2. What strategies can teachers employ to inform parents of why and how the teachers are using technology?

One strategy is to attack this problem proactively by explaining the reasons behind teaching strategies at the beginning of the school year, either in a newsletter or during back-to-school night. Teachers also might do this via e-mail, sharing the assignments they give the children or their work products.

3. How will these strategies need to be adapted for different teaching settings, for example, urban versus rural or high-SES versus low-SES students?

Different teaching settings might require different communication strategies for two reasons. First, different settings might result in different rates of parents' exposure to and knowledge about technology. Teachers might have to adapt accordingly. Second, different settings might influence parents' ability to come to school, so teachers might have to use more proactive strategies like messages and newsletters to homes.

Classroom Windows: Questions and Feedback
Technology in Classrooms

1. Did Suzanne Brush's use of technology reflect more of a hardware or a process view? Explain.

Her use of technology reflected more a process view. Rather than using it to deliver information, she used it to extend learning, ensure transfer, and develop thinking skills.

2. How effective was Suzanne's use of technology as a problem-solving tool? What could she have done to make it more effective?

She used technology as a problem-solving tool in several ways. One problem presented students with a race and asked them to decide which student ran faster. A second problem-solving use was to decide which pizza was cheapest. In both instances her instruction could have been improved by actively talking about the process afterwards to help students reflect on what they did and why.

3. In what ways did Suzanne use technology as support tools to complement her students' learning? How effective were these uses, and what might she have done to increase their effectiveness?

Students graphed birthday data as well as the information about the most common ways that students traveled to schools. In both instances talking about the process afterwards would have helped students understand the logic of the process.

4. How could Suzanne use technology as an assessment tool? What advantages and disadvantages would there be over pencil-and-paper measures?

To assess their ability to organize data, Suzanne could present unorganized information and have students graph it on computers. She could also present information on graphs on computers and assess whether students could interpret the information. In both instances students could see how technology could be used to solve real-world problems.

Self-Assessment
(Note: Students have access to these questions and their feedback on the text's Companion Website.)

1. As opposed to a hardware view of technology, a process view
   a. emphasizes the teaching of academics through drill and practice.
   b. stresses connections between academic areas.

    c.   integrates technology into instruction.

    d.   attempts to remediate learner difficulties through technology.

2. A major difference between drill and practice and tutorials is that tutorials
    a.   provide practice with feedback.
    b.   are designed for stand-alone instruction.
    c.   are aimed at basic skills.
    d.   emphasize the active involvement of students.

3. Drill-and-practice software programs can be highly motivational and are most appropriate when the teacher's goal is to
    a.   develop higher-level thinking skills.
    b.   enhance fact and skill learning.
    c.   simulate real-life situations in the classroom.
    d.   provide practice in using technology.

4. The most effective types of problem-solving software
    a.   present a problem and provide opportunities for practice.
    b.   guide learners as they attempt to solve a problem.
    c.   provide continual feedback so learners don't make mistakes.
    d.   are open-ended so students get experience in problem finding.

5. Which of the following has **NOT** been proven true of the benefits of word processing technologies for teaching writing?
    a.   Students write more.
    b.   Students revise more thoroughly.
    c.   Students have more positive attitudes toward writing.
    d.   Students produce better products.

6. Databases are most often used to
    a.   edit information.
    b.   present problems.
    c.   organize data.
    d.   process information.

7. Mrs. Williams is a middle school social studies teacher who wants her students to understand how physical features and climate influence where people live and how they make a living. To do this, students visit an uninhabited island and have to decide where they would live and what they would do to live. Mrs. Williams is utilizing
    a.   drill-and-practice software.
    b.   tutorial software.
    c.   simulation software.
    d.   spreadsheet software.

8. Chatrooms differ from bulletin boards in that they allow
    a.   students to talk over longer distance.
    b.   students to discuss the same topic.
    c.   students to talk at the same time.
    d.   students to record messages before responding.

9. Which type of computer organization format is most expensive for a school?
    a.   Computers distributed in classrooms
    b.   Computer labs

c. Classroom clusters

d. Computers available for check-out by teachers

10. Which of the following has **NOT** been linked to computer access and use?

a. Gender

b. Income

c. Ethnicity

d. Location (e.g., urban versus rural)

Self-Assessment Feedback

1. c A process view of technology attempts to integrate technology into the total instructional process.

2. b Tutorials differ from drill and practice in that they are designed to be stand-alone, both presenting new information and providing practice with feedback.

3. b Drill-and-practice programs are most valuable for teaching facts and enhancing skill learning.

4. d The most effective problem-solving technologies are purposefully left open-ended to provide students with practice in problem finding.

5. d The research here is mixed; it hasn't been conclusively proven that the products are better.

6. c Databases are most often used to organize data for subsequent analysis.

7. c Simulations allow students to experience real-world situations vicariously.

8. c Chatrooms are synchronous, allowing students to talk to each other at the same time.

9. a Computers in classrooms are most expensive because enough computers must be provided for students in each classroom to use.

10. d Location has not been clearly linked to computer access and use.

PRAXIS Practice: Questions and Feedback

1. Did Maria's lesson plan reflect a hardware or a process view of technology use? Explain.

Maria's lesson plan reflected a process view of technology because her use of technology was integrated into the lesson.

2. Did Maria's lesson focus more on problem solving or problem-based learning? Explain.

Maria's lesson focused more on problem-based learning because her goals were more divergent and open-ended. Had her lesson focused on the computation of total calories expended, for example, it would have been more oriented to problem solving.

3. Which of the following instructional issues did Maria wrestle with as she planned her lesson: instructional goals, quality of software, curricular match with instructional goals, curricular press, preparation-time constraints, plagiarism and cheating, and Internet access?

Maria wrestled with virtually all of these issues. She considered learning goals first, then thought of how technology could further those goals, and also checked to see if her goals matched the district's curricular goals. She also was concerned about the quality of available software and whether it could be used to produce spreadsheets. She also considered time, both from a personal perspective and from the amount of time the lesson would take students. She wasn't concerned with plagiarism or Internet access.

4. How did Maria address equity issues in her planning?

Maria addressed equity issues in several ways. First, she reminded herself to assign equal numbers of girls and

151

students of different abilities to each group. She also assigned rotating roles in each group to ensure that all students had opportunities to participate. Finally she made sure that students could complete their assignments at school because she knew that many of them did not have computers at home.

Useful Web Site Addresses

Web Links for Chapter Terms

assistive technology
http://www2.childrenssoftware.com.
http://www2.edc.org/NCIP/default.htm
http://www.nichcy.org/pubs/newsdig/nd13txt.htm
http://sac.uky.edu/~jszaba0/QIAT.html
http://www.resna.org/taproject/at/statecontacts.html
http://atto.buffalo.edu/
http://www.pluk.org/AT1.html

bulletin boards
http://www.ldonline.org/bulletin_boards/bb2.html
http://fedbbs.access.gpo.gov/
http://peacecorpsonline.org/messages/messages/2629/1010639.html
http://www.teachernet.com/bulletinboard/index.tmpl?command=showpage&bbn=Early%20Childhood
http://www.teachernet.com/bulletinboard/index.tmpl?command=showpage&bbn=Gifted
http://www.aera.net/anews/resource/wr00-002.htm

chatrooms
http://paws.wcu.edu/westling/discussion_groups/chatrooms.htm
http://www.siec.k12.in.us/~west/edu/chat.htm
http://www.teachers.net/
http://www.media-awareness.ca/english/teachers/wa_teachers/safe_passage_teachers/chatrooms_safety_t.cfm

computer literacy
http://www.futurekidsfla.com/sfla/more_info/media/97.03-Principal.html
http://www.iste.org

databases
http://www.indiana.edu/~ensiweb/lessons/p.tut.db.html
http://www.gcflearnfree.org/gcf_classes/access/index.asp

distance education
http://www.uwex.edu/disted/definition.html
http://www.uidaho.edu/eo/distglan.html

electronic mail (e-mail)
http://www.cs.queensu.ca/FAQs/email/etiquette.html
http://www.rand.org/publications/MR/R3283/
http://www.webfoot.com/advice/email.top.html
http://safety.ngfl.gov.uk/schools/pdf/d34.pdf
http://www.epals.com/

hypermedia
http://www.webpages.uidaho.edu/~mbolin/kapoun.html

http://www.readingonline.org/electronic/JAAL/3-01_Column/
http://ole.tp.edu.sg/courseware/teaching_guide/resources/article/Grace/icce98a.pdf
http://www.sci.sdsu.edu/multimedia/workshops/netppt/

icons
http://www.iconbazaar.com/
http://www.kidsdomain.com/icon/

Internet
http://www.fbi.gov/publications/pguide/pguidee.htm
http://k12science.ati.stevens-tech.edu/internetsafety.html
http://www.ala.org/ala/washoff/WOissues/civilliberties/washcipa/cipa.htm

problem-based learning
http://www2.imsa.edu/programs/pbl/problem.html
http://www.samford.edu/pbl/

simulations
http://www.samford.edu/pbl/
http://www.cet.edu/research/papers/cogreason/AERA01SMElYunque.pdf
http://www.economics.ltsn.ac.uk/events/games.htm

software
http://teacher.scholastic.com/activities/classroomscare/
http://edservices.aea7.k12.ia.us/edtech/classroom/workshops/software/

spreadsheets
http://www.microsoft.com/education/?ID=Excel2002Tutorial
http://www.sabine.k12.la.us/class/excel_resources.htm

technology
http://www.kidsolr.com/index.html
http://www.techedlab.com/define.html
http://nces.ed.gov/pubs2003/tech_schools/

Web Links for "Teaching in an Era of Reform: The Censorship Issue"

ALA on CIPA: http://www.ala.org/ala/washoff/WOissues/civilliberties/washcipa/cipa.htm

ACLU on Censorship: http://archive.aclu.org/issues/cyber/hmcl.html

Center for Democracy and Technology: http://www.cdt.org/

Information on Internet Censorship: http://www.isoc.org/internet/issues/censorship/

Internet Censorship: http://www.epic.org/free_speech/censorship/

Internet Censorship Around the World: http://www.efa.org.au/Issues/Censor/cens3.html

Libraries and the Internet Toolkit: http://www.ala.org/ala/oif/iftoolkits/litoolkit/librariesinternet.htm

Plain Facts About Internet Filtering Software: http://www.ala.org/ala/pla/plapubs/technotes/internetfiltering.htm

Resolution on Using Internet Filters in Libraries
http://www.ala.org/Template.cfm?Section=IF_Resolutions&Template=/ContentManagement/ContentDisplay.cfm&ContentID=13076

UCLA Online Institute for Cyberspace Law and Policy: http://www.gseis.ucla.edu/iclp/hp.html

Web Links for "Exploring Diversity: Employing Technology to Support Learners with Disabilities"

Assistive Technology, Inc.: http://www.assistivetech.com

Children and Adults with Attention Deficit Disorders (C.H.A.D.D.): http://chadd.org/

Disability-Related Resources on the Web: http://www.thearc.org/misc/dislnkin.html

Learning Disabilities Association: http://www.ldanatl.org/

National Association for Attention Deficit Disorder: http://www.add.org/

Profiles of Children with Disabilities: http://nces.ed.gov/pubs97/97254.html

Technical Assistance Documents from the Office of Special Education
http://www.state.sd.us/state/executive/deca/special/taguide.htm

Additional Chapter Web Links

Digital Divide

Americans in the Information Age: http://www.ntia.doc.gov/ntiahome/digitaldivide/
Bridging the Digital Divide
http://news.bbc.co.uk/1/hi/special_report/1999/10/99/information_rich_information_poor/466651.stm
Digital Disconnect: http://www.pewinternet.org/reports/toc.asp?Report=67
Digital Divide?: http://ksghome.harvard.edu/~.pnorris.shorenstein.ksg/book1.htm
Digital Divide and Digital Equity: http://www.edu-cyberpg.com/Teachers/digitaldivide.html
Digital Divide Data: http://www.digitaldividedata.com/index.asp
Digital Divide: Gender: http://www.pbs.org/digitaldivide/gender-main.html
Digital Divide Network: http://www.digitaldividenetwork.org/content/sections/index.cfm
Digital Divide's New Frontier: http://www.childrenspartnership.org/pub/low_income/
Europe and US on Different Sides in the Gender Divide: http://news.earthweb.com/stats/article.php/3095681
Gender and the Digital Divide: http://www.worldbank.org/gender/digitaldivide/
Global Digital Divide Initiative
http://www.weforum.org/site/homepublic.nsf/Content/Global+Digital+Divide+Initiative
Internet Gender Divide Grows Rapidly in Asian Countries: http://adtimes.nstp.com.my/jobstory/oct30f.htm
PBS Digital Divide: http://www.pbs.org/digitaldivide/
Resolution of the Gender Divide
http://www-cse.stanford.edu/class/cs201/projects-99-00/digital-divide-gender/solutions.html

Copyright and Plagiarism

Checklist for Compliance with the TEACH Act: http://www.copyright.iupui.edu/teachlist.htm

Cut and Paste Plagiarism: http://alexia.lis.uiuc.edu/~janicke/plagiary.htm
Detecting Online Plagiarism: http://oasis.unc.edu/documentation/plag.html
Distance Education and the TEACH Act
http://www.ala.org/Template.cfm?Section=Distance_Education_and_the_TEACH_Act&Template=/ContentManage
ment/ContentDisplay.cfm&ContentID=25939
Online Plagiarism: http://www.techtv.com/cybercrime/digitaldisputes/story/0,23008,3000901,00.html
Online Plagiarism: How to Prevent It, How to Detect It: http://www.citadel.edu/library/plagiarism.htm
PL 107-273: http://www.copyright.gov/legislation/pl107-273.html
TEACH ACT Toolkit: http://www.lib.ncsu.edu/scc/legislative/teachkit/
TEACH Resources: http://www.arl.org/info/frn/copy/TEACH.html

Technology in Schools

International Society for Technology in Education: http://www.iste.org
ISTE National Educational Technology Standards for Students: http://cnets.iste.org/students/s_stands.html
ISTE National Educational Technology Standards for Teachers: http://cnets.iste.org/teachers/t_stands.html
National Educational Technology Standards for Administrators: http://cnets.iste.org/administrators/a_stands.html
Technology Integration: http://www.education-world.com/a_tech/
NetLearn: Internet Learning Resources: http://www.rgu.ac.uk/~sim/research/netlearn/callist.htm
Reinventing Schools: The Technology is Now!: http://www.nap.edu/readingroom/books/techgap/index.html
Edutech's Online Resource for Education and Technologies: http://tecfa.unige.ch/info-edu-comp.html
National Center for Technology Planning: http://www.nctp.com/

Lesson Plan Sites for Teachers

Apple Learning Interchange: http://www.ali.apple.com/ali/
Educator's Reference Desk: http://www.eduref.org/
Teachers First: http://www.teachersfirst.com/matrix.htm
PBS TeacherSource: http://www.pbs.org/teachersource/
Eisenhower National Clearinghouse: http://www.enc.org/
NASA Education Program: http://education.nasa.gov/
Awesome Library K–12 Education Directory: http://www.neat-schoolhouse.org/awesome.html
Blue Web'n: http://www.kn.pacbell.com/wired/bluewebn/
Federal Resources for Educational Excellence: http://www.ed.gov/free/
WWW4Teachers: http://www.4teachers.org/
Discovery School: http://school.discovery.com/
The Library in the Sky: http://www.nwrel.org/sky/
SEIR*TEC List of Lesson Plans: http://www.seirtec.org/k12/lessons.html

Chapter 13
Developing as a Professional

Overview

This chapter examines lifelong teacher development from multiple perspectives. The chapter begins with a look at beginning teachers. Learning to teach is described from both a process (e.g., observing, interviewing, journal writing) and a content perspective. Becoming an expert teacher is described in terms of a professional continuum that requires different kinds of knowledge.

This last chapter of the book helps the prospective teacher understand how to become licensed and investigate, apply for, and obtain a teaching position. Different licensure routes are described in the text , and the advantages and disadvantages of these programs are examined. The chapter concludes with a section on surviving the first year of teaching.

Chapter Goals

This chapter examines

- Beginning teachers and what happens to them
- Beginning teachers' beliefs and how these beliefs influence their behavior
- The kinds of knowledge teachers possess and how this knowledge influences their thinking
- How teachers are licensed and efforts being made to increase teacher professionalism
- What preservice teachers can do to make themselves marketable and how they can secure their first job
- How preservice teachers can prepare for their first year of teaching.

Chapter Outline

I.   Characteristics of Beginning Teachers
    A.   The Beginning Teacher Population
    B.   What Happens to New Teachers?
    C.   Beliefs of Beginning Teachers
II. Knowledge and Learning to Teach
    A.   The Development of Expertise
    B.   Domain-Specific Knowledge in Teaching
        1.   Knowledge of Content
        2.   Pedagogical Content Knowledge
        3.   General Pedagogical Knowledge
            a.   Instructional Strategies
            b.   Classroom Management
        4.   Knowledge of Learners and Learning
    C.   Knowledge and Decision Making
III. Into the Real World
    A.   Traditional Licensure
    B.   Finding a Job
        1.   Becoming Marketable
        2.   Developing a Professional Reputation
        3.   Where Jobs Are
        4.   Building a Portfolio and Résumé
            a.   Preparing a Résumé
            b.   Creating a Credentials File

Transparencies

T 13.1 (Table 13.1) Making Yourself Marketable

T 13.2 (Table 13.2) Projected Changes in Public School Enrollment by Geographic Area and Level, 1998–2008

T 13.3 (Figure 13.2) Sample Résumé

T 13.4 (Table 13.3) Guidelines for Interviewing Effectively

T 13.5 (Table 13.4) Propositions of the National Board for Professional Teaching Standards

Teaching Suggestions

I. Characteristics of Beginning Teachers

The purpose of this section of the chapter is to help students understand beginning teachers and the challenges facing them.

- **Robert Bullough wrote two groundbreaking books about the life of a beginning teacher. The first, *First-Year Teacher: A Case Study*, is a very readable account of the trials and tribulations of a first-year teacher. The second (Bullough & Baughman, 1997) revisits that same teacher 8 years later.**

- **This section contains a questionnaire about beginning teachers' beliefs. You might want to duplicate this and administer it to students before they read the chapter. Then either collect and compute a class average, or allow students to discuss their responses individually.**

II. Knowledge and Learning to Teach

The purpose of this section of the chapter is to help students understand the different kinds of knowledge needed to become an expert teacher.

- **Point out that these different forms of knowledge were introduced in Chapter 1, when the question of a knowledge base for the teaching profession was raised.**

- **This chapter's *Classroom Windows* shows teachers at different grade levels demonstrating the different kinds of professional knowledge.**

- To start a discussion on the different forms of knowledge, ask students to rank order them in terms of their importance, and then share this ordering with the class. Ask if the order changes with grade level. Does it change with content area?

- The Berliner (1994) chapter contains an excellent overview of the expert-novice teacher literature. He used videos in much of his work to investigate expert-novice differences. Use one of the *Classroom Windows* videos to demonstrate this methodology to your students.

III. Into the Real World

The purpose of this section of the chapter is to help students understand the steps necessary to make a successful transition from student to beginning teacher.

- Find out what the licensure requirements are for your state, and share these with students. Ask students who are planning to teach in another state to do the same.

- *Increasing Understanding 13.9* asks students to analyze the National Board standards in terms of the different dimensions of professional knowledge described in this chapter.

- *Transparency 13.1* "Making Yourself Marketable" contains concrete suggestions on how to fill the résumé in *Transparency 13.4* with worthwhile information.

- *Transparency 13.2* "Projected Changes in Public Enrollment by Geographic Area and School Level, 1998–2008" contains basic demographic information on jobs nationwide. Contact your school's placement office for specific geographic information in your state or region, as well as information on specific areas like special education and ELL.

- *Transparency 13.3* "Sample Résumé" can be used in several ways. One is to use it to help students plan ahead so they can fill their résumés with valuable and worthwhile information. The second is to use it to analyze several résumés that you've obtained from graduating seniors.

- *Transparency 13.4* "Guidelines for Interviewing Effectively" can be used to frame mock interviews. Ask for volunteers, and ask them the same questions that are in the text (as well as others that you add). Have the class critique each interview.

- *Reflect on This* asks students to respond to a mock interview situation. Use this as an opportunity to discuss the characteristics of a good school described in this section.

- *Journal Starter #2* asks students to evaluate themselves in terms of personal assets that will increase their marketability.

IV. Succeeding in Your First Year of Teaching

The purpose of this section of the chapter is to encourage students to begin preparing now for their first year of teaching.

- Revisit the statistics at the beginning of the chapter on new-teacher attrition rates. Emphasize that the time to start preparing for their first year is NOW.

- There are a number of good books on classroom management (several are listed in this chapter). Locate some management dilemmas or cases to provide a concrete frame of reference for the topic of management.

- Invite a first-year teacher in to describe his or her first year on the job. Ask what he or she would have done differently during the teacher preparation program.

- *Journal Starter #1* asks students to evaluate themselves in terms of personal characteristics and experiences that will contribute to their effectiveness as a teacher.

V. Career-Long Professional Development

The purpose of this section of the chapter is to encourage students to begin thinking about professional development throughout their teaching careers.

- Brainstorm some possible topics as foci for action research. If available, bring in some action research projects that other students have done.

- *Transparency 13.5* "Propositions of the National Board for Professional Teaching Standards" contains five propositions or principles, along with their corresponding descriptions. Share these with students, and have them compare them to INTASC standards.

Journal Starters

1. Encourage students to think about the strengths and potential weaknesses they bring to the teaching profession: What personality traits will be assets to you as a beginning teacher? What traits will be liabilities? Will your age be an asset or a liability? How will your gender influence your effectiveness as a new teacher? What kinds of past experiences will contribute to your effectiveness? What kinds of things can you do in the next few years to increase your effectiveness?

2. Encourage students to think about personal factors that can help increase their marketability: What personal characteristics (e.g., age, experience) will make you more marketable? Which will make you less marketable? Is the teaching position you'll be seeking one for which there is a high demand? What kinds of things can you do in the next few years to make yourself more marketable?

Increasing Understanding: Questions and Feedback

13.1
Of the factors listed here, which can teachers best control? What might they do to improve the situation with respect to the other factors?
13.1
Teachers can best control students' behaviors. While some students are disruptive, a well-organized, effective teacher is usually able to create an orderly learning environment.

13.2
What concept is being illustrated by teachers believing they are capable of helping all students to learn and achieve? What do teachers who take responsibility for the success or failure of their instruction do differently from teachers who blame failure on students' lack of intelligence or home environments?
13.2
Personal teaching efficacy is the concept being illustrated by this belief. Teachers high in personal efficacy work harder, interact more effectively with students, and are more likely to hold students accountable for their understanding than are teachers who blame failure on lack of intelligence or home environments.

13.3

Offer two reasons why students who go through traditional teacher preparation programs are more successful and more satisfied in their work than those who experience less-formal preservice education.

13.3

Students in traditional programs have much more experience in acquiring the pedagogical content knowledge, general pedagogical knowledge, and knowledge of learners and learning that teachers need to be successful. Alternative programs select people who have knowledge of content, but they provide limited experiences in the other forms of knowledge that are required to be successful. Satisfaction is an outcome of success. People who are successful are more likely to be satisfied with their work than people who are not successful.

13.4

Describe the pedagogical content knowledge that Sheila demonstrated in her lesson on longitude and latitude. Be specific in your response.

13.4

Evidence of Sheila's pedagogical content knowledge was indicated by the fact that she represented the topic with a lined styrofoam ball combined with a globe. This made the topic understandable for the students.

13.5

Explain why questioning is such an essential teaching skill. Explain specifically how questioning and knowledge of learners and learning are related.

13.5

Questioning is an essential teaching skill–because all teachers regardless of content area, topic, or grade level must be skilled with questioning to be effective. Questioning and knowledge of learners and learning are related because the kinds of questions teachers ask depend on the background knowledge and level of development of the students.

13.6

Explain these job patterns. Why, for example, are more jobs available in the inner city than in the suburbs? Why are more jobs available in math than in English?

13.6

The job patterns relate to supply and demand, or the number of people choosing to work in these areas. For instance, more people prefer to teach in suburban schools than in inner-city schools. As a result more jobs are available in the inner city. Similarly, more people choose English as a major than choose math, so more jobs are available in math.

13.7

Explain how a portfolio and a résumé are different. Be specific in your explanation. What is the purpose of each?

13.7

A portfolio is a collection of work that is used to verify a teacher's knowledge and skills, whereas a résumé is a written document that provides an overview of background and experience. A résumé will be included in a portfolio, for example, but the portfolio will include other items, such as videotapes of the teacher's actual teaching episodes to document skills.

13.8

What will determine how able you are to provide a clear and concrete response to an interviewer's question? (Hint: Think back to the second major topic of the chapter.)

13.8

Your background knowledge will determine how able you are to provide a clear and concrete response to an interviewer's question. The more knowledge of content, pedagogical content knowledge, knowledge of learners and learning, and general pedagogical knowledge you have, the clearer and more concrete your response to the interviewer's question will be.

13.9

Identify an example of pedagogical content knowledge, general pedagogical knowledge, and knowledge of learners and learning in the descriptions of the propositions. Take information directly from the descriptions for your response.

13.9

Part of the description of Proposition 2 says, "Accomplished teachers know to make subject matter understandable to students, and they are able to modify their instruction when difficulties arise." The ability to make subject matter understandable reflects pedagogical content knowledge. Part of Proposition 3 says, "Accomplished teachers are able to use a variety of effective instructional techniques, and they use the techniques appropriately," which reflects general pedagogical knowledge. Part of the description of Proposition 1 says, "Accomplished teachers understand how students develop, and they use accepted learning theory as the basis for their teaching." This description focuses on knowledge of learners and learning.

13.10
Identify at least three similarities between the INTASC principles and the descriptions of the NBPTS propositions. Take information directly from each in identifying the similarities.

13.10

Both emphasize that teachers are knowledgeable about their subjects and how to teach them. For instance, a description of INTASC Principle 1 says, "The teacher . . . can create learning experiences that make these aspects of subject matter meaningful for students," and NBPTS Proposition 2 says, "Accomplished teachers know how to make subject matter understandable to students ."

Both emphasize that teachers understand the way students learn and develop. For instance, a description of INTASC Principle 2 says, "The teacher understands how students learn and develop and can provide learning opportunities that support their intellectual, social and personal development," and NBPTS Proposition 1 says, "Accomplished teachers understand how students develop, and they use accepted learning theory as the basis for their teaching."

Both emphasize that teachers are skilled in a variety of instructional strategies. For instance, a description of INTASC Principle 4 says, "The teacher understands and uses a variety of instructional strategies," and NBPTS Proposition 3 says, "Accomplished teachers are able to use a variety of effective instructional techniques."

Reflect on This: Questions and Feedback
(These can also be found on the Companion Website: www.prenhall.com/kauchak .)

Interviewing for a Position

1. Based on your total experience–the interview with the administrators and the tour–what is your impression of the school?

With the exception of the principal's behavior, the school looks good. The assistant principal's questions were probing and professional, and his willingness to spend time with you indicates a caring and personalized orientation toward teachers. Also, a clean physical plant and polite students are indicators of a positive school climate.

2. What might explain the principal's behavior? Offer at least two different possibilities.

Principals are very busy people, and one possibility is that he might have had pressing school-related commitments. A second possibility is that interviewing a teacher might not have been a high priority for him. Regardless of the reason, the principal's behavior is a worrisome indicator about the school.

3. Suppose you had another interview for a job in a second inner-city school, and the principal's behavior was warm and inviting in the interview, but the students appeared to be less well behaved in the hallways. Which job would you take if you were offered both? Provide a basis for your decision. (Assume that other factors, such as the distance from your home, are similar.)

This decision, as with many decisions in teaching, is difficult. The behavior of students is important; they are the people with whom you'll spend most of your time. And the principal of the first school may have a leadership style that involves delegating a considerable amount of leadership to other members of the leadership team. On the other hand, the principal sets the tone for the school, so the behavior of the principal is important.

4. What might you do to help with your decision about which job to take?

We would try and talk to teachers in both schools. If a pattern exists in their comments, you have some valuable information about the working environments of the two schools.

Classroom Windows: Questions and Feedback

Demonstrating Knowledge in Classrooms

1. Which of the four types of professional knowledge–knowledge of content, pedagogical content knowledge, general pedagogical knowledge, or knowledge of learners and learning–were best illustrated in the segment with Jenny Newhall? Explain.

Every expert teacher demonstrates aspects of each of the four types of professional knowledge in his or her instruction. For example, Jenny knew that her students needed a warm emotional environment in order to learn most effectively, which demonstrates knowledge of learners and learning. However, she most displayed an ability to organize her classroom and actively involve her students with questioning. These are the components of general pedagogical knowledge, which involves an understanding of instruction and management that transcends specific topics.

2. Explain how Richard Nelms demonstrated knowledge of learners and learning in the segment dealing with the concept of symmetry.

Knowledge of learners and learning demonstrates an understanding of principles of learning and development. Richard understood that students need concrete examples in order to understand abstract concepts, and personalized examples are more effective than those more distant. Because of this understanding he used one of his students to demonstrate the concept of bilateral symmetry. He also understood that students learn most effectively when they're actively involved in the lesson, so he developed the lesson with questioning to promote their involvement.

3. Explain how pedagogical content knowledge was illustrated in Didi Johnson's lesson on Charles's law?

Pedagogical content knowledge involves the ability to represent abstract ideas in ways that are understandable to students. Didi best demonstrated this type of knowledge with her demonstration that provided a concrete example of Charles's law. The students could see that the heated balloon had the greatest volume and the balloon in the ice had the least volume. This provided a visual example of the law to which solutions to problems could be linked.

4. Assess DeVonne Lampkin's lesson on arthropods with respect to general pedagogical knowledge, knowledge of learners and learning, and pedagogical content knowledge.

DeVonne actually demonstrated all four types of knowledge in her lesson. Her knowledge of content allowed her to conceptualize the lesson and select appropriate examples. She demonstrated knowledge of learners and learning by designing the lesson to actively involve each student. Her understanding of pedagogical content knowledge was evidenced in her use of interesting and engaging examples. Her classroom was orderly and well managed despite the use of a hands-on activity, which can demand careful management, and the ability to create an orderly learning environment is one characteristic of general pedagogical knowledge. In addition, she used extensive questioning, which is another aspect of general pedagogical knowledge.

162

Video Discussions: Questions and Feedback

1. Dr. Urie Triesman is a professor of mathematics at the University of Texas at Austin and Director of the Charles A. Dana Center for Math and Science Education. He believes teacher professional development is central to school reform. From Dr. Triesman's perspective how can professional organizations and colleagues complement each other in fostering teacher professional development? What implications does this have for beginning teachers?

Teachers need to be active and involved in professional organizations and must also use this knowledge to improve teaching and learning in their schools. This suggests that beginning teachers should join professional organizations and not be hesitant about serving on school curriculum committees.

2. Dr John Goodlad is professor emeritus and codirector of the Center for Renewal at the University of Washington and president of the Independent Institute for Educational Inquiry. He views technology as a potentially liberating force for teachers. In what ways does Dr. Goodlad believe that technology might free up teachers to engage in alternate instructional strategies? Do these alternate instructional activities reflect a hardware or a process view of technology? Explain.

Dr. Goodlad recommends using technology as a substitute for the teacher as information disseminator. With technology acting in this role, the teacher can then work one on one with students to tutor them and help with individual problems. Interestingly, this suggestion reflects a hardware view of technology since it acts as a standalone substitute for the teacher and is not integrated tightly into other instruction.

Self-Assessment Questions
(Note: Students have access to these questions and their feedback on the text's Companion Website.)

1. Of the following the best description of beginning teachers' confidence is
   a. they aren't initially confident about their competence, but their confidence quickly increases.
   b. they are initially very confident about their teaching ability, but their confidence decreases as they gain experience.
   c. they aren't initially confident about their teaching ability, and their uncertainty remains until about their third year of experience.
   d. they are confident about their teaching ability when they begin, and their confidence remains high at the end of their first year.

2. From which of the following sources do beginning teachers believe they will learn most of what they need to know to be effective teachers?
   a. Their university classes
   b. Their university classes combined with pre-internships
   c. Classroom experience
   d. Their university classes combined with internships

3. Which of the following statements best describes the importance of knowledge of content (such as knowledge of history) in being an effective teacher?
   a. Knowledge of content is a necessary and sufficient condition for becoming an effective teacher.
   b. Knowledge of content is a necessary but not sufficient condition for becoming an effective teacher.
   c. Knowledge of content is valuable but not essential for being an effective teacher.
   d. Knowledge of content isn't necessary for becoming an effective teacher.

4. Which of the following best describes pedagogical content knowledge?

a. Understanding of ways of representing content so that it's comprehensible to others
b. Understanding relationships between topics (such as understanding how the French and Indian War relates to the American Revolutionary War)
c. Understanding how to create and maintain orderly and efficient classrooms for learning
d. Understanding how young people learn, grow, and develop

5. Which of the following best represents general pedagogical knowledge?
   a. Knowledge of specific topics (such as understanding how to solve algebra equations in math)
   b. Knowing that most students, including older ones, think concretely instead of abstractly
   c. Knowing how to create examples that make topics meaningful to learners
   d. Teacher questioning

6. Which of the following is best described as "the process by which a state evaluates the credentials of prospective teachers to ensure that they meet the state's professional standards"?
   a. Tenure
   b. Licensure
   c. Efficacy
   d. Certification

7. Which of the following best describes the attrition rate of people who go through alternative licensure programs compared to those who go through traditional licensure programs?
   a. About the same
   b. Slightly lower (about 5% lower)
   c. Slightly higher (about 10% higher)
   d. Nearly three times higher

8. Which of the following is best described as "special recognition by a professional organization indicating that an individual has met certain requirements specified by the organization"?
   a. Licensure
   b. Certification
   c. Tenure
   d. Efficacy

9. Which of the following best describes a professional teaching portfolio?
   a. A collection of work products (such as written papers and videotapes of teaching) from the course of a teacher-preparation program
   b. Experiences that extend beyond taking paper-and-pencil tests
   c. An assessment of a prospective teacher's knowledge and skills
   d. A description of a prospective teacher's professional goals and philosophy of education

10. Which of the following most accurately describes the importance of a teacher candidate using standard English and grammar during a job interview?
    a. Not important
    b. Desirable but not essential
    c. Desirable for cultural minorities but essential for nonminorities
    d. Essential for all candidates

Self-Assessment Feedback

1. b Research indicates that beginning teachers are initially very confident, but their confidence decreases as they gain experience.
2. c Beginning teachers believe they will learn most of what they need to know to be successful teachers in classrooms.
3. b Knowledge of content is essential, but, alone, it isn't sufficient to become an effective teacher.
4. a The ability to represent topics in ways that are understandable to others is the definition of pedagogical content knowledge.
5. d General pedagogical knowledge is knowledge that applies to all teaching situations, such as the ability to establish and maintain orderly classrooms and highly developed questioning skills.
6. b Licensure is he process by which a state evaluates the credentials of prospective teachers to ensure that they meet the state's professional standards.
7. d The attrition rate of people who go through alternative licensure programs is much higher than the attrition rate for first-year teachers in general.
8. b "Special recognition by a professional organization indicating that an individual has met certain requirements specified by the organization" best describes certification.
9. a A professional portfolio is a collection of work products (such as written papers and videotapes of teaching) from the course of a teacher-preparation program. (Portfolios are assessed during the job-application process.)
10. d The language and grammar that job applicants use create an immediate impression in the interviewer, and using inaccurate or inappropriate language and grammar creates a negative impression.

PRAXIS Practice: Questions and Feedback

Remind students that ratings of this sort are not exact. However, the ratings will give a general picture of the assessment. If their ratings are similar to these, they are demonstrating a good understanding of the information studied.

The following are the ratings for Judith Thompson on each of the forms of knowledge:

Knowledge of Content:
Judith demonstrated adequate knowledge of the Civil War content based on the kinds of questions she asked and the range of topics she discussed with the students in the lesson.
Rating = 4

Pedagogical Content Knowledge:
This was one of Judith's weaker areas. Because her objectives weren't clear (to her), she didn't know what examples and representations to use to help her students understand the topics. For instance, she used a small map that showed the United States but illustrated virtually nothing about the concept of sectionalism. And virtually all of her lesson was conducted at a verbal level with no other examples or representations of any of the other topics.
Rating = 1

General Pedagogical Knowledge:
Judith's lesson was out of alignment. She said her objectives were for the students to understand the geography and dynamics of the war, but the learning activity dealt with topics such as how slaves might have felt, abolitionists, Lincoln, and the respective advantages of the North and the South during the war. Then her seatwork assignment dealt with the vocabulary words, which hadn't been discussed in the lesson. Finally, her homework assignment didn't relate to her learning activity or seatwork assignment. However, her students were very orderly, and she asked a number of questions during the lesson.
Rating = 2

Knowledge of Learners and Learning:
In order to understand topics in depth, learners need effective examples and other representations of content; they need information presented as concretely as possible; and they need to be actively involved in learning activities. Judith used virtually no examples, and the lesson was conducted at an abstract and verbal level. The students were quite involved in the lesson.
Rating = 2

Useful Web Site Addresses

Web Links for "Teaching in an Era of Reform: The Alternative Licensure Issue"

AASA: Bureaucratic Barriers Not the Only Impediment to Developing a Highly Qualified Teaching Force
http://www.ncate.org/newsbrfs/houston_article.htm

Alternative Certification: http://www.ncei.com/

Alternative Certification: A Review of Theory and Research
http://www.ncrel.org/policy/pubs/html/altcert/intro.htm

Alternative Certification for Teachers: http://www.ericfacility.net/databases/ERIC_Digests/ed266137.html

Alternative Routes: Do You Get There in One Piece?: http://www.education-world.com/a_admin/admin252.shtml

Are Alternative Certification Programs the Answer to the Teacher Shortage?
http://www.sedl.org/pubs/sedletter/v13n02/2.html

National Association for Alternative Certification: http://www.alt-teachercert.org/index.asp

National Council on Teacher Quality: Alternative Certification: http://www.nctq.org/issues/alternative.html

Teacher Quality and Alternative Certification Programs: http://www.ncei.com/Testimony051399.htm

Who Prepares Your Teachers? The Debate over Alternative Certification
http://www.aasa.org/issues_and_insights/issues_dept/alternative_certification.pdf

Web Links for "Exploring Diversity: The Competition for Minority Teachers"

Recruitment and Retention of Minority Teachers: http://www.nea.org/recruit/minority/

NEA Offers Tips to Recruit Minority Teachers: http://www.education-world.com/a_admin/admin171.shtml

Demand and Supply of Minority Teachers: http://www.ed.gov/databases/ERIC_Digests/ed316546.html

The Importance of Diversity: http://www.recruitingteachers.org/findteachers/diversity.html

Recruiting and Retaining Minority Teachers: Programs That Work!
http://www.educationworld.com/a_admin/admin213.shtml

Recruiting Teachers for the 21st Century: The Foundation for Educational Equity
http://www.teachingquality.org/resources/pdfs/RecruitingTeachersforthe21stCentury.pdf

Supply and Demand of Teachers of Color: http://www.ericfacility.net/databases/ERIC_Digests/ed390875.html

Teachers for Today and Tomorrow: http://www.ascd.org/publications/ed_lead/200105/bintrim.html

Additional Chapter Web Links

Professionalism

American Federation of Teachers: http://www.aft.org
National Education Association: http://www.nea.org
National Board for Professional Teaching Standards: http://www.nbpts.org/
State Certification Requirements: http://www.education-world.com/jobs/state_certification.shtml
Summary Data on Teacher Effectiveness, Teacher Quality, and Teacher Qualifications
http://www.ncate.org/resources/factsheettq.htm
Teacher Quality: Teacher Licensure: http://www.ncsl.org/programs/educ/TLice.htm

Job Search

Are You Ready for the Job Interview?: http://www.education-world.com/a_issues/issues091.shtml
Characteristics Count: What Principals Look for When Hiring New Teachers
http://www.education-world.com/a_admin/admin257.shtml
Education Career Center: http://www.education-world.com/jobs/
Links to State Education Agencies: http://www.ncate.org/resources/statelinks.htm
National Teacher Recruitment Clearinghouse: http://www.recruitingteachers.org/channels/clearinghouse/
National School Jobs Bulletin Board: http://www.school-jobs.net
Preservice Teacher Electronic Portfolio Examples
http://education.wichita.edu/m3/models/content_area/electronic_portfolios.htm#stteachers
Principals Offer Advice to Job Seekers: http://www.education-world.com/a_admin/admin222.shtml
State Certification Offices: http://www.ub-careers.buffalo.edu/aaee/certoffice.shtml
Teacher Licensure: http://www.aft.org/edissues/teacherquality/tealic.htm
Teachers-Teachers.Com: http://www.teachers-teachers.com/
Teaching Jobs.Org: http://www.teaching-jobs.org/
What's Wrong with Teacher Certification?: http://www.ncate.org/newsbrfs/wrong_cert.htm

First-Year Teachers

Mentoring Beginning Teachers: http://www.sedl.org/pubs/policy23/welcome.html
Advice for First-Year Teachers–from the "Sophomores" Who Survived Last Year!
http://www.education-world.com/a_curr/curr152.shtml
A Survival Kit for New Teachers: http://www.education-world.com/a_curr/curr086.shtml
Back-to-School Guide for Beginning Teachers (and Not-So-New Teachers Too)!
http://www.education-world.com/a_curr/curr264.shtml
New Teacher Resources: http://www.nvo.com/ecnewletter/newteacherresources/
Teacher Knowledge: http://www.sit.edu/tkp/
What to Expect Your First Year of Teaching: http://www.ed.gov/pubs/FirstYear/foreword.html
A Homepage for New Math Teachers: http://people.clarityconnect.com/webpages/terri/terri.html

Teacher Salaries and Performance Pay for Teachers

NEA Average Salaries: http://www.nea.org/publiced/edstats/salaries.html
School Systems and Teachers Unions Mull over Performance Pay
http://www.educationworld.com/a_issues/issues135.shtml
Should PTAs Be Allowed to Fund Teacher Salaries?: http://www.education-world.com/a_admin?admin028.shtml
Sweetening the Pot: http://www.edweek.com/sreports/qc00/templates/article.cfm?slug=recruit.htm
Teachers at the Bottom of the Class for Professional Pay: http://www.education-world.com/a_issues/issues106.shtml
Teacher Salary Homepage: http://www.aft.org/research/salary/home.htm
Teaching Bonus System Criticized: http://www.s-t.com/daily/02-00/02-19-00/a05sr037.htm
US Teacher Salaries: http://resource.educationamerica.net/salaries.html

Media Guide:
Introduction

Media ancillaries for this text exist in four formats: Classroom Windows (also available on the CD-ROM that accompanies the text), Video Perspectives, Video Discussion, and the text's Companion Website, which also contains clips from Video Discussion. Each of these formats is described briefly here and then in greater detail in the pages that follow.

About *Classroom Windows*

These eight videos provide students with realistic glimpses of teachers working in real classrooms. This boxed feature in the text contains a short summary of an unscripted and unrehearsed video episode that shows a real teacher working in an actual classroom. In addition, each *Classroom Windows* feature contains questions that can be used to stimulate discussion and focus students' analysis. Feedback for the discussion questions in the text is available on the Companion Website and in this Instructor's Manual in the appropriate chapters. *Classroom Windows* videos are found in Chapters 1, 2, 6, 7, 10, 11, 12, and 13.

About *Video Perspectives*

These five videos are integrated with chapter topics and allow students to investigate these topics through ABC News video segments focusing on controversial educational issues. Each *Video Perspectives* section in the text offers a short summary of the episode and asks students to think about and respond to questions relating to the video and chapter content. A short description of each of these videos, along with feedback to the discussion questions, can be found in the *Video Perspectives* section of the Media Guide. In addition, *Video Perspectives* is cross listed in the *Teaching Suggestions* section of the appropriate chapters–Chapters 3, 4, 5, 8, and 9.

About *Video Discussion*

These videos feature interviews with John Goodlad, Theodore Sizer, and Urie Triesman. Discussion questions focusing on chapter-relevant topics can be found near the end of Chapters 1, 2, 4, 7, 8, 10, and 13 in the section *Video Discussion Questions*. These questions are connected to short excerpts from the videos which are found on the text's Companion Website.

About the *Companion Website*

Technology is a growing and changing aspect of education that is creating a need for resources. To address this emerging need, Prentice Hall has developed an online learning environment for both students and professors to support this textbook. In creating the Companion Website, http://www.prenhall.com/kauchak, our goal is to embellish what the textbook already offers. For this reason the content is organized by chapter and provides the professor and the student with a variety of meaningful resources.

Classroom Windows

These video segments show real teachers teaching actual students. The segments exist on the CD-ROM that accompanies this text and also appear as boxed features in Chapters 1, 2, 6, 7, 10, 11, 12, and 13. Following is a brief description of each segment, as well as feedback for the discussion questions that also appear in the text.

Chapter 1
The Real World of Teaching (Video #1, 00–24:50)

This video segment looks at three teachers at three different levels.

    <u>First Grade</u>. This interactive lesson shows Rebecca, a first-grade teacher, using questioning to explore the topic of planting a garden with a class of inner-city students. Several aspects of the lesson are noteworthy. One is the positive attitude of the teacher; she obviously enjoys working with young people and shows it in her teaching. She also is effective at accessing students' background knowledge, linking new concepts and ideas to what students already know. Finally, she uses questioning effectively to actively involve a large number of students in the lesson.

    <u>Middle School</u>. Scott Sowell, a seventh-grade science teacher at Kirby Smith Middle School, wants his students to understand Bernoulli's principle, the physical law that explains why airplanes can fly. He begins by reviewing the concept of force and reminds students that when opposing forces meet, movement occurs in the direction of the one of greater magnitude. To illustrate Bernoulli's principle, he first has his students blow over the top of a piece of paper. Then he has students blow between two pieces of paper held closely together. Finally, he places a Ping-Pong ball in a funnel and blows out; surprisingly, the ball remains in the funnel. On the board he reviews each of these experiments, in each case asking students where the force was greater. To conclude the lesson, he introduces the term *Bernoulli's principle.*

    <u>High School</u>. Sue Southam is a high school English teacher at Highland High School, a large (2,200 students) high school located in a major western metropolitan area. The class is focusing on Nathaniel Hawthorne's *The Scarlet Letter,* and in previous sessions the class has discussed the setting for the novel and its heroine, Hester Prynne. In this session Sue is attempting to help students understand the character of Reverend Dimmesdale, the secret father of Hester's illegitimate child. Sue begins by briefly reviewing the book and then asks students how they know that Dimmesdale is the father of the child. After some discussion she asks students to create a portrait or picture of Dimmesdale in their writing journals. Following this assignment, she asks students to pretend they are directing a film and to suggest whom they might cast in Dimmesdale's character.
    After discussing students' suggestions, Sue reads a scene from the book in which Reverend Dimmesdale, in front of the whole congregation, exhorts Hester to identify the father of the child, her illegitimate lover. Following this passage, Sue assigns half the class to be Hester and half to be Dimmesdale and asks them to record their feelings line-by-line during Dimmesdale's speech. She then breaks the students into groups of four with two Hesters and two Dimmesdales in each and asks them to role-play the characters, responding to each other's reactions. After the small-group work Sue brings them back together, and the students discuss their reactions in a whole-group setting. Students can't decide whether Dimmesdale is a tragic character to be pitied or a cowardly one to be scorned.

Discussion Questions and Feedback

1. For which of the three teachers are the emotional rewards likely to be the greatest? Explain.

Although emotional rewards are important for each level–elementary, middle, and secondary teachers–they are likely to be the greatest for Rebecca, the kindergarten teacher, because young children are spontaneous, open, and genuine. Comments such as "I like to play in the mud," which one little boy said in the episode, illustrate these characteristics. On the other hand, a great many emotional rewards exist for middle and secondary teachers as well. They simply weren't as observable in these episodes.

2. For which of the three teachers are the intellectual rewards likely to be the greatest? Explain.

The intellectual rewards can be important for both Scott, the middle school teacher who taught Bernoulli's Principle, and Sue, the high school teacher who was working with her students on The Scarlet Letter. *Bernoulli's Principle has a great deal of real-world application, and* The Scarlet Letter *is a classic piece of literature. Studying either or both can be very stimulating. It is difficult to say that the intellectual rewards will be greater for Scott than for Sue, or vice versa.*

3. Based on what you saw in the episodes, which teacher do you believe has the most difficult job? Explain.

As with many topics and issues in education, people's opinions with respect to a question such as this one will vary. For instance, attracting and maintaining the attention of small children is difficult, so in this regard Rebecca's job is demanding. With respect to planning, Scott probably had the most difficult job, since he had to gather the funnels and balls, distribute them to the students efficiently, so time wasn't wasted, and then teach a challenging topic. Sue's job was probably least demanding physically since she had no materials to gather. All three teachers' jobs were demanding in the sense that they needed to think clearly about their goals and the means of helping students reach the goals.

4. For which teacher is knowledge of content most important? Pedagogical content knowledge? General pedagogical knowledge? Knowledge of learners and learning? Explain why you think so.

Knowledge of content was probably most important for both Scott and Sue. He needed to thoroughly understand Bernoulli's Principle, and Sue needed to have a deep understanding of the novel. Pedagogical content knowledge was most important for Scott. He understood that he could illustrate Bernoulli's Principle by having the students blow over and between the papers and blow through the funnel. General pedagogical knowledge was important for all three teachers. All needed to be skilled in organizing their lessons, using their time efficiently, and questioning. Knowledge of learners and learning was also important for all three teachers. Rebecca needed to understand the way kindergartners think, Scott needed to realize that, for middle school students, concrete examples are essential for comprehending a challenging topic, and Sue needed to know that her students had to be in active roles to learn as much as possible about the novel.

5. How much autonomy do you believe each teacher had in designing and conducting his or her lesson? Explain.

Each teacher had virtually total autonomy in designing and conducting his or her lesson. Selecting the topics and deciding how the topics would be taught were decisions the teachers alone made.

6. To what extent do you believe each teacher demonstrated the characteristics of a professional? Explain.

Based on the evidence we have from the video episodes, each of the teachers demonstrated the characteristics of professionals. They demonstrated specialized knowledge, each was a licensed teacher (although we don't have evidence for that conclusion from the video), and most importantly, they demonstrated a great deal of decision making and autonomy in their teaching.

Chapter 2
Working with Parents: A Parent-Teacher Conference (Video #1, 24:55–32:40)

Having examined barriers to parental involvement as well as strategies for involving parents, you now have the chance to observe a teacher conducting a parent-teacher conference. In this episode DeVonne Lampkin, a fifth-grade teacher, conducts a conference with a parent of a student who is struggling in her class. The parent is somewhat defensive at different points in the conference, and DeVonne attempts to simultaneously support and disarm the parent by grounding her discussion with specific facts about the student's performance.

Discussion Questions and Feedback

1. What did DeVonne do to prepare for the conference? Why was this important?

DeVonne gathered all the information she had with respect to the student's performance, which was to be the topic of the conference. She went into the conference armed with factual data.

2. In an attempt to break the ice in the conference, what did DeVonne do to put the parent at ease?

DeVonne thanked the parent for coming in, and she began the discussion by saying some positive things about the student. Beginning a conference on a positive note is important in setting the tone for a conference.

3. When the parent became somewhat defensive and attempted to divert responsibility for the problems from the student to DeVonne, what did DeVonne do in response?

DeVonne used her factual data to support the conclusions she had made about the student. Having data available that can be shared with parents is probably the most effective mechanism for dealing with parents who are defensive or even potentially hostile.

4. Offer an assessment of DeVonne's handling of the conference. Provide a rationale for your assessment based on your observations of the episode.

DeVonne handled the conference well. She planned carefully, she had ample data to support her conclusions, and she maintained a positive tone throughout the conference.

Chapter 6
Examining Philosophies of Teaching (Video # 1, 33:14–53:00)

This video segment uses philosophy as a lens to look at two secondary social studies teachers, one at the junior high level and the other at the high school level.

Junior High. Judy Holmquist is a ninth-grade geography teacher at Lakeside Junior High School in Orange Park, Florida. Lakeside is a large suburban junior high that serves a lower-middle- to middle-class student population. Judy has 27 students in her second period geography class. She is beginning a unit on the different climate regions of the United States. To introduce students to the unit, she assigns them to four different groups to investigate the influence of geography on four states–Florida, California, New York, and Alaska. Each group is responsible for describing one of these states in terms of geography, economy, ethnic composition, and future issues. When students have completed their investigation, Judy assists them in placing the information into a matrix with the states along the vertical axis and the dimensions–geography, economy, ethnic composition, and future issues–along the top.

Judy begins the lesson by asking students to find a partner and identify three similarities and differences among the states in terms of geography. After several minutes Judy calls the class back together and asks the groups to share their conclusions with the whole class, in the process writing their findings on the board. She then asks the groups to do the same with the Economy column, listing similarities and differences among the states. After discussing the economic similarities and differences, Judy asks the class to compare the two columns and explain connections between them. Finally, she has the students summarize their findings by making generalizations about the influence of climate on economics in different regions.

<u>High School.</u> This veteran teacher is beginning a unit on the Vietnam War and uses this lesson to provide historical background knowledge. He begins by introducing students to the geography of Southeast Asia, explaining that the artificial division of Vietnam into North and South Vietnam was the result of the French withdrawal from the region in the mid-1950s. In his lecture he also talks about Ho Chi Minh and his role in the French withdrawal, which sets the stage for his leadership during the Vietnam War. The lesson is very organized, with the teacher using outlines and maps to illustrate main points. The lesson is also very teacher-centered with minimal interaction with students.

Discussion Questions and Feedback

1. Which of the traditional philosophies is most nearly reflected in Judy's teaching? Explain.

Of the traditional philosophies Judy's teaching most nearly reflects pragmatism. Pragmatism emphasizes direct experiences and problem solving, and Judy's students were directly involved in gathering the information that appeared on her matrix, and they were involved in a form of problem solving as they searched for patterns and relationships in the information.

2. Which of the traditional philosophies is most nearly reflected in Bob's teaching? Explain.

Of the traditional philosophies, Bob's teaching most nearly reflects realism. An understanding of our world is an important goal for realists, and an understanding of the causes of the Vietnam War helps us understand our world. Also, his focus was on information as opposed to practical problem solving, which would be more nearly aligned with pragmatism.

3. Which of the educational philosophies is most nearly reflected in Judy's teaching? Explain.

Of the educational philosophies Judy's teaching most nearly reflects progressivism. Her lesson was learner-centered, her students collaborated in the activity, and she guided their learning with her questioning. These are all characteristics of progressivism.

4. Which of the educational philosophies is most nearly reflected in Bob's teaching? Explain.

Of the educational philosophies Bob's teaching most nearly reflects essentialism. Essentialism is grounded in the belief that important knowledge exists that all people should understand. Understanding the causes and outcomes of the Vietnam War would be viewed by essentialists as important to understanding today's world as an American citizen.

5. Which teacher, Judy or Bob, most clearly reflects your own personal philosophy of education? Explain.

The answer to this question depends on the individual. Our personal philosophies are more nearly aligned with Judy's than with Bob's. This is based on the belief that students need to be active participants in lessons in order to learn as much as possible. We also believe that essential knowledge exists that all teachers should know. In that regard our thinking is also guided by essentialism.

Chapter 7
Within School Coordination: A Grade-Level Meeting (Video #1, 53:15–1:03)

In this episode DeVonne Lampkin, a fifth-grade teacher, leads a grade-level meeting with her colleagues as they discuss various issues related to their duties as teachers in an elementary school.

Discussion Questions and Feedback

1. At what time of the day did the meeting appear to be conducted? Why do you suppose it was conducted at this time?

The meeting appeared to be conducted before school. Teachers are well rested in the morning, and meetings tend to focus on issues that influence but don't directly relate to teaching and learning, such as student placement, scheduling, communication with parents, and coordination of programs. Because meetings occur before students and parents arrive, teachers are often better able to focus on topics such as these.

2. On what topics did the meeting focus? Why do you suppose the teachers focused on these topics?

As suggested in the answer to Item 1, the meeting tended to focus on topics and issues that weren't directly related to teaching and learning. This is common in grade-level meetings in elementary schools and in department meetings in middle and high schools.

3. What topics were conspicuously absent in the meeting's discussions? Why do you suppose this was the case?

The teachers didn't discuss topics or issues related to teaching and learning in their classrooms. Instead, the teachers tended to focus on topics that were more schoolwide or gradewide.

4. How effective was the interaction in the meeting? Provide a rationale for your assessment of the effectiveness of the interaction.

The interaction in the meeting was quite effective. The teachers remained focused on the topics they intended to discuss, and each of the teachers appeared to feel comfortable offering opinions.

Chapter 10
The Math Curriculum in Elementary Schools (Video #2, 0–13:33)

Suzanne Brush is a second-grade teacher at Webster Elementary School, located in a lower- to lower-middle class neighborhood and serving a variety of students from different ethnic backgrounds. Suzanne begins the lesson by explaining that she is planning a party for the class and needs to know what kinds of jelly beans she should buy. After some discussion the class agrees that one way to find out would be to give each student a sample of different kinds of jelly beans and have each student vote for his or her favorite. Suzanne then gives a bag containing seven different-flavored jelly beans to each student and asks each to choose his or her favorite. After the tasting, Suzanne asks students how they could organize this information. After considerable discussion they arrive at the idea of graphing the information by having each student place a colored cardboard rectangle in the appropriate column of the graph.

After each student "votes," Suzanne prompts students to begin interpreting the graph by asking questions such as, "What does the graph tell us?" Suzanne encourages students to analyze the graphed information by asking questions that require them to compare the information in the columns (i.e., the numbers of students choosing each color). Suzanne then asks students to pose similar problems of their own. As students discuss their problems, Suzanne emphasizes student understanding of problem-solving strategies by repeatedly asking, "How did you get that?" To provide additional practice with problem solving, Suzanne then assigns students to different learning-center activities, where they work in small groups to apply their problem-solving and graphing strategies to new problems.

Discussion Questions and Feedback

1. You considered the implicit curriculum in Suzanne's classroom earlier in the chapter. Based on what you have seen in the video, describe the implicit curriculum in her classroom in more detail.

The following include some of the ideas that Suzanne's students are learning through the implicit curriculum: making mistakes is part of the learning process, being actively involved is valuable and important, acquiring math skills is practical and part of the real world, and teachers and students work together to promote learning.

2. Which of the educational philosophies is most nearly reflected in Suzanne's teaching? Explain why you think so.

Suzanne's teaching most nearly reflects progressivism. Her instruction was learner-centered and focused on real-world problems.

3. Consider the forces that influence the curriculum: philosophy, textbooks, the local district, the national government, and professional organizations. Then rate the influence you believe each had on Suzanne's curriculum. Use the following scale for your rating: 4 = very strong influence, 3 = strong influence, 2 = weak influence, 1 = no influence.

- Philosophy   1   2   3   4
- Textbooks   1   2   3   4
- Local district   1   2   3   4
- National government   1   2   3   4
- Professional organizations   1   2   3   4

Explain your rating in each case.

We recognize that assessing influences is highly subjective, but with that note of caution we would rate the influences on Suzanne's curriculum as follows:

Philosophy	*4*	*Suzanne described her beliefs about the importance of students being involved in their learning activities and math being practical. These beliefs were part of her personal philosophy of education.*
Textbooks	*2*	*While textbooks influence teachers in general and they also influenced Suzanne's teaching, they had a minor influence in the video episode.*
Local district	*3*	*The philosophy of Suzanne's district promoted student-centered learning.*
National government	*1*	*No evidence of national government influence was observable in the episode.*
Professional organizations	*3*	*The National Council of Teachers of Mathematics strongly endorses the kind of learning that was evident in the video episode.*

4. To what extent did Suzanne display professionalism in the episode you saw? Explain your analysis.

Suzanne demonstrated the characteristics of a professional. She displayed a great deal of professional knowledge, she was a licensed teacher, and she demonstrated a high level of decision making and autonomy.

Chapter 11
Learning About Balance Beams in Fourth Grade (Video #2, 14:04–24:30)

Jenny Newhall, a fourth-grade teacher, wants her students to know how to solve problems involving a balance beam and weights. Jenny starts by dividing students into groups and giving each group of students a balance beam and weights. She begins the lesson by directing each group to put 4 weights 8 places, or notches, from the center on the righthand side and 1 weight 2 places from the center on the left side. She then asks each student in the different groups to come up with as many different ways as possible to balance the beam without moving the original weights. After students work for awhile on their individual solutions, they then share them with other members of their group and test the different solutions on the balance beam.

Different students in the focal group that was interviewed after the lesson offer different solutions:

- One suggests adding 3 weights to the 10 place and explains it this way: 3 x 10 + 2 x 1 = 8 x 4.
- A second suggests adding 5 weights to the 6 place and explains it in this way: 6 x 5 + 2 x 1 = 8 x 4.
- A third student suggests adding 3 weights to the 10 place and justifies that by noting there will then be 4 weights on each side. This same student also suggests adding 2 weights to the 10 and 1 to the 6.

When Jenny visits this group, she encourages students to share their thinking. Two of the students understand the logic behind balancing the beam (i.e., number x distance) while two others believe that the number of weights alone, without consideration of their distance from the center, determines whether the beam will balance.

The whole class then discusses the solutions the different groups produced. Jenny encourages students to use number sentences like 8 x 4 = 32 = (10 x 3) + 2 = 32 to explain their answers. She then asks the groups to generate different solutions to balance a beam that has 1 weight 2 places from the center on the left and 3 weights 5 from the center and 1 weight 6 from the center on the right. As students share their answers, it is evident that many still don't understand the principle of length x weight needed to solve the problem.

Discussion Questions and Feedback

1. Was Jenny's instruction based primarily on behaviorism or on cognitive views of learning? Explain your reasoning.

Jenny's instruction was based primarily on cognitive views of learning. The lesson focused on thinking and understanding, not on observable responses to specific and isolated questions.

2. To what extent did Jenny display the personal characteristics of effective teachers, the strategies of effective teachers, and effective classroom management? Cite specific evidence from the lesson to support your conclusions.

Jenny displayed many of the personal characteristics and teaching strategies as well as classroom management of effective teachers. Her behavior suggested that she believed all the students could learn and she expected them to do so. She developed her lesson with questioning rather than explaining, she represented her topic effectively (with her balances), the students were orderly, and they all participated in the lesson.

3. Which of the educational philosophies (described in Chapter 6) was most nearly reflected in Jenny's teaching? Explain why you think so.

Jenny's instruction most nearly reflected progressivism. The lesson was student-centered and focused on a practical, real-world problem.

4. We examined the explicit and implicit curricula in Chapter 10. Describe both the explicit and implicit curriculum implied in Jenny's lesson. Cite specific evidence from the lesson to support your conclusions.

The explicit curriculum in Jenny's lesson focused on the principle for making a balance beam balance. She wanted her students to understand that the number of tiles times the distance on one side of the fulcrum was equal to the number of tiles times the distance on the other side of the fulcrum. The implicit curriculum implied in the lesson was that students should learn to cooperate and solve problems in school and that school is a place where students are actively involved in learning.

5. To what extent did Jenny display professionalism in the episode you saw? Explain your analysis.

Jenny displayed the characteristics of a professional. She demonstrated knowledge of content, pedagogical content knowledge, general pedagogical knowledge, and knowledge of learners and learning, which are characteristics of a professional. She demonstrated a great deal of decision making and autonomy in planning and conducting her lesson.

Chapter 12
Technology in Classrooms (Video # 2, 25:00–28:50)

Suzanne Brush, the teacher in the video segment in Chapter 10, uses technology in a variety of ways to reinforce her students' developing understanding of graphing. In one segment students call different pizza restaurants to find the price of pizza and graph their results. In another, students watch a laser disk video clip of students racing through alternate routes on an obstacle course, and they time and graph the runners' results. In another, students use computers to graph the results of a student survey on students' soft drink preferences.

Discussion Questions and Feedback

1. Did Suzanne Brush's use of technology reflect more of a hardware or a process view? Explain.

Her use of technology reflected more a process view. Rather than using it to deliver information, she used it to extend learning, ensure transfer, and develop thinking skills.

2. How effective was Suzanne's use of technology as a problem-solving tool? What could she have done to make it more effect?

She used technology as a problem solving tool in several ways. One problem presented students with a race and asked them to decide which student ran faster. A second problem-solving use was to decide which pizza was cheapest. In both instances her instruction could have been improved by actively talking about the process afterwards to help students reflect on what they did and why.

3. In what ways did Suzanne use technology as support tools to complement her students' learning? How effective were these uses, and what might she have done to increase their effectiveness?

Students graphed birthday data as well as the information about the most common ways that students traveled to schools. In both instances talking about the process afterwards would have helped students understand the logic of the process.

4. How could Suzanne use technology as an assessment tool? What advantages and disadvantages would there be over pencil-and-paper measures?

To assess their ability to organize data, Suzanne could present unorganized information and have students graph it on computers. She could also present information on graphs on computers and assess whether students could interpret the information. In both instances students could see how technology could be used to solve real-world problems.

Chapter 13
Demonstrating Knowledge in Classrooms (Video # 2, 28:53–50:00)

Having examined the different kinds of knowledge that expert teachers possess, students now have the chance to see this knowledge displayed in four teaching segments with students of different ages. In the first segment Jenny Newhall, a kindergarten teacher, explores the properties of air with her children. In the second, Richard Nelms, a seventh-grade teacher, illustrates the concept of symmetry for his students. The third shows Didi Johnson, a chemistry teacher, attempting to help her students understand Charles's law of gases; and in the final episode DeVonne Lampkin, a fifth-grade teacher, uses real and live examples to teach the concept of arthropod.

Discussion Questions and Feedback

1. Which of the four types of professional knowledge–knowledge of content, pedagogical content knowledge, general pedagogical knowledge, or knowledge of learners and learning–were best illustrated in the segment with Jenny Newhall? Explain.

Every expert teacher demonstrates aspects of each of the four types of professional knowledge in his or her instruction. For example, Jenny knew that her students needed a warm emotional environment in order to learn most effectively, which demonstrates knowledge of learners and learning. However, she most displayed an ability to organize her classroom and actively involve her students through questioning. These are the components of general pedagogical knowledge, which involves an understanding of instruction and management that transcends specific topics.

2. Explain how Richard Nelms demonstrated knowledge of learners and learning in the segment dealing with the concept of symmetry.

Knowledge of learners and learning demonstrates an understanding of principles of learning and development. Richard understood that students need concrete examples in order to understand abstract concepts, and personalized examples are more effective than those more distant. Because of this understanding he used one of his students to demonstrate the concept of bilateral symmetry. He also understood that students learn most effectively when they're actively involved in the lesson, so he developed the lesson with questioning to promote their involvement.

3. Explain how pedagogical content knowledge was illustrated in Didi Johnson's lesson on Charles's law?

Pedagogical content knowledge involves the ability to represent abstract ideas in ways that are understandable to students. Didi best demonstrated this type of knowledge with her demonstration that provided a concrete example of Charles's law. The students could see that the heated balloon had the greatest volume and the balloon in the ice had the least volume. This provided a visual example of the law to which solutions to problems could be linked.

4. Assess DeVonne Lampkin's lesson on arthropods with respect to general pedagogical knowledge, knowledge of learners and learning, and pedagogical content knowledge.

DeVonne actually demonstrated all four types of knowledge in her lesson. Her knowledge of content allowed her to conceptualize the lesson and select appropriate examples. She demonstrated knowledge of learners and learning by designing the lesson to actively involve each student. Her understanding of pedagogical content knowledge was evidenced in her use of interesting and engaging examples. Her classroom was orderly and well managed despite the use of a hands-on activity, which can demand careful management, and the ability to create an orderly learning environment is one characteristic of general pedagogical knowledge. In addition, she used extensive questioning, which is another aspect of general pedagogical knowledge.

Video Perspectives

Chapters 3, 4, 5, 8, and 9 contain a *Video Perspectives* feature that briefly describes the video segment and includes discussion questions. These descriptions and questions are reproduced here together with feedback for the questions.

Chapter 3
Safe Haven: Helping Emotionally Troubled Kids Get Back on Track

The trend in special education is inclusion, but some students require extra structure and support to cope with the demands of schooling. This ABC News video examines a day school that assists teens with serious emotional problems.

1. How well would these students function in regular schools and classrooms?

Based on their past experiences, it is highly unlikely they would be able to function in regular schools or classrooms. The demands of classroom life plus stresses caused by other students would be overwhelming.

2. What are the advantages and disadvantages of this approach to helping students with special needs versus inclusion?

A self-contained day school provides the structure and nurturing that these students need to survive. What this approach lacks is opportunities for these students to learn to function in the real world. A major goal of the curriculum at this school would focus on transitioning into regular schools, colleges, and jobs.

3. How could schools and classrooms be adapted to help these students make a successful transition back into a regular classroom?

Inclusion suggests that students spend as much time as possible in regular classroom settings. It does not rule out supplementary instruction, such as small-group sessions with similar students to ease the transition. In addition, the teacher would have help from an IEP team in designing the classroom to maximize student adjustment and success. School counselors, psychologists, and social workers would be valuable to the teacher in this process.

Chapter 4
Action, Reaction, and Zero Tolerance

This ABC News video examines the effects of zero tolerance policies on schools and students. It first visits an elementary school in Irvington, New Jersey, where an 8-year-old boy was expelled for playing cowboys and Indians with a paper gun. Next the video focuses on a high school in Virginia where the school mascot, a Spartan, is not allowed to wear a cardboard sword.

1. What are the major goals of zero tolerance policies?

Zero tolerance policies in schools have two major goals: to make schools safer and change student behavior.

2. What are the advantages and disadvantages of zero tolerance policies?

The major advantages of zero tolerance policies are that they clearly outline rules for acceptable and unacceptable behavior and clearly define consequences for violating these rules. The major disadvantages are that there isn't clear research evidence that these policies work and their misapplication not only causes individual students problems, but also makes students doubtful about the validity of other rules.

3. What could schools do to minimize the negative effects of zero tolerance policies?

In implementing zero tolerance policies, schools should make a special effort to clearly explain the reasons for specific rules. In addition, administrators should use sound judgment and flexibility in applying these rules.

Chapter 5
God and Evolution in Kansas Classrooms

This ABC News video examines a recent controversy in Kansas in which the Kansas Board of Education decided to drop the teaching of evolution from the required coursework in the state's public schools. The video features interviews with Sue Gamble, a candidate for the Board of Education, who questions this decision, as well as two experts on the topic.

1. What are some reasons that religion is such a hotly debated topic in American education?

One major reason is historical; from colonial times there has been an ongoing tradition of religion influencing our schools. In addition, religion plays a central role in many Americans' lives, as do families and children. When these two areas overlap, controversy is probably inevitable.

2. What areas of the curriculum are most likely to encounter problems with religious issues?

Virtually all areas of the curriculum have overlap with religious topics and concerns. The humanities, including literature and art, continually deal with the meaning of life. The social sciences, including history and anthropology, attempt to explain the human condition. Even the sciences, especially biology, deal with human origins. Areas like math and grammar seem relatively safe.

3. What are the advantages and disadvantages of including religion in our schools?

A definite advantage is that integrating religion would link school to many homes and allow the teaching of values. However, the inclusion of religious advocacy is forbidden by the U.S. Constitution. In addition, the diversity of the U.S. in terms of differing religions makes the inclusion of any one religion impractical and counterproductive.

Chapter 8
Home Room: One Last Chance

This ABC News video describes a unique kind of school, SEED Public Charter School, a public urban boarding school in Washington, DC. The video interviews the founders of the charter school, as well as teachers and students. These interviews provide insights into the promises and challenges of this innovation.

1. How is this charter school different from ones that you've read about?

The biggest difference is that it is a residential facility. Although other charter schools target-inner city African American students, this is the only one that has a residential program.

2. Why aren't there more charter schools like this across the country?

Cost is probably the major factor. A residential school is probably at least four or five times more expensive than a regular school. In addition, many parents might not want their children living away from home at a young age.

3. What positive features of this school could be transported to other schools?

Probably the most beneficial aspects of this school are its emphasis on academics and positive expectations for student success. The curriculum clearly identifies essential knowledge, called Gates, and expects each student to master the content.

Chapter 9
Affirmative Action

This ABC News segment examines the issues around the recent U.S. Supreme Court decision on affirmative action policies at the University of Michigan. The video features a short clip of President George W. Bush opposing the University of Michigan policy as a quota system, as well as the president of the University of Michigan defending its policies.

1. What are the arguments for and against affirmative action policies in admissions?

Proponents of affirmative action contend that it is an effective mechanism for righting past wrongs and for recruiting a diverse student body. Opponents contend that it unfairly punishes nonminorities, in essence arguing that two wrongs don't make a right.

2. How is a point-based formula system different from a quota system?

Quota systems allocate a certain number of slots to minorities, disregarding qualifications for the most part. Formula systems don't create quotas but instead allocate extra points for desired aspects of diversity such as race, gender, geographic origins, or socioeconomic status.

3. What might be some potential educational benefits of a diverse student body?

Having diversity in a student body exposes students to different opinions and perspectives. It also provides opportunities for students to learn about other cultures and to learn how to interact with different types of people.

Discussion Videos

Three videos that accompany the text feature interviews with John Goodlad, Theodore Sizer, and Urie Triesman. Discussion questions focusing on chapter-relevant topics can be found near the end of Chapters 1, 2, 4, 7, 8, 10, and 13 in a section titled *Video Discussion Questions*. The questions are connected to short excerpts from these videos, which are found on the text's Companion Website. Following is a brief description of each of these videos.

Theodore Sizer (approximately 16 minutes)

Theodore Sizer is the director of the Coalition for Effective Schools, which attempts to reform high schools. Dr. Sizer believes that the high school curriculum needs to be focused on essential knowledge, emphasizing depth over breadth. This would allow teachers to focus more on critical thinking versus content acquisition. This emphasis should also be reflected in the ways we assess student learning. In emphasizing critical thinking, teachers should continually encourage students to ask why. Dr. Sizer also believes that parents should play an active, integral role in their children's education and that they should have choice in where their children attend school.

John Goodlad (approximately 12 minutes)

John Goodlad is professor emeritus and codirector of the Center for Renewal at the University of Washington and president of the Independent Institute for Educational Inquiry. In his work he emphasizes the critical role that people–principals and teachers–play in school reform and renewal. Though districts play a role in influencing schools, principals are the educational leaders at the school level and exert a powerful influence. Parents can also have a powerful and positive influence on learning. Goodlad is optimistic about the power of technology to play a liberating role in freeing up teachers to work with students either one-on-one or in small groups.

Urie Triesman (approximately 9 minutes)

Urie Triesman is a professor of mathematics at the University of Texas at Austin and director of the Charles A. Dana Center for Math and Science Education. He believes that schools should be held accountable for student learning but that they should also have autonomy to design learning experiences that fit the needs of students within a particular community. He also believes that both teachers and principals play a critical role in improving learning at the school level. Principals should provide dynamic leadership; teachers need to be involved in a community of learners that continually examines practice. In addition, beginning teachers need to actively seek out mentors, effective teachers who can assist them in their journey towards professional growth and development.

The Companion Website (CW)–**http://www.prenhall.com/kauchak**–contains resources for both the instructor and the students.

For the Instructor

Syllabus Manager™ –Syllabus Manager™ is an online syllabus creation and management instrument with the following capabilities:

- Syllabus Manager™ provides you, the instructor, with a step-by-step process to create and revise syllabi with direct links the Companion Website and other online content without having to learn HTML.

- The completed syllabus is hosted on our servers, allowing convenient updates from any computer on the Internet. Changes you make to your syllabus are immediately available to your students at their next log-on.

- Students may log on to your syllabus at any time. All they need to know is the web address for the Companion Website and the password you've assigned to your syllabus.

- By clicking on a date, the student is shown the list of activities for that day's assignment. The activities for each assignment are linked directly to text content, saving time for students.

- Adding assignments consists of clicking on the desired due date, then filling in the details of the assignment.

- Links to other activities can be created easily. If the activity is online, a URL can be entered in the space provided, and it will be linked automatically in the final syllabus.

For the Student

The CW provides students with resources and immediate feedback on exercises and other activities linked to the text. These activities, projects, and resources enhance and extend chapter content to real-world issues and concepts. Each chapter on the CW contains the following modules, or sections, unless specified otherwise:

- Chapter Overview–an outline of key concepts and issues in the chapter

- Self-Assessment–multiple-choice quizzes with automatic grading to provide immediate feedback for students

- Web Links–links to www sites that relate to and enhance chapter content

- Increasing Understanding–the margin questions from the text with immediate feedback available

- Reflect on This–reflection questions that extend chapter content

- Exploring Diversity–links to multicultural/diverse content and Web sites

- Portfolio Activities–activities and projects that give students the opportunity to begin building their professional portfolios

- Virtual Field Experience–projects and activities that create a virtual field experience for students who do not have a formal field experience as part of the course

- Video Perspectives–thought-provoking questions that correspond to the issue-based ABC News video segments offered with the text (Chapters 3, 4, 5, 8, and 9)

- Classroom Windows–critical-thinking questions and feedback that connect the video and the chapter (Chapters 1, 2, 6, 7, 10, 11, 12 and 13)

- Video Discussion–streaming video with discussion questions (Chapters 1, 2, 4, 7, 8, 10, and 13)

- Communications: Message Board–a virtual bulletin board to post or respond to questions or comments to/from a national audience, allowing anyone who is using the text anywhere in the country to communicate in a real-time environment; ideal for discussion and study groups, or class projects

- Other Resources–access to PowerPoint Transparencies, the INTASC Standards as they are connected to chapter content and activities, and links to professional organizations

Reference List of Transparencies:
PowerPoint slides/acetate transparencies that accompany
Kauchak and Eggen, *Introduction to Teaching: Becoming a Professional*, Second Edition

NOTE: The transparencies listed below and referenced throughout this Instructor's Manual are included as downloadable files on the Companion Website, as PowerPoint slides on CD, and as acetate transparencies.

CHAPTER 1 *Why Become a Teacher?*

Transparency 1.1	Table 1.1: Responses to Interest in Teaching Inventory
Transparency 1.2	Table 1.2: Beginning Teacher Salaries for Each State
Transparency 1.3	Figure 1.1: Dimensions of Teacher Professionalism
Transparency 1.4	Table 1.3: The INTASC Principles

CHAPTER 2 *The Teaching Profession*

Transparency 2.1	Table 2.1: How Teachers Spend Their Time
Transparency 2.2	Table 2.2: Public School Teachers' Gender by Assignment

CHAPTER 3 *Learner Diversity: Differences in Today's Students*

Transparency 3.1	Figure 3.2: Changes in School-Age Population, 2000–2020
Transparency 3.2	Table 3.1: Different Programs for ELL Students
Transparency 3.3	Figure 3.3: Sexual Harassment in U.S. Schools
Transparency 3.4	Table 3.2: Gardner's Eight Intelligences
Transparency 3.5	Table 3.3: Acceleration and Enrichment Options for Students Who Are Gifted and Talented

CHAPTER 4 *Changes in American Society: Their Influences on Today's Schools*

Transparency 4.1	Figure 4.2: Poverty Levels by Ethnicity
Transparency 4.2	Figure 4.3: Changes in the Student Population
Transparency 4.3	Figure 4.4: Student Drug and Alcohol Use: Percentage of High School Seniors Reporting Use in the Previous 30 Days
Transparency 4.4	Table 4.1: Characteristics of Students Placed At-Risk

CHAPTER 5 *Education in the United States: Its Historical Roots*

Transparency 5.1	Table 5.1: Changes in Educational Thought in Europe
Transparency 5.2	Table 5.2: A Summary of Historical Periods in American Education
Transparency 5.3	Figure 5.1: The Evolution of the American High School
Transparency 5.4	Table 5.3: Major Provisions of the Goals 2000 Act

CHAPTER 6 *Educational Philosophy: The Intellectual Foundations of American Education*

Transparency 6.1	Figure 6.1: Philosophy and Professionalism
Transparency 6.2	Table 6.1: The Traditional Schools of Philosophy
Transparency 6.3	Table 6.2: Classroom Applications of the Educational Philosophies
Transparency 6.4	Table 6.3: An Analysis of Allie's Philosophy of Education